# SHECKY'S BAR, CLUB & LOUNGE GUIDE 2000

Move over New Testament, there's a new Bible in town!

Now in its third edition, *Shecky's Bar Club & Lounge Guide* is still the most comprehensive guide to New York City nightlife! With more than 700 reviews and a staff of writers who are on a mission to unearth every cool bar in town, *Shecky's* is, plain and simple, your salvation.

What makes *Shecky's* so unique (besides the name), is that it caters to an audience who has a healthy sense of humor, needs to hear the "real truth" about New York City's bar scene. From warning you about annoying door policies to raving about the new, hot scenes, *Shecky's* tells it to you straight.

Say goodbye to wandering the streets hoping to stumble across a "find." That's our job, so rest easy. We've done all the dirty work, now it's your turn to go out and have fun!

Grab it, read it, live it...enjoy it!

Shecky

GW00497192

Published by
Hangover Productions, Inc.
65 Reade Street, 5B
New York, NY 10007

**212-420-BARS**
**e-mail: sheckys@hotmail.com**
**http://www.sheckys.com**

**President/Publisher** Chris Hoffman

**Editorial Staff**
**Editor-In-Chief** Chris Hoffman
**Editor/Copy Editor** Jennifer Sendax
**Reviewers** Steve M. Altiere, Nicky Beer, Caroline Colston,
Lisa Cramp, Chris Hoffman, Miles Kahn, Michelle McCrary,
Colleen O'Keefe, Connie Pantone, Dina Schonfeld, Jennifer
Sendax, John Sullivan, Christopher Walsh.

**Marketing Director** Lisa Cramp

Cover Design by Chris Hoffman and Automated Graphics, Inc.
The images used herein were obtained from IMSI MasterClips
Collection, 1895 Francisco Blvd. East, San Rafael, CA 94901-
5506.

Publishers note: No fees or services were rendered in
exchange for inclusion in this book.

Please note that while every effort was made to ensure the
accuracy of phone numbers, addresses, hours, policies, prices
and details at the time of publication, any of the criteria is
subject to change so please call ahead.

**Special thanks to Dina Schonfeld who co-founded
Shecky's Bar Club & Lounge Guide.**

Copyright © 1999 by Hangover Productions, Inc.

Third Edition.
ISBN 0-9662658-4-X

Printed in the United States of America

# MANHATTAN MAP

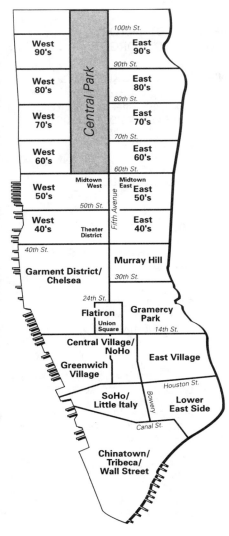

# TABLE OF CONTENTS

# ICON KEY

**LOUNGE / SWANKY/ UPSCALE**

**NEIGHBORHOOD BAR**

**DIVE BAR / NO FRILLS / INEXPENSIVE**

**CLUB/ DANCING**

**SPORTS BAR**

**LIVE MUSIC**

**FRAT / COLLEGE BARS**

**FOOD**

**GAY BARS**

**SHECKY'S PICK**

# ALPHABETICAL LISTING OF BARS

**ABBEY TAVERN**
**354 3rd Avenue (At. 26th St.)**
**532-1978**

*ALL MAJOR CREDIT CARDS*

A more fitting name might be the "Shabby Tavern." This neighborhood watering hole doesn't have much to offer besides bland food and beer. They serve a full diner-type menu at red and white checker tablecloth tables reminiscent of an Italian restaurant. The long and narrow bar is decorated with a bunch of clutter and knickknacks. It wouldn't be that bad if it weren't for the surly service. Daytime finds the Abbey packed with construction workers from Baruch College. At night the after work locals hang out, grab a few beers, and watch the games. There's never too much excitement here.

**ACE BAR**
**531 E. 5th St. (bet. Aves. A & B)**
**979-8476**

*ALL MAJOR CREDIT CARDS*

The healthy mix of downtown yuppies and tattooed vagrants has sadly turned to the dark side. Yuppies in collared shirts and Dockers have unfortunately swarmed and taken over the Ace. The bar's décor is a combination of '70s retro, gothic haunted house and a smarmy pool hall. Pool, darts and pinball keep a lively group of talkative singles busy in between cheap pints of Guiness and Jager shots. Despite the invasion of conservative types, the jukebox still plays a great mix from headbanging Sabbath to the punk rock sounds of Television and The Ramones. If you're looking for a better-than-a-dive but less-snooty-than-a-lounge type of atmosphere, this is a great pick. With plenty of seating, it's especially good for meeting up with groups. For the hardcore drinkers, a second happy hour kicks in after 2 am.

## ACME UNDERGROUND
**9 Great Jones St. (bet. B'way & Lafayette)**
**420-1934**

*ALL MAJOR CREDIT CARDS*

Beware! You are now entering the official dietary hell. As for those of you who are not thwarted by the potential risk for full-blown artery collapse, mosey on down and inhale some of the greasiest yet most delightful southern fare in town. This large party barn adorned with old Sunaco signs, photos of Elvis and countless bottles of hot sauce, packs in a crowd of neighborhood singles. Below the restaurant, the Acme Underground showcases live bands on various evenings for a $6 — $10 cover. Although there is no Happy Hour, half price appetizers are offered at the bar daily from 4 pm — 7 pm. Open Monday — Thursday from 11:30 am — 11:30 pm and Friday and Saturday from 11:30 am — 12:30 am, Acme Underground is a good casual spot for dinner and drinks with a group of friends.

## ADLIB
**50 W. 33rd St. (bet. 5th Ave. & B'way)**
**971-3819**

*ALL MAJOR CREDIT CARDS*

Somewhere between an airport lounge and a supper club is New York's newest jazz bar, Adlib. This Korean-owned venture, still very much in need of an identity, is nestled right between two strip clubs. The Korean/American menu is a little pricey: Entrees range from $8-$25; beer and wine is $5-$6; cocktails are $7. Look for the Owen Hart, Jr. Trio, which hosts a jam session on Wednesdays. On other nights they feature all-Korean jazz acts. Although there is no cover, there is a $10 drink minimum for the music that runs Monday through Saturday. Korean pop music plays over the sound system between sets, and the projection TV shows

'70s rock concerts and Spanish soap operas. Catering primarily to Korean businessmen and tourists, it's obvious that the owners have never run a jazz club before — at least not in New York.

## ALCHYMY
**12 Ave A (bet. E. Houston & 2nd Sts.)**
**477-9050**

### ALL MAJOR CREDIT CARDS

Alchemy, meaning "turning lead into gold," is a perfect definition of what happened to this bar. Formerly known as Spoon, Alchymy has, well, grown up. Once a haven for young pot smoking hip-hop kids, this culturally-infused bar is now courting an older, more mature crowd. Minimally decorated with a lot of red lights, this two-story bar hosts an open mike every Thursday with local talent performing anything from comedy to jazz to poetry readings. Beginning on a monthly basis, Alchymy will host Wednesday night art exhibits with free wine and cheese from 7pm - 9pm. A jukebox provides a mixed musical selection while guest DJs spin techno, house and urban party mixes on any given night of the week. Open daily from 5pm - 4am. Happy hour is served daily from 5pm-9pm with ½ price drink specials. No cover.

## ALIAH
**59 5th Ave. (bet. 12th & 13th Sts.)**
**242-9710**

### ALL MAJOR CREDIT CARDS

A resounding "thank you!" to the Baldwin brothers! Yes, those famous acting heartthrobs have stepped up to plate and created a small oasis in a neighborhood void of all things good and social. Forecasted by many to mimic "scene cuisines" like Moomba and Veruka, Aliah is just as cool but half as pretentious. The split-level space is seductive, chic and comfortable, making it an excellent date spot. The lower level offers a rather nondescript dining area while the upper level boasts a large bar area with beautiful glass ceilings, plush textures and romantic lighting. The music is quite good too. Although not an obvious pickup scene, the pa-

8

trons are young, sophisticated and good-looking. Drinks are pricey yet generous and there are appetizers available at the bar. Like all downtown scenes, weekends tend to attract the Upper East Side crowd with a few Bridge-and-Tunnelers mixed in. Dress to impress...for the velvet rope.

## ALLIGATOR ALLEY
**485 Amsterdam Ave. (bet. 83rd & 84th Sts.)**
**873-5810**

*CASH ONLY*

Despite the offensively cheezy green neon sign outside, Alligator Alley is a down-to-earth postgrad bar. The décor, which is minimal, will remind you of a poorly refurbished Midwestern basement. You will find a bevy of clean-cut young singles playing pool and swilling one of the 14 bottled beers and 5 beers on tap. The jukebox boasts a collection of 1970s disco, so be prepared for a white man's overbite dance party to break out at a moments notice. Happy hour, from 5 pm — 8 pm, offers $2 beers and well drinks.

## ALVA
**36 E. 22nd St. (bet. B'way & Park Ave. S.)**
**228-4399**

*ALL MAJOR CREDIT CARDS*

Named after Thomas Alva Edison, Alva is more of an upscale restaurant than a bar. During the weekend, and after work, you can barely see the restaurant over the sea of single yuppies who clog up the small bar in front. The crowd leans towards a mix of upscale Gramercy Parkers and out-of-towners. Either way, both groups come for the funky '70s music, delicious fare, cigar-friendly atmosphere and the mellow vibe of the space. Mixed drinks are $6, served in large tumblers and give the three-second pour a new meaning. Open for lunch and dinner, the bar remains open daily until 4 am.

9

**AMERICAN SPIRITS**
**1744 2nd Ave. (bet. 91st & 92nd St.)**
**289-7510**

***ALL MAJOR CREDIT CARDS***

You're at college again attending one of those fraternity parties...no, wait a minute, you're at American Spirits! This two-story bar decorated with stickers and beer posters is certain to bring back a few memories—some of which you probably don't want to re-awaken. If you're young, a frat boy, or think "Animal House" is the best movie ever made, this is like the Disneyland of bars for you. With karaoke on Tuesday nights, a pool table, an Internet consul, 10 beers on tap and loud top forties music screaming from the juke-box, one can spend endless hours at American Spirits. Open for two years, this ridiculously loud college bar is open every day from 4pm-4am. A daily happy hour from 4pm to 8pm offers $1 drafts, $5 pitchers, and $1.75 margaritas. Make sure to bring your ID—they're strict at the door. Along with the extensive indoor space, there are a few plastic tables and chairs out front for those who can't deal.

**AMERICAN TRASH**
**1471 1st Ave. (bet. 76th & 77th Sts.)**
**988-9008**

***CASH ONLY***

Covered in kitschy ornaments, old surfboards, fishnets and women's bras, American Trash is a place that both stock-brokers and Hell's Angels call home. This "professional drinking establishment" keeps patrons occupied until the wee hours with extreme sports videos, darts, pool tables and drink specials. The men are on the prowl, making this a great pickup joint for women who need an ego boost. The friendly staff and non-frat boy crowd makes this watering hole a refreshing choice for heavy boozing. A daily happy hour offers $2 pints of Fosters and Bud Lites and $3 imported pints and Guiness from 12 pm – 7 pm.

## ANGELO & MAXIE'S
**233 Park Ave. S. (At 19ᵗʰ St.)**
**220-9200**

*ALL MAJOR CREDIT CARDS*

If your goal of the evening is to be gawked at by Wall Street banker-types drinking scotch on the rocks and smoking fat cigars; pull up a chair. This beautiful art deco steakhouse could be so much more, but for some reason it fell into the pit of mediocrity. You'll find that B&T types overrun the place on the weekend ruining the otherwise serene atmosphere. Even the food seems to have suffered a bit from all of this decadence. The portions are large, but leave you feeling completely unsatisfied. This stretch of Park Ave. South is loaded with wonderful places to eat and drink—it's a shame Angelo & Maxie's doesn't cut the mustard.

## ANGEL'S SHARE
**8 Stuyvesant St. (bet. 2ⁿᵈ & 3ʳᵈ Aves.)**
**777-5415**

*ALL MAJOR CREDIT CARDS*

Hidden in the back room of a Sushi joint, this chic art deco lounge overlooks 10ᵗʰ Street from the second floor. Adorned with a large Michelangelo-type painting of Asian angels in the clouds, the predominately Asian clientele peacefully sit at the bar or at tables in the corner. While listening to soft piano music, choose from an extensive menu of drinks including grappa, sake, Scotch and deliciously unique daiquiries. With a touch of tradition and exactness, the bartender has his technique down. There are a few odd rules to follow at Angel's Share: No cigar smoking, no standing and no more than four people in the bar at once. Hours: 6 pm – 3 am daily.

## ANNIE MOORE'S
**50 E. 43ʳᵈ (bet. Vanderbilt & Madison)**
**986-7826**

*ALL MAJOR CREDIT CARDS*

A commuter's dream, Annie Moore's is conveniently located right across the street from Grand Central Station. The large Irish pub has a sprawling bar in front and a small restaurant in the back. So as not to miss your train while grabbing a cold one, television screens flash the Metro-North schedules in between sporting events. Thursday nights seem to draw the young banking analysts who come here not because they live in the burbs, but because it is one of the better places to drink in the area. While there is no happy hour, the bar is open daily from 11 am to 12 am.

## ANSEO (CLOSED)
**126 St. Marks Pl. (bet. 1ˢᵗ & A)**
**475-4145**

## ANTARCTICA
**287 Hudson St. (bet. Spring & Dominick Sts.)**
**352-1666**

*ALL MAJOR CREDIT CARDS*

Welcome to the Upper East Side on the outskirts of SoHo. Open for about two years, Antarctica attracts a young collegiate crowd who work in the neighborhood. This large space houses a lengthy wooden bar, church pews, tables and a Yates poem hanging on the wall. Antarctica is your basic run- of-the-mill bar with a pool table, cheap drinks and a jukebox playing everything from Neil Diamond to Radiohead to your grade school fave, "School House Rock." Open daily from 5pm – 4am, Monday and Wednesday nights offer a $2 discount on pitchers. The coolest event occurring here is the nightly "Name Game." If your name is written above the bar, then you drink free from 5pm-11pm.You might want to call ahead to check that it's your name night before you make the long trek to Antarctica.

## AQUAGRILL
**210 Spring Street (At 6th Ave.)**
**274-0505**

*ALL MAJOR CREDIT CARDS*

Relax in the lovely underwater-like atmosphere while sipping a glass of wine. The bar area is rather tiny with a few stools and one couch in the front alcove. If you're one of the lucky few to grab a spot early on, do yourself a favor and indulge in a sampling from the raw bar. Aquagrill offers over a dozen varieties of oysters from across the United States that are absolutely sublime. If you have the opportunity to be seated on the outside patio, you'll be able to do some wonderful people watching from the comfort of this prime piece of real estate. Aquagrill is a real find for seafood lovers because its reasonably priced menu affords one the luxury of fine dining without the hefty tab.

## AQUAVIT
**13 W. 54th St. (bet. 5th & 6th Aves.)**
**307-7311**

*ALL MAJOR CREDIT CARDS*

After 12 years, this super-attractive, Euro classic still has swank. Great for a first date, (you'll impress her/him *and* get them drunk), Aquavit is a *little* romantic and a *lot* civilized. Bring your boss, your clients—hell, bring your parents! This Scandinavian standard has a pedigree all its own. Situated in the former townhouse of Nelson Rockefeller (he died upstairs...oops), it has great lighting and a wonderful, cozy, elegant charm. The bar/café is on the main floor and serious dining is downstairs along with a cavernous, 7-story atrium and a towering, remarkably quiet wall of water and stone that goes two floors underground. The real deal is the Aquavit menu: Scandinavian, mostly potato-based vodkas infused during the distillation process with everything from caraway seeds to gooseberries are deadly and delicious. All the best things are. You can order them in flights from the pleasant and professional bartender, Jack. They serve 10 bottled Aquavits and 14 homemade flavors. You could be boring and order beer or wine. Smoking is permitted (no cigars or pipes) and they serve food till 10:30 pm. The crowd is sophisticated and subdued, international, attractive and chilled-out.

## ARLENE GROCERY
**95 Stanton St.**
**(bet. Ludlow & Orchard Sts.)**
**358-1633**
*CASH ONLY*

Cheap and grungy, there is no better place to see loud bands such as Lesion and Bay of Pigs for free. Yep, there is never a cover charge and there is always a band. Housed in a space that was once a Spanish bodega, Arlene's is the quintessential dirty and cramped hole in the wall offering live music and cheap drinks. The crowd is young and determined by the type of band showcasing. Although there is no happy hour, the Butcher Bar, which is attached to Arlene's, offers one daily. Definitely a great addition to the downtown live music scene, A&R scouts frequent the place to find the next big thing to hit the music scene. Hours: 6 pm – 4 am daily.

## ART BAR
**52 8th Ave. (bet. Jane & Horatio Sts.)**
**727-0244**

*ALL MAJOR CREDIT CARDS*

This longstanding neighborhood bar has attracted a young and cute ad-exec crowd throughout the years. A large mural in the front room hangs above a noisy wall of banquettes that are chock-full of young singles looking for love in the West Village. The larger back lounge offers a more calm and sexy scene. With plush couches and candle-lit tables, you might have to sell your soul to get a seat. Those seatless ones hover like hawks waiting to attack a free spot on a couch. The cushy lounge is always well stocked with smoking artist wannabe's drinking Cosmo's amidst brick and a gas fireplace. Although the place is always packed, it's worth stopping by to take advantage of their 2 for 1 happy hour, daily from 4 pm – 7 pm.

## ARTHUR'S TAVERN
**57 Grove St. (bet. 7th Ave. & Bleecker St.)**
**675-6879**

*CASH ONLY*

Ever walk into a place and feel like a haystack in a pile of needles? Try poking your head into this place for a minute or two and you'll see what we mean. Arthur's Tavern caters to an older theatre type so don't be surprised to see men in their 50's still sporting bell-bottoms and sheepskin coats. The corny backround music and off-the-wall décor might make you think twice about poking your head in this place for a second time. Bring cash; credit cards are not accepted.

## ASIA DE CUBA
**237 Madison Ave. (bet. 37th & 38th Sts.)**
**726-7755**

*ALL MAJOR CREDIT CARDS*

Ian Schrager, the official king of swank, knows that the right combination of fabric, texture and lighting is all it takes to get the new money and celeb crowd chucking money at him by the fistfull. This once trend of all trends, now "been there done that" money vacuum, is a hip little China-meets-the-Caribbean paradise that caters primarily to people who like to be in the center of the action. Attracting a wealthy clientele with about as much soul as a stale twinkey, one can sit at long communal tables drinking overpriced Mai Tai's while eavesdropping on conversations about $3000 backpacking trips throughout the Himalayas. Nonetheless, the spectacular décor equipped with a huge indoor water-fall makes for a romantic drink. It's also a perfect spot for ass-kissing client dinners. Hours: Sun – Wed 12:30pm-11pm, Thurs-Sat, 5:30pm- 12am.

**ASTOR**
**316 Bowery (At Bleecker St.)**
**253-8644**

*ALL MAJOR CREDIT CARDS*

Reminiscent of the bar in the movie Casablanca, this Moroccan-inspired lounge is a comfortable and swanky little spot to bring a date for a quick drink. Adorned with lovely tiles and ancient leather French club chairs from the '30s, the crowd here tends to be attractive, painfully in search of a personality, and in their thirties. The space is beautiful but seems to lack a soul. Don't be surprised if during the week you spot tumbleweed blowing across the floors — the staff to patron ratio is 2 to 1. While the bar is open till 4 am on the weekends, the dinner, brunch and bar hours vary during the week.

**AU BAR**
**41 E. 58th St.**
**(bet. Madison & Park Aves.)**
**308-9455**

*ALL MAJOR CREDIT CARDS*

Oh Lord won't you buy me a Mercedes Benz...so I can get into the Au Bar! One part supper club, one part disco, 50 parts Euro-Trash; the Au Bar is one of the first mega lounges to hit the New York scene. The décor is striking and tasteful, with gothic candelabras, comfortable couches, beautiful paintings, and of course, beautiful people. The vibe however remains somewhat stuck in the late 1980s: One out of every two men drive a Porsche and the Euro-Trash factor is off the Richter scale. Don't come unless you are well travelled, sporting a pair of Valentino shoes, and plan to blow a lot of cash. A hefty cover charge of $25 on Sat. night keeps the riffraff away from this very upscale meat market.

**AUBETTE**
**119 E. 27th St.**
**(bet. Lex. & Park Aves.)**
**686-5500**

*ALL MAJOR CREDIT CARDS*

This dual personality bar takes a little getting used to. Furnished in all leather, Aubette is draped in a post-French modern industrial look. In the swanky front section you'll find a veritable Euro-posing double-kiss extravaganza rife with bridge and tunnel sales assistants drinking on daddy's dime. If you continue past this scene you'll find the generally unpopulated club-chaired cigar room and heave a sigh of relief. With an oak bar, cozy tables and a fireplace, it's somewhat of an oasis. The appetizers suffice as meals and are served till closing at 4am. Aubette has an impressive drink selection with a knowledgeable bartender to educate you on their 20 wines by the glass, 10 champagnes and wide selection of Scotch. If you're looking for the signature drink, try the Apple Martini which tastes like a Jolly Rancher. Aubette's logo reads: "We provide the toys to pleasure yourself." Huh?

## AUCTION HOUSE
**300 E. 89th St. (bet. 1st & 2nd Aves.)**
**427- 4458**

*ALL MAJOR CREDIT CARDS*

Despite a somewhat crappy location, the Auction House is going on its sixth glorious year. With a minimal dress code and reasonably priced drinks, the two rooms glow with warm flickering candlelight, fresh flowers and old-fashioned chandeliers. With the hint of cigar smoke in the air, the exposed brick, quiet music and oriental rugs attract a chic and unpretentious Upper East Side group of 25-year-olds and over only! (They check ID to keep the *really* young ones out.) The only eyesore is the televisions showing extreme sports events. Other than that, this bar is small, charming and personal. In order to keep the frat riffraff away, a happy hour is not offered.

## AUSTRALIA
**1733 1st Ave. (At 90th St.)**
**876-0203**

*ALL MAJOR CREDIT CARDS*

Although not exactly the place you'd find Crocodile Dundee, Elle MacPherson or the crew from "Men at Work" hanging out, Australia is one of the better dives in the city. With egg carton ceilings, low lighting, candles and two pool tables, the vibe is cool and laid back. The back of the bar offers two quiet and comfortable lounge areas where mature twenty-somethings pile atop plenty of over-stuffed couches and sing along with the jukebox to the likes of "Brick House" and "Let's Get it On." Framed photographs of naked scuba divers and a picture of a young Mel Gibson are the bar's only homage to down under. Open daily until 4 am, this is a great place to chill out on the Upper East Side, mate.

## AUTOMATIC SLIMS
**733 Washington St. (At Bank St.)**
**645-8660**

*VISA/MASTERCARD*

This tiny dive bar in the West Village is cheap, loud and caters to a weekend monsoon of baseball cap and khaki pants clad frat buffoons. The male dominated post-college crowd that gathers here likes to drink as they did back in the day. Small piles of puke that line the sidewalk out front are evidence that some Phi Delta Theta's can't hold their liquor like they used to. During the week the bar is a whole different world and serves as a good place for some finger food and catching up over a beer. The music is usually decent as are the bartenders.

## AVENUE B SOCIAL LOUNGE (CLOSED)
**99 Ave. B (6th/7th St.)**
**674-7957**

## B BAR (AKA BOWERY BAR)
**358 Bowery (At 4th St.)**
**475-2220**

*ALL MAJOR CREDIT CARDS*

A revival of sorts seems to be taking place at the "B" Bar. Notorious for drawing models, moguls, and pretentious assholes from all over the world, this place serves as a catwalk for the young and the hip. Although it's the bar that people love to hate, the B-bar has managed to keep afloat longer than most celebrity hangouts. Despite how many positive or negative things you've heard, this venue is large, comfortable, expensive and still draws a very fabulous and good-looking crowd. The best thing about B-bar is the large outdoor space (formerly a Gulf gas station) where people flock like lemmings in the springtime for after work drinks in the sun. Beware of the pilgrimages of Jersey folk who ruin the place on the weekend. Cocktails are not cheap, the actor/bartenders are not very accommodating, and the bouncers are in need of velvet rope strangulation. But despite all the hurdles, once you're in you'll probably have a great time. If nothing else, it's great for people watching. The B Bar hosts Beige on Tuesday nights. Filled with gay studs all sporting the same beautiful look, come here to rub elbows with fashion people, movie stars, pop stars and drag queens. What's the dress code? Just don't wear cargo pants...you'll see.

## BABY JUPITER
**170 Orchard St. (At Stanton St.)**
**982-BABY**

*VISA/MASTERCARD*

This wacky little bar/restaurant/performance space is somewhat of an eyesore from the outside. Variety seems to be the theme here where the vibe changes from night to night based on the creative performances that take place in the back room. Working bohemians and in-the-know arty yuppies come here to chow down on reasonably priced Cajun delights while a DJ spins trip-hop and funky dance tunes. It's hard to get a pulse on this place but it's worth stopping into.

## BACK FENCE
**155 Bleecker St. (At Thompson St.)**
**475-9221**

*ALL MAJOR CREDIT CARDS*

This rock and roll stomping ground has rhythm with a friendly demeanor. Open for 35 years, this tiny corner bar rocks the night away daily until 4am. For a small cover charge, the transient music-loving crowd can enjoy live music with reasonably priced drinks: $3.75 for a Bud, $4.25 for cider and $4.50 for cocktails. Listen to Bruce Springsteen on the jukebox while the hippie-chick patron next to you recounts the days when Bleecker Street was taken over by free love, spirituality and rocking music, man!

**BAGATELLE**
**12 St. Mark's Pl. (bet. 2nd & 3rd Aves.)**
**674-1011**

***ALL MAJOR CREDIT CARDS***

If you see an obviously lost yuppie wandering around St. Marks, send them straight to Bagatelle. Only opened for 6 months, Bagatelle's aim is to draw in the yuppies. (There goes the neighborhood.) This vast restaurant /bar hosts different live musical acts as well as a DJ at night. Some of the live entertainment includes jazz bands, comedy nights, reggae nights on Fridays and a soon-to-be '80s night. Entertain yourself with a couple of video games and a jukebox offering tunes from Neil Young to Pat Benetar or mingle with celebs such as the Duchess of York and Meg Ryan. With no happy hour, Bagatelle is open daily from 12pm - 4am. With 16 beers on tap, drinks are relatively inexpensive. The décor is beautiful, with glossed wood floors, two bars, circling ceiling fans and mood-enhancing red lighting. Although it's a nice space, Bagatelle's clientele seems out of place amongst the typical St. Mark's Place crew of punks, metal heads and true rock 'n' rollers.

**BAGGOT INN**
**82 W. 3rd St.**
**(bet. Thompson & Sullivan Sts.)**
**477-0622**

***ALL MAJOR CREDIT CARDS***

If you are waiting around for the show at the Boston Comedy Club upstairs, this is a good place to get a pint. The Baggot Inn hosts a crowd of locals with a couple of tourists thrown into the mix. Roomy and dark with a nice stage space and plenty of seating, expect to pay a $5 cover for the live local bands that are featured nightly.

## BAHI
**274 3rd Ave. (bet. 21st & 22nd Sts.)**
**254-5466**

*ALL MAJOR CREDIT CARDS*

A welcome addition to the otherwise drab strip of 3rd Avenue, Bahi attracts a hip East Side crowd. The surprisingly large bar offers a young, friendly and lounge-like atmosphere along with expertly mixed drinks. Guest bartender nights spice things up a bit for the after work crowds that congregate here. You can choose from a beanbag room, a blue room, and a red room, depending on your mood. If you ever find yourself on a date that needs a quick pick-me-up, an intimate drink in the Beanbag Room will certainly jumpstart some activity.

## BAILEY'S CORNER (CLOSED)
**1607 York Ave. (At 85th St.)**

## BAKTUN
**418 W.14th**
**(bet. 9th Ave. & Washington St.)**
**206-1590**

*ALL MAJOR CREDIT CARDS*

Located right next to Cooler, this lounge/club is a nice addition to the rat infested streets of the meat-packing district. The long thin space is filled with sleek, modern couches, a long metal bar and a large projection TV displaying photographs and new age films. It feels like a very raw loft that was quickly turned into a bar. The crowd is young, hip and multicultural. A DJ spins hip-hop and acid jazz to a crowd that is eager to bust some moves. (Although dancing, thanks to Rudy G., is officially not allowed.) Didn't he see "Footloose"? This is a nice change from the somewhat tame and conservative West Village. On weekends there may be a cover charge.

## BALTHAZAR
**80 Spring St. (bet. B'way & Crosby St.)**
**965-1414**

### ALL MAJOR CREDIT CARDS

A beautiful and bright large space, Balthazar bar and restaurant can be intimidating from the outside with its frosted glass windows and stretch limos parked out front. A reproduction of a French bistro, the conscientious design deserves an A+ as well as a few gold stars. The bar area is a place to "see and be seen" and harbors a collection of well coifed men and women on the prowl. An impressive 160 wines line the bar to amplify the European ambiance. Now on its third year, the popularity is starting to die down making it easier to get a reservation these days. Nonetheless, Balthazar is one of the top scenes in the city and continues to attract the young and the well dressed by the truckload. It may be a hangout for the Michael Jordan's of the world, but it's not exactly the place to sport your Adidas unless, of course, your Adidas were made by Prada.

## THE BANK
**225 E. Houston St. (At Essex St.)**
**505-5033**

### CASH ONLY

Was that Marilyn Manson or are we on another Jenny Jones Gothic makeover show? The Goth scene is back in full force at The Bank on Friday and Saturday nights. For those of you who want to relive the '80s, shell out the $12 cover and enter this labyrinth of decadence. Inside you'll find heavily lipsticked young gothic kids hanging out with older Limelight graduates. Dance in the shadows of dry ice smoke on the main dance floor to Peter Murphy, Prodigy and Tones on Tail or lounge at the upstairs bar where girls in wedding dresses and black make-up pose with boys in latex and dog collars. Travel to the back room onto the tiny dance floor into a sea of '80s freaks. The energy at The Bank is remarkable, the style is dark and creative and the hair dye is plenty. When was the last time you actually danced in public to Madness, Softcell or Cindy Lauper? Certain nights host an array of bands, so call ahead for the line-up.

**THE BANK CAFÉ**
**431 3rd Ave. (At 30th St.)**
**725-5999**

*ALL MAJOR CREDIT CARDS*

Looking for an eclectic crowd in an unusual setting and a chance to meet someone who actually has something intelligent to say? Sorry, you've stumbled across the wrong place. This is what you'd call one of the many generic frat pubs in Murray Hill. This spacious two-room bar/café supplies your typical bar food and drinks for a relatively decent price. While the jukebox spits out Bob Marley and '70s disco, big drunken boys clad in Gap and Eddie Bauer watch sports on television while shooting pool. Its saving grace? The Victorian furniture and art deco sconces make it a bit more upscale than the other Irish pubs in the area.

**BAR D'O**
**29 Bedford St. (At Downing St.)**
**627-1580**

*CASH ONLY*

This sexy, intimate lounge caters to a young and intellectual crowd who can be seen sipping cocktails through mini straws while lounging on pillow-style seating. While patrons discuss their latest angst-inspired film projects, soothing hip tunes ebb and flow throughout the candle and lava lamp lit cave. Famed for their transvestite shows and Billy

Holiday impressionist on Tuesday, Saturday and Sundays ($5 cover), Bar D'O offers great music, a good vibe, a good-looking crowd, and an all around fun time. Call ahead for show times.

## BAR 54
**701 B'way (bet. 53th & 54th St.)**
**247-0720**

*ALL MAJOR CREDIT CARD*

Hey kids, lost on your way back to Jersey? Stop in for a cold one at Bar 54, where you'll fit right in as long as you haven't updated your fashion statement since 1986. Guys in vests abound at this charm-less, brightly-lit midtown hang-out where their idea of comfort and class is an old box fan propped on a chair (read: air-conditioning). 18 beers on tap and sports on the 'boob tube' keep the 25-40-ish, very straight, mainstream, more-male-than-female crowd happy while an odd mix of predictable disco and bad '80s tunes drowns out all possibility of conversation. The weird thing is the "sort of okay" décor, with the attractive, upscale cherry wood paneling and recessed lighting, looks like the owners were trying to do something classy, realized halfway through they didn't get it, and gave up. It's all about t-shirts from suburbia at Bar 54, where one of the few redeeming qualities is the cool location right next to the Ed Sullivan Theater. Look out David Letterman.

## BAR 85
**504 W. 16th St. (At 10th Ave.)**
**645-2207**

*ALL MAJOR CREDIT CARD*

This nightclub/lounge located in West Chelsea delivers different DJ's nightly. On Wednesdays Deep House and Global Fusion groove you until 4 am. Fridays you can dance to classic underground with Guest DJ's and Saturday delivers with DJ Robe Lowe giving you classic Reggae, House, Salsa, and Meringue.  On Sunday they have the famous Buddha Bar, an amazing "Ladies Only" night. The clientele is a serious upscale crowd who love to dance, drink, and dress to kill.  (The dress code entails no jeans, no baggy clothes, and absolutely no sneakers.) Drinks range from $5-7. Cover is $20, but call ahead to get on the guest list.

### BAR 89
**89 Mercer St.**
**(bet. Spring & Broome Sts.)**
**274-0989**

*ALL MAJOR CREDIT CARDS*

Most will say the reason they flock to this lofty, futuristic bar in the heart of SoHo is because of the hip scene. Whatever! It's for the bathrooms! In fact, they're so cool that we're not going to spoil it...you'll have to check them out for yourself. The drinks are strong, the food is good and the space is spectacular with its high vaulted ceilings and sleek curving bar.  The youngish crowd ranges from Euro-poser's to Jerseyites to Wall Streeter's. A word of advice — keep your drink order simple.  The bartenders are a bit shaky on the complicated drinks.

### BAR 9
**807 9th Ave.  (Bet. 53rd & 54th Sts.)**
**339-9336**

*ALL MAJOR CREDIT CARDS*

Grandma?  Has anyone seen my grandma? She's got to be here somewhere,  maybe napping on one of the dozens of old sofas covered in that thin plastic spill-guard she loves so much.  Or maybe she's hidden behind one of the hundreds of odd light-fixtures, lava lamps, and other trinkets worthy of the flea markets she shops at.   Grandma? Are you in here? I can't see you, it's too dimly lit (despite the hundreds of light fixtures), too smoky, and too damn hot. Someone better get some air conditioning in here before my Grandma dies of heatstroke. Maybe she's alright, I mean, she does have two bars to grab a drink from, 6 beers on tap, and a decent bar menu from which to nourish her old bones. Wait...maybe she's in the bathroom getting laid—Grandma always did like the type of neighborhood frumpy guys and frizzy-haired girls this place is filled with. Grandma...you okay?

## BAR NONE
**98 3rd Ave. (bet. 12ᵗʰ & 13ᵗʰ Sts.)**
**777-6663**

*CASH ONLY*

This surprisingly huge space is home to frat boys, guidos, and bridge and tunnelers who are not afraid to scream the lyrics to "Louie, Louie" at the top of their lungs. The sports/frat bar feel is complete with a host of dartboards, pool tables and televisions. With an assortment of shot specials to accommodate even the most finicky of drinkers, this is a 21-year-old's wet dream! On the weekend there's a cover charge and what could pass as the cast from "Animal House" chugging beer by the truckload and hitting on everything that moves. Bouncers are very strict checking ID's so beware.

## BAR ON A
**170 Ave. A (bet. 10ᵗʰ & 11ᵗʰ Sts.)**
**353-8231**

*ALL MAJOR CREDIT CARDS*

This cozy and nondescript bar is easy to miss. Although certainly not a destination point, it's a good place to start the ball rolling, or wind down. Its décor is quietly upscale and dreamy with a relaxed atmosphere. The crowd — if there is one — is made up of mostly locals who seem to enjoy the fact that the place has yet to be run over and ruined by uptown slummers. Try the fried calamari and the house red wine.

**BAR SIX**
**502 6th Ave. (bet. 12th & 13th Sts.)**
**691-1363**

*ALL MAJOR CREDIT CARDS*

This popular swanky French bistro with its brassy bar, large golden-framed mirrors, and tiny tables looks like the twin sister of Lucky Strike in SoHo. A romantic spot, Bar Six serves a well-rounded menu along with a decent selection of wine available by the glass. The crowd is young, flamboyant, cigarette smoking and well dressed. By far one of the better places to dine and drink in this area. A great date spot and subtle pick up place as well.

**BARAZA**
**133 Ave. C (bet. 8th & 9th Sts.)**
**539-0811**

*CASH ONLY*

And you thought hanging out on Avenue B was as bad-ass as it gets. Baraza is the latest of the brave souls to set up shop along one of New York's most "non-fuzzy" strips of real estate, Avenue C. Inside, brick walls adorned with Barbie doll parts and a plate glass bar play host to neighborhood "trendoids" and a few curious in-the-knows from other parts of town. Homemade spiked punches are ladled out to patrons by cute bartenders sporting pop culture t-shirts. If you're in the hood, check out Baraza – a subtle artsy meat market tucked away in the heart of Alphabet City.

**BARCLAY'S BAR & GRILL**
**111 E. 48th St. (bet. Park & Lex. Aves.)**
**755-5900**

*ALL MAJOR CREDIT CARDS*

Unless you're staying at the Hotel Intercontinental, you have no reason to come here. Although, if you prefer bars located in hotel lobbies that serve expensive drinks to an older, conservative, married clientele, then you might be happy here. Even the hotel patrons agree that it's lame, as the bar is usually empty.

## BARFLY
**244 3rd Ave. (At 20th St.)**
**473-9660**

### ALL MAJOR CREDIT CARDS

This casual sports bar attracts the twenty to thirty something suburban preppie out for a night of sports and beer. Cheap drinks with an all-American menu of hamburgers, fries and wings help to keep the place packed on the weekends. There are seven TV monitors and a jukebox playing pop and classic rock. Men outnumber the ladies making it more of a place to pig out, drink a few beers and cheer for your favorite football team.

## BARMACY
**538 E.14th St. (bet. Ave. A & B)**
**228-2240**

### CASH ONLY

Barmacy can only mean one thing...annoying theme bar! Yes indeed, the "remedy" here is (yawn) alcohol and the decor, unless you're still in college, seems ridiculous. Some cute gimmicks like bartenders being dressed like nurses and beer served in beakers are novelties that will wear off sooner than you can say "get me the hell out of here!" In its defense, Barmacy actually has a lot of cool stuff to look at. Glass cases in the back are filled with 1950s medical remedies and old pharmaceutical items. There's lots of seating, making it a great place to come with a group. In the back there's a DJ who's sure to get your butt moving at some point during the evening to classics from the '50s through the '90s.

**BARRACUDA**
**275 W. 22nd St. (bet. 7th & 8th Aves.)**
**645-8613**

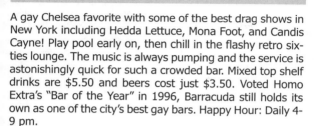

*CASH ONLY*

A gay Chelsea favorite with some of the best drag shows in New York including Hedda Lettuce, Mona Foot, and Candis Cayne! Play pool early on, then chill in the flashy retro sixties lounge. The music is always pumping and the service is astonishingly quick for such a crowded bar. Mixed top shelf drinks are $5.50 and beers cost just $3.50. Voted Homo Extra's "Bar of the Year" in 1996, Barracuda still holds its own as one of the city's best gay bars. Happy Hour: Daily 4-9 pm.

**BARRAMUNDI**
**147 Ludlow St.**
**(bet. Stanton & Rivington Sts.)**
**529-6900**

*CASH ONLY*

This dimly lit little number on the Ludlow strip is a perfect spot for prime chillin'. Though the bar itself is small, the music and the crowd is great. Groups of friends convene on metal patio furniture while the soothing sounds of acid jazz and heavy bass quell the 20-something singles crowd. While the Caesar's Palace columns and gas fireplace in the cozy back room are cheezy, the decor of the bar is like that of hanging out in a surreal underground cave. Note: there is a "door guy" and it does get crowded on the weekends so get there early. Try the Mundi-Martinis, they're really tasty. If you are looking for a solid spot that's also a great place to meet up, look no further.

**BARROW STREET ALE HOUSE**
**15 Barrow St.**
**(bet. W. 4th St. & 7th Ave. S.)**
**206-7302**

*VISA/MASTERCARD*

Are you fed up with dressing up to go sit on a velvet couch in some pretentious lounge? Do you need a place where you can do a back hand spring and no one will look twice? Come play keno and a game of pool in this dual level, pub-like hole in the wall. Just a few doors in from bustling Bleecker Street, you will be whisked away and made to feel like you are in the middle of the Blue Ridge Mountains. As the juke-box plays Jewel and Seal, patrons sit at checkered tables eating fresh hot pizza while drinking cheap beer. While you almost expect to see a hog go running through the joint, the bar owner and patrons are awfully friendly. You can hang out with the local yokels every day for happy hour and maybe you'll even get lucky and score a date with the Daisy Duke look-a-like serving the drinks behind the bar. Beware: weekends are a mob scene.

## BEACON HILL ALE HOUSE
**1471 1st Ave. (bet. 76th & 77th Sts.)**
**744-8992**

*ALL MAJOR CREDIT CARDS*

Open for 13 years, this neighborhood Irish pub is said to have the best bartenders in all of New York. A very diverse crowd listens to an Irish influenced jukebox while sitting at the cozy bar, or playing pool on the second floor. Attracting a mid-twenties crowd of yuppies, the bar is decorated with many large televisions, beer-brand mirrors and a black jack video game. There are eight beers on tap with 1/2 price drinks daily from 4-8 pm.

## BEAR BAR
**1770 2nd Ave. (bet. 92nd & 93rd Sts.)**
**987-7580**

*ALL MAJOR CREDIT CARDS*

If a prep school teacher went out on a Saturday night, came here, and got drunk, he would definitely run the risk of hooking up with one of his students. The bras hanging all over the place, as well as the Beavis and Butthead posters, pretty much spell out the story here on weekend nights. Teenyboppers and frat boys fresh out of college flock here for the likes of "bear juice" shots and funnel ready beer. The rest of the week finds this bar filled with adults in playland enjoying the likes of a whole festival of games including pool, darts, foosball, video games and basketball, as well as sporting events on big screens. There is picnic table style seating downstairs to accommodate all the people crowding in here for some of the best wings available on the Upper East Side.

## BEAUTY BAR
**231 E. 14th St. (bet. 2nd & 3rd Aves.)**
**539-1389**

*VISA/MASTERCARD*

Manicures at happy hour? Cool. This former beauty salon located on New York's breathtaking 14th street strip is 1960s to the core. The dark red lighting, old chandeliers and old fashioned steel hair dryers are no doubt interesting to look at, but make for a somewhat unsociable atmosphere. The music is very nondescript and dull but luckily the seating is so uncomfortable that it makes it difficult to fall asleep from boredom. This tourist trap hosts a very unique happy hour on Thursday and Friday nights from 5pm to 10pm when its 80-year-old original owner of the salon brings her talents to the bar by giving $7 manicures with a free drink. Her name is Flora and rumor has it that her manicures are favored by the drag queens from Lucky Chengs! A definite incentive for us women who like our manicures with a cold one.

## THE BEEKMAN
**15 Beekman St. (bet. Nassau & William Sts.)**
**732-7333**

*ALL MAJOR CREDIT CARDS*

A refreshing change from some of the other dingy, financial district bars, The Beekman has a friendly staff that serves worn-out traders and brokers their afternoon beer or shot.

The up-to-date jukebox sputters out tunes that make you forget the woes of the working man's drudgery. This strictly after work bar serves continental fare and the mostly male clientele seem to enjoy themselves.

**BEEKMAN BAR & BOOKS**
**889 1st Ave. (At 50th St.)**
**980-9314**

***ALL MAJOR CREDIT CARDS***

The midtown location of this bar is an upscale meeting place that offers premium liquors, wines, cocktails, caviar and cigars. The jazz music in the background, dim lighting, and book-lined walls politely whisper "swank." The few patrons present have a touch of silver in their hair and an air of conservative stuffiness. It's no wonder that jackets are required. Good pick for a client drink.

**BEER BAR AT CAFÉ CENTRO**
**200 Park Ave. (Met Life Building)**
**818-1333**

***ALL MAJOR CREDIT CARDS***

If for nothing else, at least come here to check out the tallest hamburger you have ever seen in your entire life. Located just down the street from Grand Central, the Beer Bar is a commuter pit stop that offers an extensive selection of foreign beers and a full bar. In the summer an outdoor beer garden emerges, offering a midtown equivalent to Wall Street's famous yuppie meat market, "Moran's." The crowd is young, fresh-faced and has money. Join their Beer Club and get a round of drinks for you and your friends on your birthday.

**BEER HALL**
**29 2nd Ave (bet. 1st and 2nd Sts.)**
**375-1449**

***ALL MAJOR CREDIT CARDS***

Happy hour is every hour at Beer Hall. The space is vast with high ceilings and more than enough room to grab a beer and relax without feeling confined or smoked out by nearby patrons. This very modern space with a touch of Mediterranean decor boasts the cheapest prices around. Specializing in beer (hence the name) a Rolling Rock goes for $2 while a glass of wine begins at $3. Open from 6:30pm to 4am, the crowd is very East Village and laid back making this cheap but pleasant bar a definite start to a long evening.

## BELGO
**415 Lafayette St.**
**(bet. 4th St. & Astor Pl.)**
**253-2828**

***ALL MAJOR CREDIT CARDS***

1999 will be known as the great Belgian invasion of New York. Waterloo, Markt and now Belgo, the newest on the fries and mussels train. This European chain restaurant/bar has a great beer selection, good food, and a very cool industrial space that resembles a SoHo art gallery more than a restaurant/bar. Don't expect to cuddle up with a date to the relaxing sound of Barry White—Belgo is about as warm and fuzzy as a Klondike Bar in January. The first floor consists of a small, crowded bar area filled with Euro-hipsters and yuppies waiting to descend the long ramp to the dining room. Here you'll find a cold and stark "monastery" filled with picnic-style tables and waiters dressed like monks. Try the fries, the mussels and of course one of the 105 delicious beers. Girls—bring a sweater!

## BELMONT LOUNGE
**117 E. 15th St.**
**(bet. Park Ave. & Irving Pl.)**
**533-0009**

***ALL MAJOR CREDIT CARDS***

Belmont Lounge provides a little slice of the East Village in Gramercy. This bar/lounge caters to a different crowd during the week than on the weekend. During the week you will find young preppy Wall Street geeks and a post-college crowd hanging out either by the front bar or in the large and spacious back lounge. On the weekend, the place is swarming with beautiful young women and a Gen-X crowd that has more money to spend than your typical East Villager. With a live DJ nightly, this lounge is open from 1pm to 4am and hosts a daily happy hour from 1pm to 7pm. The hip-hop and reggae beats spun by the DJ create high energy and a hip and funky atmosphere without the pressure to look cool. Mixed drinks are $6 and beers are $5.

## BEST IN NEW YORK
**393 Canal St. (At Thompson St.)**
**334-5490**

*ALL MAJOR CREDIT CARDS*

If first impressions are deceiving, this place takes the cake. Trying to guess what this establishment is from its sketchy blue neon lights, ambiguous name and Mr. T bouncers standing guard is tough. Is it a strip joint? Gangsta' dance hall? Fly by night tourist theme bar? Nope. It's a large Karaoke bar. Do you really need bouncers outside of a place where the only offensive thing to ever take place inside is someone out of sync to "Summer Lovin?" Private booths are available for $60 per hour and the crowd is middle-aged and cheezy.

## BIG SUR
**1406 3rd Ave. (At 80th St.)**
**472-5009**

*ALL MAJOR CREDIT CARDS*

Wall Street traders used to call Big Sur home. Now, trader wanna-be's flock to ogle the very tall blonde bombshell who tends bar here. Be warned gentlemen, she is married to the owner. They have recently revamped the menu in an attempt to attract a more genteel crowd, and have for the most part succeeded. Big Sur does continue to draw crowds, and the average age is climbing as the food improves. The outside café-like seating in the summer adds a pleasant dimension to this lounge, and provides people watching opportunities for even the most jaded spectator.

## BIG BAR
**75 E. 7th St. (bet. 1st and 2nd Aves.)**
**777-6969**

Big? Very funny. Just a touch larger than a walk-in closet, the "Big" Bar is a marvelous, although cramped place to grab a beer. Its red, black and silver decor is somewhat a la '80s disco, but if you can snag one of the worn booths, it's a decent spot to catch up with an old friend. The crowd is young, cliquey, catty, and stick to themselves, so don't expect any late night renditions of "99 bottles of beer on the wall" with your arm slung around a total stranger. Check the chalkboard outside for their daily "Angry Hour" specials.

## BILL'S GAY NINETIES
**57 E. 54th St. (bet. Mad. & Park Aves.)**
**355-0243**

*ALL MAJOR CREDIT CARDS*

Originally a speakeasy, this cozy bar offers live jazz Tuesdays through Saturdays at 9 and 11pm for a $15 cover. A grandmother-type will take your coat, relieving you of its burden as you relax and enjoy the tunes with your two-drink minimum. A good male/female ratio, made up mostly of dates and married couples, keeps the atmosphere sedate and conservative.

## BIRDLAND
**315 W. 44th St. (bet. 8th & 9th Aves.)**
**581-3080**

*ALL MAJOR CREDIT CARDS*

Step into this jazz oasis named after Charlie Parker, and

35

enjoy a dinner featuring such Cajun-inspired dishes as Linguine with Shrimp Creole and Jambalaya, or just come for the jazz. Shows start at 9pm and 11pm every night. The drinks range from $5-$8 and the cover charge ranges from $15 to $40 depending on the act. The mood is intimate and decidedly relaxed, with dim lights and tables surrounding a small stage. This bar feels like an upscale jazz dinner club from the '20s and caters to an older clientele. Send the folks here for a big night out.

## BISTRO LATINO
**1711 B'way (At 54th St.)**
**956-1000**

*ALL MAJOR CREDIT CARDS*

Come on everybody now and do the rumba, come on everybody now and shake your rump-a. A pleasant but plain bar/restaurant, Bistro Latino is perfect for all your Latin butt-shaking needs. A spacious dance floor beckons, but amateurs beware—this place is filled with those who know what it means to shake their asses, and they shake 'em well. However, the crowds are on the middle-aged side, so there's a lot of cellulite shaking too. On the weekends, live Latin and Cuban bands create the beat and the dance floor really heats up. Their specialty is Cuban food and drinks, but the décor is too ordinary to really make you feel like you're having a cultural experience. In fact, aside from the dancing, Bistro Latino is strictly middle-of-the-road.

## BITTER END
**147 Bleecker St. (At Thompson St.)**
**673-7030**

*ALL MAJOR CREDIT CARDS*

For you music lovers, the Bitter End is the place to be. Since 1961, this cozy spot has hosted the likes of Billy Joel, Neil Young and Joni Mitchell. With a $5 cover charge nightly, music lovers can hear diverse grooves ranging from blues to rock and roll to hip hop. A large stage set against a backdrop of exposed brick and theatrical lighting has tables and chairs within arm's reach. Photos of the talent who debuted here adorn the walls lending to the incredible history behind this fabulous bar. The Bitter End is open weeknights until 2am and 4am on the weekend. Although there is no happy hour, drinks are inexpensive: beer is $4.25 while mixed drinks range from $4.50 - $5.50.

## BLACK & WHITE
**86 East 10th St. (bet. 3rd & 4th Aves.)**
**253-0246**

*ALL MAJOR CREDIT CARDS*

The owners of Niagra and Spy combined to bring you their newest creation. Recently opened the end of July, this American bistro and bar promises to be one of the trendier spots in the East Village. With its laid back atmosphere and music that is not too loud, Black & White is a great place to bring a date. There is no annoying door policy as of yet, however, don't expect to just waltz in wearing jeans and a tee shirt. The owners obviously are trying to establish a certain status for their new spot.

## BLACKFINN'S
**994 2nd Ave. (bet. 52nd & 53rd Sts.)**
**355-6993**

*ALL MAJOR CREDIT CARDS*

Thar she blows! Okay, well maybe later after you get her drunk at this frat-infested post-college meat market scene in mid-town. Jam-packed on weekend nights with recent grads of the Gap and J. Crew variety, Blackfinn's is the perfect pick up spot for the early twenties crowd. A jukebox and several TV's offer entertainment, but these folks are more interested in scoping out potential breakfast partners for the morning.

**BLACK STAR**
**92 2nd Ave. (bet. 5<sup>th</sup> & 6<sup>th</sup> Sts.)**
**254-4747**

*ALL MAJOR CREDIT CARDS*

Somewhat personality-free, this little spot is still trying to figure out its crowd and will accept just about any type that walks through the door. Live music and reggae nights on Tuesday draw a fun, mixed crowd. As one patron noted, "this is the place where white women come to meet Rastafarian boyfriends." The décor is minimal and there is a pool table in the back. If you're looking to hook up, this might be a good place for you.

**BLARNEY COVE**
**510 E. 14<sup>th</sup> St. (bet. Aves. A & B)**
**473-7284**

*CASH ONLY*

You see the guy at the end of the bar drinking his scotch? He's been right there, in the same seat, for the past 35 years. Witness history at this friendly, neighborhood bar. Very brightly lit with wood paneling, revolving Budweiser signs and green and white striped wall paper, Blarney attracts a young crowd mixed with ex-Vegas performers and Italians from, you know, "the neighborhood." Open daily from 8am - 4am, drinks are incredibly cheap. With 6 beers on tap and assorted wine, shelf drinks are $3, Bud Light goes for $2.50 while a pint of Bass is $3.25. A great juke-box will take you "back to the day" with crooners such as Tony Bennet, Jonny Mathis and Dean Martin. Don't worry, some Doors, Talking Heads and Guns N' Roses are mixed in there too. Save your appetite for the Friday night free buffet from 2pm to 10pm. Great Italian food, straight from Brooklyn, will fill you up with ziti, ham, and lasagna...just like momma used to make. While the week attracts locals, the weekends tend to bring in the Barmacy goers who either can't get into Barmacy or just don't want to get in. The Blarney Cove is a great bar where you can sit, have a cheap drink and listen to never ending stories about "the good life."

## BLEECKER STREET BAR
**58 Bleecker St. (At Crosby St.)**
**334-0244**

*ALL MAJOR CREDIT CARDS*

Calling all Hootie fans! This bar must have slipped off the back of the truck on route to an upstate New York college town. It's a place for people who want to keep that old college feeling without making the trek to the Upper East Side. Equipped with two pool tables, dartboards, and a juke-box filled with pansy rock, it's the perfect venue for the non-artistic, sports-loving guy (lots of pool action to be had).

## BLIND TIGER ALE HOUSE
**518 Hudson St. (At 10th St.)**
**675-3848**

*ALL MAJOR CREDIT CARDS*

This popular West Village hangout offers a stupendous beer selection in a relaxed, no-frills environment. A mishmash of rocky tables and chairs and a few prime spots in the win-dow gives that neighborly, doesn't-it-feel-great-to-be-in-jeans-on-a-Saturday-night feel. If it's Apricot or Raspberry Ale that you're having a hankering for, then this is your place. And for all you beer lovers out there, if you drink 50 different beers (not in a row, don't worry) your name is placed on a plaque on the wall. Make your parents proud!

## BLUE ANGEL EXOTIC CABARET (CLOSED)
**99 Stanton St. (Ludlow Street)**

## BLUE AND GOLD
**74 E. 7ᵗʰ St. (bet. 1ˢᵗ & 2ⁿᵈ Aves.)**
**473-8918**

*CASH ONLY*

One of the finest local dive bars in the East Village, Blue and Gold attracts an array of punks, Village townies, and Indie rockers. It really picks up on the weekends where everyone rocks out to a jukebox that includes Cyndi Lauper, Frankie Vallie, Johnny Cash, and Curtis Mayfield. "Rolling Stone" dubbed it the "best indie-rock juke box in the world," and they're probably right. The beer is cheap, from $2.50 domestics to $4 cans of Boddingtons and Guinness. The liquor is poured with bottle-top ounce counters, so don't expect a drink with a heavy hand. Watch out for alternative-types making out in the side booths. The back pool table can get a little crowded, but who cares! Sit back, have a drink...have many drinks.

## BLUE NOTE
**131 West 3rd St. (bet. 6th Ave. & MacDougal St.)**
**475-8592**

*ALL MAJOR CREDIT CARDS*

Blue Note is without a doubt New York's primary jazz institution. You'll only find household names like B.B. King do sets here, making it a very pricey tourist trap. The gift shop does nothing but subtract from the whole feel of the place and make you feel like you're in Planet Hollywood or something. Saturday and Sunday they offer a jazz brunch, but the food is never as delightful as the music.

## BLUE WATER GRILL
**31 Union Square West (At 16th St.)**
**675-9500**

*ALL MAJOR CREDIT CARDS*

Open since 1996, this converted bank offers a classy, old money feel. Amid marble columns and towering bouquets of fresh flowers, you'll need your elbows to set some personal space for yourself at the bar where many are waiting for a dinner table. If you sealed the deal that day and you want to relax, head downstairs to the lounge which is surprisingly empty. Later in the evening you might be treated to the cool sounds of a live jazz combo. While you're there, try the oysters from one of the most exhaustive raw bars in the city.

## BMW
**199 7th Ave. (bet. 21st & 22nd Sts.)**
**229-1807**

**ALL MAJOR CREDIT CARDS**

No, it's not the car's initials, it actually stands for beer, music, wine. This intimate hole in the wall features live music and/or poetry readings every night of the week in a setting as comfortable as your studio apartment. As you sit back and relax with a Sunset Red listening to the sounds of free jazz, you might wish that you could stay here all night. And what luck, you can! BMW is open 24 hours, so if you're looking for that beatnik home away from home, this might just be the place.

## BOB
**235 Eldridge St.**
**(bet. E. Houston & Stanton Sts.)**
**777-0588**

**CASH ONLY**

This Lilliputian-sized gallery/club plays a mix of live jazz and a DJ'd fusion of Latin, reggae and house music. Find a space to shake your booty among the sweaty college students busting their moves. The club gets packed on Friday and Saturday nights, so expect to wait at the door for a while and pay a small cover. The doormen are friendly and the bar offers happy hour every day from 7pm to 10pm. This is an excellent alternative should you get rejected from the Sapphire Lounge down the street.

## BOCA CHICA
**13 1st Ave. (At. 1st St.)**
**473-0108**

**ALL MAJOR CREDIT CARDS**

If you're looking for excellent Latin/Caribbean food, Boca Chica is sure to please. The funky leopard print seating and thick frosty pina coladas make this a great place for a group dinner. The bar itself, if you can score a seat, is not a bad place to suck down a few with a friend, although the real draw here is the complete package meal.

## BOILER ROOM
**86 E. 4th St. (bet. 1st & 2nd Aves.)**
**254-7536**

*CASH ONLY*

The standard of the East Village gay bar scene, Boiler Room has declined from hot new thing, to old, why-are-they-playing-Fleetwood Mac-again bar. Today, it's enjoying quite a renaissance, thanks in no small part to a revamped and fantastic rock-heavy jukebox. The large space with black walls and a central pool table is dimly lit and cozy. Customers sit at the bar, lounge on the back sofa trio, parlay in the side lounge area, play pinball, shoot pool or just stand around. The hip, relaxed and relatively attitude-free crowd make it comfortable. Monday nights feature $1 mugs and weekends feature sardine-impersonating crowds.

## BOND ST. LOUNGE
**6 Bond St. (bet. B'way & Lafayette)**
**777-2500**

*ALL MAJOR CREDIT CARDS*

What could have been a cool upscale lounge, has very quickly evolved into another downtown "Glam" scene. If you plan to eat here, keep in mind that your reservation time will be pushed back by at least a half hour. The Japanese-inspired food is stylish, pricey and excellent. The lounge downstairs is filled with shallow, beautiful people loving themselves. There's a door guy making sure that only the genetically or surgically perfect are allowed in. Although, the venue is quite pleasing to the eyes, the love myself attitude leaves something to be desired. Note: If you eat here, that doesn't necessarily mean they will let you drink in the lounge. Even if it's not crowded.

## BOOMERS SPORTS CLUB
**349 Amsterdam Ave.
(bet. 76th & 77th Sts.)
362-5400**

*CASH ONLY*

This top-notch sports bar is one of the best in the city. You can barely shift your eye an inch without seeing a gigantic TV screen of some sort. In fact, there are so many here it's surprising that people don't leave the place with full-fledged radiation-induced tumors. The long narrow space has a good mix of men and women ranging in age from late 20s to 30s and fast and friendly bartenders. If you're looking for a great place to watch the game on the Upper West Side, this is it!

## BOOTS AND SADDLE
**76 Christopher St.
(bet. 7th Ave. & Bleecker St.)
929-9684**

*CASH ONLY*

This popular leather bar is one of the only places you'll find a drag queen sipping Budweiser on the rocks. The West meets gay New York at this venerable Christopher Street landmark where an awesome jukebox, friendly staff, 2 for1 drinks and a happy hour Monday through Friday from 3-9 pm attracts locals and tourists alike.

## BOTANICA
**47 Houston St. (bet. Mott & Mulberry)
343-7252**

*CASH ONLY*

Formerly the home of the Knitting Factory, Botanica opened its unlabeled doors in 1995. Known to many simply as "Bar" (the only sign in its window), Botanica is a dimly lit and inviting neighborhood hangout noted for its comfortable back room with couches. Stop in for a quick drink, or if the DJ is matching your vibe, settle in for the night.

Claustrophobics take note: On weekends it's *really* packed!

## BOTTINO
**246 10th Ave. (bet. 24th & 25th Sts.)**
**206-6766**

*ALL MAJOR CREDIT CARDS*

This Chelsea hot spot has become a favorite among the newly formed gallery scene. The interior has a 1960s flair with a beautiful garden in the rear and a popular lounge area in the front. The crowd is cool, good looking and super trendy. Bottino's food, like its décor, shouldn't be overlooked. Not only is it one of the only places in the hood to get great Italian, but it's also reasonably priced. The bartenders are friendly, attentive and mix a mean drink. (Pretty unusual for such a trendy bar.) This is a great date spot and a convenient place to meet after a gallery opening. Shecky *definitely* approves.

## BOTTOM LINE
**15 W. 4th St. (At Mercer St.)**
**228-6300**

*CASH ONLY*

Providing the village with bluegrass, country, folk, and rock music for years is very impressive. Of all the venues in lower Manhattan, Bottom Line has one of the best sound systems. The cabaret setting provides an intimate experience between the listener and the performer which doesn't exist in most other places. True, the cover charge is never cheap, usually $15-$25, but you get you money's worth and a table. Casual dining is offered at all times and the doors open at 6pm. Call ahead or drop by for a schedule of upcoming performers up to one month in advance.

**BOUSCHE BAR**
**540 E. 5th St. (bet. Aves. A & B)**
**No Phone**

This cozy bar attracts an older and artistic neighborhood crowd. As big as your friend's East Village living room, the exposed brick, dark lighting and quiet music create a safe haven away from the neighboring trendy bars. The super friendly and warm bartenders shout out "hello!" when you walk into the bar while pouring their specialty drink, the "Flim Flam." It's a great place to have a drink and a cigarette while reading your favorite novel.

**BOWLMOR LANES**
**110 University Place.**
**(bet. 12th & 13th Sts.)**
**255-8188**

*ALL MAJOR CREDIT CARDS*

Recent renovations have transformed this bowling alley into a club-like atmosphere, making it a fun alternative to going to your usual bar. Monday nights—$12 bowl till you drop night—packs the place with "too-cool-for-the-front-seat-of-the-bus" twentysomethings who strut their stuff in bell bottoms, baby tees and platform bowling shoes. When the games begin, the lights are dimmed and everyone and everything glows under the black light. Say goodbye to archaic score keeping, Bowlmor has embraced the millennium with a high tech computerized system! The DJ spinning everything from disco to show tunes and a full bar make the Bowlmor experience complete. One word of advice, get there before 9 pm on Mondays to avoid the line. It's a guaranteed good time for all!

**BOXERS**
**190 W. 4th St. (bet. 6th & 7th Aves.)**
**1485 2nd Ave. (bet. 77th & 78th Sts.)**
**633-BARK**

*ALL MAJOR CREDIT CARDS*

This friendly neighborhood bar/restaurant is a good spot to drink pitchers of beer with good homemade food. On the weekends, the bar tends to get mobbed with a young, male-dominated scene **from the towns of "up" and "outta."** Nonetheless the vibe is good, the people are cheery and it is one of the better venues in the area. Summertime outdoor seating offers spectacular people-watching during brunch.

### BRADY'S BAR
**1583 2nd Ave. (At 82nd St.)**
**650-0567**

Although most people come here to drink beer and shoot a few rounds of pool, the serious dart player knows that Brady's dart league is one of the best in New York. With the high ratio of Irish pubs in the city it's no surprise that there are several "Brady's" out there, and like most of them, this one is a typical pub. This bar attracts the sports-loving crowd who are mostly in their mid- to late twenties along with several cigar smoking, port swilling older gentlemen.

### BRANDY'S PIANO BAR
**235 E. 84th St. (bet. 2ⁿᵈ & 3ʳᵈ Aves.)**
**650-1944**

***CASH ONLY***

Hidden away on a side street in the most unlikely of places, Brandy's is one of the Upper East Side's best kept secrets. Run by the owners of Duplex and Eighty Eight's, this intimate spot showcases live talent every night of the week and has been for over 30 years. Singing bartenders and waitresses address the needs of an unbelievably eclectic clientele ranging from the gay crowd at the bar to couples and groups of yuppies at the tables near the piano. This extremely friendly and warm bar invites its patrons to participate and sing along to show tunes and old classics performed by the talented professionals. This is definitely a great spot to end an evening, especially with a date.

## BRAQUE
**775 Washington St. (At W. 12ᵗʰ St.)**
**255-0709**

### ALL MAJOR CREDIT CARDS

When is doubt, convert a garage into a bar. Well, at least in the West Village you do. Braque is one of the "converted" with a makeshift marble bar and cocktails available until the "party is over." This upscale restaurant/cocktail lounge is home to Manhattan's artists and models and their devoted entourage. Appetizers ($5-15) and entrees ($9-15), are served from 5:30 till 11:00 pm. Food usually isn't the motivation for coming here but the Prosciutto, Melon and Fig Plate ($9) with a glass of Veuve Cliquot ($11) is highly recommended and worth the trip to an otherwise less traversed part of the city. If you're looking for a more raucous evening, visit its fun neighbor, "Tortilla Flats."

## THE BREAK
**232 8th Ave. (At 22nd St.)**
**627-0072**

### CASH ONLY

This gay bar is well known for its non-stop drink specials which change nightly and a  daily 2-4-1 happy hour from 4 pm to 8 pm.  If you're gay, love gym queens and drink more than you know you should, come here.  Not only do they offer a liquid brunch on Saturday and Sunday ($2 Bloody Mary's, Mimosas, and Screwdrivers from 2-6 pm), during the week it's $4 martinis on Tuesdays, $3 Buds on Wednesdays, $1 Margaritas on Thursdays, and $3 Rolling Rocks on Fridays. Phew! A cruising neighborhood/bridge and tunnel crowd hangs by the pool table, watches videos and lounges in the back yard. Drink up boys!

## BREW'S
**156 E. 34<sup>th</sup> St. (bet. Lex. & 3<sup>rd</sup> Aves.)**
**889-3369**

### *ALL MAJOR CREDIT CARDS*

There really is no reason to come to Murray Hill unless of course you're going to Brew's. On a nondescript street located next to a movie theater, you'll find what looks like a pub that's been there for years...and it has. This inexpensive, family-owned tavern draws a crowd of folks in their 30s and 40s, many of whom are retired police officers and detectives. With its cozy decor and friendly staff, Brew's exudes history. On a blustery January day there's nothing better that popping into this neighborhood pub for a beer and a burger. A party room upstairs is also ideal for small gatherings.

## BREWSKY'S
**41 E. 7th St. (bet. 2<sup>nd</sup> & 3rd Aves.)**
**420-0671**

### *CASH ONLY*

Open since 1948, this cheezy, although popular East Village institution is a beer lover's dream. With a selection of 600 bottled "brewsky's," even Norm Peterson from "Cheers" would keel over before sampling all of them. The floors are covered with sawdust and the walls are plastered with pictures of celebrities who have stepped in for a drink. This is a pub, plain and simple, and the crowd is as varied as the beer menu. If you're looking to impress your date, there's a beer for a mere $4000. Thanks, I'll just have a Heineken.

## THE BRIDGE
**309 E. 60th Street (bet. 1<sup>st</sup> & 2<sup>nd</sup> Aves.)**
**223-9104**

### *CASH ONLY*

Disguised as an unsuspecting local watering hole next door to Scores, a frat boy probably wouldn't realize where he was at first. Various locals sip on $3 domestic beers, and $6 rum and cokes. It never gets too busy, and everyone is fairly nondescript. Even if you miss the hard body Herb Ritts poster, you will eventually notice the video tape of rippling men posing on the TV above the bar. Although seedy, the crowd is a mix of friendly gay locals, not in the mood for picking up. It stays open till 4am on most nights, and hosts monthly events and barbecues which fill up the large outdoor garden. The music varies between Blondie and VH1. If you have $10, you should be able to drink all night.

## BRITISH OPEN
**320 E. 59th St.(bet. 1st & 2nd Aves.)**
**355-8467**

### ALL MAJOR CREDIT CARDS

Upon entering, give yourself a minute to adjust to the blue lighting before you turn right back around to head elsewhere. If you're a corporate male in your late 50s who enjoys a stuffy atmosphere to down an after-work cocktail, look no further. Opened in the early 90s, the British Open's golf décor stays true to its name.

## BROADWAY LOUNGE (IN THE MARRIOTT MARQUIS HOTEL)
**1534 B'way (bet. 45th & 46th Sts.)**
**398-1900**

### ALL MAJOR CREDIT CARDS

Calling all tourists! Located on the 8th floor of the Marriott Marquis Hotel, the Broadway Lounge would normally be considered a typical tacky hotel bar if it wasn't for its crowned feature — it rotates. What's more fun than sipping pricey cocktails overlooking the lights of Times Square? Well, if you're from out of town, nothing. There's free jazz in the afternoon and a piano player at night. Locals, we suggest doing a few quick shots, snagging a comfortable chair out in the lobby, and watching the glass elevators shuttle wide-eyed and fanny-packed hotel guests to their rooms.

## BROTHER JIMMY'S BAIT SHACK
**1644 3rd Ave. (At. 92nd St.), 426-2020**
**1461 1st Ave. (At 76th St.), 288-0999**
**428 Amsterdam Ave. (bet. 80th & 81st St.),**
**501-7515**
*ALL MAJOR CREDIT CARDS*

This is where "Porky's" and the Upper East Side become one. With a neon sign flashing "eat meat," vegetarians should stay far away from this small, but comfortable party pit that smells like barbecued ribs. Decorated with chili pepper lights and sports posters, this place is for the fun at heart and could have the best drink deals around. A Bud Light is $3.50, while a Jack and Coke is $4.50. Every Saturday, Brother Jimmy's sucks in the crowd with its college hoops theme, 10 cent wings and $1 drafts. Thursday night is ladies night with free wine, liquor, and beer. And get ready for the happy hour: 50 cent oysters, $1 drafts and $2 cocktails from 5pm-8pm daily! The wait staff is super friendly and as wacky as the decor. Personality and energy is the name of the game so prepare to have fun!

## BROWNIES
**169 Ave. A (bet. 10th & 11th Sts.)**
**420-8392**

*ALL MAJOR CREDIT CARDS*

One of the few places to see good live alternative bands, cheap. This small open space with its no-frills bar is always crowded with a young audience that's not squeamish about being pressed up against a sweaty stranger. If you're looking for a cleaner alternative to CBGB's, this is the place.

## BRYANT PARK GRILL
**25 W. 40th St. (bet. 5th & 6th Aves.)**
**840-6500**

*ALL MAJOR CREDIT CARDS*

This mammoth restaurant/café/bar takes up the entire width

of Bryant Park. At first you may feel as if you are some-where other than New York—that is until you mix it up with midtown yuppies looking to score. One of the busiest after work bars in the city, The Grill was opened 4 1/2 years ago by the same folks who brought us Louisiana Grill and The Rodeo Bar. There are several different areas, all serving a standard American bistro, $5 drafts, and $6-$10 drinks. Its scenery, space and location made it *New Yorker Magazine's* "hottest pick-up spot." There are essentially four sections, so be specific when you meet someone here. "The grill" refers to the main interior, good for a spacious candlelit meal. "The garden," out front, offers a light menu under enormous umbrellas. "The upstairs terrace" overlooks all of Bryant park, and is sometimes rented out as a private space. "The café" next door serves as a crammed outdoor meat-market. They open at 11am for lunch, and close around 11pm, or until the last suit stumbles back to the Upper East Side. The summer is the best time to pay a visit, and from the terrace you can watch a classic flick show-ing at the Bryant Park film series.

## BULL'S HEAD TAVERN
**295 3rd Ave. (bet. 22nd & 23rd Sts.)**
**685-2589**

*ALL MAJOR CREDIT CARDS*

With a tacky mural of Jesus with a bison, this fraternity hell attracts a mostly male crowd. With mission-style lanterns and bad art, 20 premium beers are served on tap to the beat of a jukebox well stocked in the Van Halen depart-ment. That's the quick and dirty.

## BUBBLE LOUNGE
**228 W. Broadway (At White St.)**
**431-3433**

*ALL MAJOR CREDIT CARDS*

The first official champagne bar in the city, the Bubble Lounge is a chic SoHo mega-lounge serving over 200 types of cham-pagne along with a host of mouthwatering appetizers. The

51

large back room, with its walls of champagne bottles, offers luxurious couches and chairs where waiters mill about at your beckoned call. A downstairs grotto is even more intimate and sets the stage for intimate rap sessions. Due to its Tribeca location, it has become a popular venue for the Wall Street after work crew and for impress-your-friends get-togethers. The weekend tends to draw a large crowd mostly from the outer boroughs. It's a beautiful crowd in an equally attractive setting...perfect for a romantic champagne toast.

### BULL & BEAR (WALDORF ASTORIA HOTEL)
**301 Park Ave. (At 49th St.)**
**872-4900**

*ALL MAJOR CREDIT CARDS*

Established in the 1950s at the stunning Waldorf Astoria, the Bull & Bear attracts a suit-clad, older crowd mainly from the hotel. The quiet sounds of glasses tinkling and polite laughter are a nice reprieve from loud jukeboxes and slurred hollering at most drinking holes in the city—assuming a reprieve is what you're looking for. A rich decor and similar clientele help decorate this upscale bar. Definitely a place to take mom and dad.

### BULL MOOSE SALOON
**354 W. 44th St. (bet. 8th & 9th Aves.)**
**956-5625**

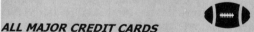

*ALL MAJOR CREDIT CARDS*

This small underground sports bar in Hell's Kitchen caters to the young, post-college fraternity brother. Like most sports bars in the city, original décor is of the utmost importance...not! This is evident when you see the neon beer signs in the window, Heineken coasters, faux stained glass lamps, a pool table and a CD jukebox. Come here to drink, shoot some pool, throw some darts and talk about sports. Anything else would simply be out of place.

## BURBON STREET
**407 Amsterdam Ave. (bet. 79th & 80th Sts.)**
**721-1332**

### ALL MAJOR CREDIT CARDS

It's Fat Tuesday every day at this Mardi Gras theme bar conveniently located on the Upper West Side. A giant black board outside with the words "Women drink free on Wednesday!" scrawled across it says it all. Inside, it's strewn bras, bead necklaces and debauchery. Thursday, Friday and Saturday offers the "Budweiser Challenge" where for a mere $5 you can drink to your heart's content. It's a decent place to come with a group but be prepared to stand...there's limited seating.

## BURP CASTLE
**41 E. 7th St. (bet. 2nd & 3rd Aves.)**
**982-4576**

### CASH ONLY

If the name doesn't cry "date spot," well really, what does? Run by Trappist Monks (or so they want you to believe), this theme bar, equipped with bartenders clad in dark brown robes, offers a top notch beer selection. Open for five years, this bar draws tourists who find the whole theme thing hysterical, especially when they have the Harley Davidson Café and the Hard Rock Café to compare it with. Despite its non-East Village vibe, the beer selection is phenomenal and obviously the service is unobtrusive...they're Monks!

## C3 LOUNGE
**103 Waverly Place (Washington Square Hotel)**
**254-1200**

### ALL MAJOR CREDIT CARDS

This lounge in the heart of Greenwich Village caters to hotel guests at the historic Washington Square Park Hotel. Brass tables lit with candles, cushy couches and paintings of Marlene Dietrich hanging on the walls transport you into the 1930s. That is until you realize that C3 is suffering from a major theme crisis. It's way too bright for a jazz lounge and the music is a "subtle" mix of jazz, elevator music and cheesy Motown. Drink prices are relatively cheap and happy hour (Monday through Friday from 5pm till 7pm) offers two-for-one draft beers, wine and house liquor. Open from 4pm till midnight, live jazz is played from 8pm-11pm on Tuesday nights. If you can manage to ignore the bizarre choice in music, the C3 Lounge is a great place to relax and have a drink before retiring to your room.

## C-NOTE
**157 Ave. C (At 10th St.)**
**677-8142**

**ALL MAJOR CREDIT CARDS**

Now that Avenue A and B have been "yuppified," C is now the latest strip to gentrify faster than Pamela Anderson changes breast size. This swanky music spot is host to live salsa and jazz bands almost every night of the week and caters to an older East Village crowd. The club, with its exposed brick walls, bistro tables and soft lighting captures every aspect of what you would expect in a beatnik neighborhood haunt.

## CAFÉ CARLYLE (AT THE CARLYLE HOTEL)
**35 E. 76<sup>th</sup> St. (At Madison Ave.)**
**744-1600**

**ALL MAJOR CREDIT CARDS**

Sometimes, and that's sometimes, swilling back a few frosty ones at your local pub just won't do. That's why there's the Café Carlyle. For more than 25 years, this nightspot has offered cabaret acts and delicious French cuisine. Don't expect to see your friends from the bowling league here, this is a class act, and supposedly you are too if you drop in for a martini at the bar or slap down 50 bucks for a bite to eat before listening to Bobby Short. The crowd is typically over

40-years-old and looks *really* comfortable in this upscale setting. With the accommodating staff and infectious class prevailing the hotel, you're sure to have an enjoyable evening.

## CAFÉ NOIR
**32 Grand St. (At Thompson St.)**
**431-7910**

*ALL MAJOR CREDIT CARDS*

On any given night this popular French/Moroccan bar is standing room only. It's all about having an attitude at Café Noir. What a spectacle it is as the crowd—Euro thirty-somethings looking to score—are waited on by bartenders who ignore them. Your best bet is to go for brunch during the summer when the windows open onto the street. Or stop by for dinner before dancing the night away at "Naked Lunch" across the street. Try their specialty, a $12 Margarita made from a rare, blue tequila that's pricey but potent.

## CAFÉ PIERRE
**2 E. 61st St. (At. 5th Ave.)**
**940-8195**

*ALL MAJOR CREDIT CARDS*

This elegant bar, located in one of the most expensive and prestigious hotels in Manhattan, draws a very sophisticated clientele that tends to be in their 40s. Not a bar to travel to, but a nice choice if you are in the hotel or in the area.

## CAFE REMY
**104 Greenwich St. (bet. Rector & Carlisle Sts.)**
**267-4646**

*ALL MAJOR CREDIT CARDS*

Travel way downtown to this split-level venue and experience everything from after work Wall Street parties to hot salsa weekends. Downstairs the bar is dark, plush and comfortable with flickering candles setting off the red and black decor. Upstairs, there are always live Latin bands plus DJs

Alex and Binho spin Salsa, Merengue, Latin rock, Brazilian and House. Although many come here after work to take advantage of the free open bar from 5-6pm, Saturday night is the night at Cafe Remy. The dancing is great and the crowd is young, hip and full of energy. Saturday night's cover charge goes like this: $15, $10 w/ invite, $5 w/ mention of Tony (huh?), women free until midnight with invite. (For reduced admission call 252-4363.) The dress code prohibits sneakers so put on your dancing shoes and salsa the night away!

## CAFETERIA
**119 7th Ave. (At 17<sup>th</sup> St. )**
**414-1717**

### *ALL MAJOR CREDIT CARDS*

Cafeteria will go down in history as the biggest comeback...ever! Originally blacklisted as one of the most attitude-laden bars in Chelsea, Cafeteria had made the big mistake of hiring assholes as staff. The bitchy hostess was notorious for, well, being bitchy. After being panned by EVERYONE, Cafeteria did something really smart—they decided to get an attitude makeover! Now, Cafeteria is busting at the seams with a loyal crowd of customers who eagerly eat the delicious food at almost cafeteria prices. The waiters have a tendency to be a bit flaky but they're so nice in that spaced-out sort of way that you find yourself brushing it off that they forgot your drink...for the 4<sup>th</sup> time! Frequented mostly by locals, the gay vibe is so thick you could cut it with a dull knife. But hey, everyone is dressed so fabulous! Everything seems so New York, so downtown, until you notice the blond bombshell sitting next to you has been on her cell phone for the past hour. "That's not in my contract! I never agreed to take off *all* my clothes!" How weird, now you're in LA and Steve Martin is ordering a double no-foam decaf café late with a lemon twist. Aaaaghh! What the hell happened? Hollywood has procreated with Chelsea and its offspring is Cafeteria! But as scary as that may seem, New Yorkers have learned to love this sterile, contemporary bar and restaurant that always manages to serve as a home away from home.

**CALIENTE CAB CO.**
**61 7th Ave. S. (At Bleecker St.), 243-8517**
**21 Waverly Pl. (At Greene St.), 529-1500**

***ALL MAJOR CREDIT CARDS***

A return to Spring Break Cancun, Jersey-style. At the Cab, Chess King is in fashion and spandex is the material of choice. It's here that you can enjoy some of the most non-authentic Mexican food on earth with some of the trashiest people on the East Coast. If you're from Manhattan you wouldn't be caught dead in here. It's the type of place where Americans must bow their heads in shame. Cheap margaritas, cheap food, cheap people...enough said. Caliente Cab specializes in $5 margaritas, while beers are as little as $4. A daily happy hour provides cheaper drinks from 3pm to 8pm. With the tasteless atmosphere filled with annoying touristy ploys, it is a good idea to stay in your cab and pass by. Is there *anything* okay about this place, you ask? Well, the summertime offers top notch outdoor seating perfect for an afternoon group booze-fest.

**CANDELA'S**
**116 E. 16th (bet. Irving Pl. & Park Ave. S.)**
**254-1600**

***ALL MAJOR CREDIT CARDS***

If goatees and black turtlenecks are out, nobody told this crowd. The movers and shakers are nowhere in sight in this cavernous Union Square haunt jam-packed with the tragically fashionable advertising go-getters. The décor is Dungeons and Dragons meets Bonanza and the menu, though diverse, delivers only so-so food. Drinks are adequate and pricey and the dull roar of flamboyant conversation can be overwhelming. If it's a quiet romantic dinner you're after, head to the back. Otherwise, the bar area has pick-up spot potential, although most people seem too engrossed in themselves to leave the crowd they came with. Overall, the place is aesthetically pleasing but offers little else.

**CANDLE BAR**
**309 Amsterdam Ave. (At 74th St.)**
**874-9155**

*CASH ONLY*

One of a few on the Upper West Side, Candle Bar remains the ultimate gay neighborhood bar. Drinks are cheap, service is friendly and the crowd tends to be a little reminiscent of the Village People. Monday through Friday from 2-9 pm offers $2 Buds and Rolling Rocks or rack drinks for $3.50. If you happen to be on Amsterdam Ave. and you're thirsting for a beer, step inside, step back in time, down a beer and reminisce about the good old days. Sunday's drinks are cheap and Go-Go boys are there to entertain the masses who show up here after church.

**CANDY BAR**
**131 8th Ave. (bet. 16th and 17th Sts.)**
**229-9702**

*ALL MAJOR CREDIT CARDS*

This Chelsea favorite has all the makings of a solid and happening scene. They serve wonderful food, the décor is chic and modern and the crowd is hip and predominantly gay. Drinks are strong and creative with such originals as the Tina Louise and the Vampires Kiss, while the menu is simple yet full of flavor. The bar scene doesn't get going till 9 pm, but the restaurant is packed all night. If you're looking for a nice start to an evening, this place will definitely do. If you're looking to "party like a rock star," try Rebar down the block.

**CARBON**
**605 W. 55th ST. (11th/12th Ave.)**
**582-8282**

*ALL MAJOR CREDIT CARDS*

This mega club formerly known as Mirage, sports three floors of full action-packed disco dancing and techno-clubbing. The first level, equipped with a huge dance floor, is filled with everything from hip hoppers to drag queens. On the second floor you can look over the balcony and catch a glimpse of the sea of dancing fools from overhead. The real treat, however, is the roof garden which is VIP only but worth trying to get onto. Thursday is "Rich Bitch" night, which usually draws a model-esque crowd. The weekends are almost completely Bridge & Tunnel and the door policy is your usual pain in the ass with a $20 dollar cover charge.

## CARNEGIE HILL BREWING CO.
**1600 3rd Ave. (At 90th St.)**
**369-0808**

*ALL MAJOR CREDIT CARDS*

A microbrewery with very bad beer is not a good combination. However, Carnegie Hill makes up for its bad beer by having some of the best people watching on the Upper East Side. The wide windows open up onto the sights of evening strollers making their way back home up 3rd Avenue's restaurant/bar row. The outdoor seating adds a resort-like feel to this tight-laced neighborhood. The huge old fashioned wood bar provides plenty of seating and access to friendly bartenders, as well as a good view of the many TVs for sporting events. All in all, the seating and people-watching make up for the mediocre food and bad beer.

## CAROLINE'S COMEDY CLUB
**1626 B'way (bet. 49th & 50th Sts.)**
**757-4100**

*ALL MAJOR CREDIT CARDS*

Caroline's is by far the most professional, nicest looking, and best taken care of comedy club in Manhattan. There are always household names appearing on the stage as well as comics you may not have heard of...yet. Caroline's has an eye for talent that most other clubs don't. They put the funny guys on stage and provide a full evening of entertainment. The cover charge varies according to the act, and whatever the price, it's always worth it. There is always a two drink minimum and a full menu with finger foods, salads, and burgers. This is not your ordinary, dingy, smoky, club room with uncomfortable chairs. There is no smoking in the main room and the large velvet banquettes provide good cushioning for an entire evening of laughing your ass off. Book in advance and get to the show early for up-front seating. Caroline's is also a great change of pace for after work drinks. Instead of going to a noisy pub where you complain about your job, watch some comedy and laugh away your miserable day.

## CASA LA FEMME
**150 Wooster St. (bet. Houston & Prince Sts.)**
**505-0005**

*ALL MAJOR CREDIT CARDS*

"Ishtar" meets SoHo at this ultra-swank, rarely packed lounge/restaurant. With its heavy Egyptian/Moroccan theme you might feel like you are on the set of a Cecil B. de Mille epic. In the front, soft flickering candlelight illuminates comfy pillow seating while in the back, tented private tables provide an intimate setting for dates and groups. Due to its SoHo location the crowd tends to be good looking, thin and dressed in designer duds. The drinks are fairly expensive, but it's definitely a good place to bring a date for a romantic after-dinner drink. Sit at one of the tented tables so you can smooch the night away. During the summer they line the floor with real grass...definitely worth checking out!

## CAVIARTERIA
**310 W. B'way (At Grand St.)**
**925-5515**
**502 Park Ave. (At 59th St.)**
**759-7410**
*ALL MAJOR CREDIT CARDS*

An elegant restaurant, bar, and retail store created by the high-priced catalog of the same name, Caviarteria is a caviar-lovers dream. Prices are extremely high and portions are tiny, but, remember, we're talking caviar here, not potato knishes. Sip fine champagne, vintage wines and top-shelf alcohol while sucking down dozens of varieties of fetal fish and other odd delicacies you can spread on a cracker. The décor is luxurious and refined, but the whole package is a bit on the pretentious side. But then again, what could be more pretentious that eating a fish before it even has the fighting chance to grow fins and swim away?

## CBGB'S
**315 Bowery (At Bleecker St.)**
**982-4052**

### *CASH ONLY*

It stands for "Country Blue Grass Blues," but if you know anything about this nasty hole-in-the-wall you'll understand that's about the last type of music you'll find playing here. The entrance to this landmark music venue is so encrusted with graffiti and band stickers that you may want to put on surgical gloves before entering. Mosh pits and armpits are everywhere in this dark music dungeon where bands like the Police, Blondie and the Talking Heads got their start. With its great sound system and rough demeanor, the crowd is generally young, wayward and groupie-like. If you're feeling really brave, check out "Open Mike" Sundays. This place oozes history and fungus.

## CEDAR TAVERN
**82 University Pl. (bet. 11ᵗʰ & 12ᵗʰ Sts.)**
**741-9754**

### *ALL MAJOR CREDIT CARDS*

The Cedar Tavern is a beautiful old-fashioned pub/tavern located in the heart of Greenwich Village. The food is consistently good, the drinks are moderately priced and the service is prompt and friendly. Primarily a local hangout for the nearby NYU students and local post-college yuppies, it's a perfect place to go and talk with a friend over a beer and burger.

## CHAOS (CLOSED)
**23 Watt St. (bet. W. B'way & Thompson)**

## CHAZ AND WILSON'S
**201 W. 79th St. (bet. Amsterdam & B'way)**
**769-0100**

*ALL MAJOR CREDIT CARDS*

This is not the old Chaz and Wilson's. Now a mature, stylish restaurant and bar, it caters to an older, thirtysomething and up crowd. With subtle lighting and pleasant jazz music in the background this is a great place to bring a date and enjoy oversized martinis and cosmopolitans. It definitely fills a void created by the uptown sea of kiddy bars. If you go on Wednesday or Friday you are in for a night of excellent Motown music as this is the home base of one of the best bands around—the "Stingers." Sundays you might find yourself star struck on open mike night with the likes of Charles Oakley, John Starks and other Knicks regulars. The large and beautiful space is worthy of a visit and a good place to bring the parents for a meal.

## CHEETAH
**12 W. 21st St. (bet. 5th & 6th Aves.)**
**206-7770**

*ALL MAJOR CREDIT CARDS*

Like many of New York's more upscale dance clubs, Cheetah has a full scale army of people working the door whose mission is to keep your ego in check until they decide you're cool enough to let in. The crowd inside on the weekends is young, clubby and has most likely come to Manhattan either by bridge or by tunnel. Like animals of prey, packs of horny muscle-bound men wearing gold chains slither across the dance floor hunting for babes. If you're not up for dancing to a 20-minute version of "White Lines," sit at one of the large inviting cheetah print booths and have a drink amongst the waterfall column centerpiece and hundreds of little disco balls dangling from the ceiling. The dance floor is smaller than expected, and the theme changes nightly so call ahead. The VIP "Red Room" opens later in the evening for the cooler in-the-know. Prepare to drop some cash here: $20 cover on weekends; $3 coat check; and criminally overpriced beer and cocktails served in plastic cups.

## CHELSEA BREWING COMPANY
**Chelsea Piers, Pier 59**
**23rd St. & the Hudson River**
**336-6440**

*ALL MAJOR CREDIT CARDS*

This large brewery overlooking the Hudson is a great place to unwind after shooting hoops or practicing your golf swing over at Chelsea Piers. Although you may have time to write a complete novel while waiting for your waiter to appear, the beer is delicious and the food is equally pleasing and served in enormous portions. The triplex space, reminiscent of a ski lodge, offers views of the large steel brewing casks. It's best to go in the summer when you can sit outside and bask in the sun.

## CHELSEA COMMONS
**242 10th Ave. (At 24th St.)**
**929-9424**

*ALL MAJOR CREDIT CARDS*

Chelsea Commons may be at its best in the summer. With great bar food and a small but satisfactory selection of beers on tap, they also feature an outdoor courtyard. Its quiet, relaxing atmosphere and view of the trees (yes, trees) might just make you forget how close you are to the West Side Highway. In the winter months, Chelsea Commons is still an ideal neighborhood refuge. Assuming the string of marionettes that decorate the bar doesn't make you edgy, you'll be able to relax in its exposed brick interior and enjoy the sounds of the jukebox or catch up on the score from either of the two TVs.

## CHEZ ES SAADA
**42 E. 1st St. (bet. 1st & 2nd Aves.)**
**777-5617**

*ALL MAJOR CREDIT CARDS*

As predicted, the popularity of this place has become offensively annoying. Nonetheless, it remains one of the more decadent hot spots in New York and makes for a perfect little date spot. A flower petal-lined staircase descends into a Moroccan-inspired cavern with a series of eating and drinking nooks that are intimate and beautifully appointed. The downstairs restaurant transforms into a bar/lounge area after 11pm which prior to its discovery was comfortable and mellow but is now filled with the young and tragically hip from every part of the city. Despite the crowds, it is definitely worthy of a visit. Try one of their fabulous signature cocktails.

### CHIBI'S SAKE BAR
**242 Mott St. (At Prince St.)**
**274-0025**

***ALL MAJOR CREDIT CARDS***

Welcome to a slice of eccentricity in Little Italy. This small, elegant sake bar with an art deco/French twist is warm and comfortable. Rest at cozy tables with an older, arty neighborhood clientele. An amazing 1970s flower chandelier illuminates the small wooden bar that is decorated with 1950s vintage glasses. Listen to soulful music while choosing between 10 different high end sakes. Even if you're not a sake fan, this place will hook you in instantly. (Sake goes for $7 a glass, while beer and wine are $6 a glass.) An array of favorable appetizers such as the Dumplings of the Day or Kunanoto Oysters go for about $10. Open from 6pm-1am during the week and until 2am on the weekend, Chibi's has soul and flavor with a warm, personal touch. If you're curious about the inspiration behind the name, just gaze above the bar at the huge, framed painting of Chibi...the dog!

### CHICAGO B.L.U.E.S.
**73 8th Ave. (bet. 13<sup>th</sup> & 14<sup>th</sup> Sts.)**
**924-9755**

A nice large space to see live music in the West Village. The decor definitely has a Chicago feel to it with its cleaner-than-your-usual-New-York-music-dive feel. Nice little tables in the back near the stage provide for an intimate (and loud) viewing of some great live bands. It's a place for an older (30s to 40s) neighborhood crowd.

## CHINA CLUB
**268 W. 47ᵗʰ St. (bet. 7ᵗʰ & 8ᵗʰ Aves.)**
**398-3800**

### *ALL MAJOR CREDIT CARDS*

Anyone who is familiar with the guys on Saturday Night Live who bob their greased heads to "Baby Don't Hurt Me" will realize, almost immediately, that this is the place they were looking for. There is a lot of cheap leather in this space that looks like a multi-leveled series of hotel conference rooms. Bright lights everywhere and stackable chairs around circular tables makes for a bad wedding banquet vibe. Decor aside, the music is pretty good and the young and energetic patrons seemed to be getting along and enjoying each other's company. There is a door policy and a $20 cover on the weekends.

## CHUMLEY'S
**86 Bedford St. (bet. Barrow & Grove Sts.)**
**675-4449**

### *CASH ONLY*

Formerly a speakeasy, Chumley's is a popular bar that's tough to find. (There's no sign outside.) Once you walk through the people-were-much-smaller-back-then door you'll find an unexpected cavern filled with the delicious smells of pub food and people jammed into every ounce of space available. If you can squeeze your way towards the bar you'll find an impressive array of over 20 beers on tap. Get there early and grab a table to hang out with friends. The mood is always friendly, unpretentious and talkative, and though its a bit heavy on the J.Crew-barn-jacket-wearin'-type, it's a great place to meet new people.

**CIBAR**
**56 Irving Pl. (bet. 17th & 18th Sts.)**
**460-5656**

*ALL MAJOR CREDIT CARDS*

If you can find the Cibar, you might just have the opportunity to blow your whole paycheck in one sitting. Underneath the Irving Place Inn, this small cigar lounge with low marble tables and close seating is designed for those interested in stogies and the like. If you have cash to burn, the drinks are well worth it. Watch out for the $40 beers! Wealthy middle-aged lounge lizards of all varieties seem to saunter in around elevenish, packing the place to the gills. The only pocket of sunlight in the place is the lush garden in the rear. If you can't stand the smell of smoke, stay far away. Good spot for taking clients for drinks.

**CIEL ROUGE**
**176 7th Ave. (bet. 20th & 21st Sts.)**
**929-5542**

Oh what a dignified place! Ciel Rouge offers a bit of French paradise smack in the middle of Chelsea. The sign above the door is hard to see, but you will notice the place by its great French doors and red velvet curtains. The atmosphere is warm, unobtrusive and very casual. Vases filled with flowers, old antique mirrors and a large baby grand piano compliment the rosy lighting creating a romantic vibe perfect for a first date. The music varies from quiet classical to David Bowie and Iggy Pop. While drinks are a bit overpriced, the service is top-notch. Ciel Rouge is the perfect start, middle and end to an evening.

**CIRCA**
**103 2nd Ave. (At 6th St.)**
**777-4120**

*ALL MAJOR CREDIT CARDS*

This big and beautiful 1940s style bar/restaurant is a great place to bring a date for drinks and dinner. Sit at either the wraparound bar or the cozy sitting area in the front window and people-watch over a couple of overpriced martinis. The crowd is artsy and model-esque, but seems to be refreshingly unpretentious. The bar does get crowded so get there as early as you can so you can snag a seat.

**CIRCA TABAC**
**32 Watts St. (bet. 6th Ave. & Thompson St.)**
**941-1781**

***ALL MAJOR CREDIT CARDS***

As far as theme bars go, this is the most authentic, original, and truly enjoyable one in the city. A newcomer to the lower SoHo area, Circa Tabac is a wonderful interpretation of the art deco period. From the lighting fixtures to the furniture you will feel transported to another era, an era when smoking was chic and the three martini lunch was the norm. There is something magical here that makes you feel like a movie star. 150 brands of cigarettes are offered along with a nice selection of wine and beer. For those anti-smokers among us, please don't stay away for fear of your clothes and hair reeking of smoke. The owners have spent hundreds of thousands of dollars on a state of the art air filtration system that constantly and silently pumps all of the air in the place out, replacing it with fresh air. This is a good date place, after work spot, business meeting place, or a spot to impress just about anyone.

**CITRUS BAR AND GRILL**
**320 Amsterdam Ave. (At 75th St.)**
**595-0500**

***ALL MAJOR CREDIT CARDS***

A little tequila never hurt anyone, but what about a flight of tequila? This large jam-packed Tex-Mex bar and grill is one of the more dynamic venues on the Upper West Side. Geared towards the serious "ta-kill-ya" drinker, Citrus offers over 100 different kinds of tequila with plans to import up to 150 down the road. Inventive margaritas populate the drink menu with everything from pear cactus, pomegranate, kiwi and mango. The ambiance gets its punch from the mango and celadon colored walls and overgrown cactus. One flight down is the Squeeze Lounge equipped with a southwestern patio feel and a neon fiber optic bar that changes colors. Expect singles nights and private parties to take over this lounge. Come early, stay late and try not to overdo it on the margaritas. This place packs it in!

**THE CITY GRILL**
**269 Columbus Ave. (bet. 72ⁿᵈ & 73ʳᵈ Sts.)**
**873-9400**

*ALL MAJOR CREDIT CARDS*

If you're not an Upper West Side local in your mid-forties looking to booze the night away by yourself watching the Yankees game, pass right through the bar and sit down for a meal. This saloon-type operation used to be named Ruppert's, and it hasn't changed much from those days. Their weak attempt at making this a more upscale establishment by using white tablecloths is almost laughable. The full American menu is very tasty and the service is attentive, but there's just something about the gold rush décor that's holding it back.

**CITY HALL**
**131 Duane St. (At Church St.)**
**227-7777**

*ALL MAJOR CREDIT CARDS*

More of a restaurant than a bar, City Hall definitely gets special mention because of the beautiful space, spectacular art deco décor and great food. The bar area is inviting with flowers placed all around, a great oyster bar and a friendly and attitude-free staff. The drinks aren't cheap, but it's worth it. A great spot for a post Wall Street dinner or a pre-club snack, City Hall attracts a crowd that's well dressed and not afraid to spend some cash. Whether you're looking for a steak night out with the guys or an intimate evening with your date, City Hall's vibe is suitable for either.

68

## CITY WINE AND CIGAR (CLOSED)
**62 Laight St. (At Greenwich St.)**

## CLEMENTINE
**1 5th Ave. (At 8th St.)**
**253-0003**

*ALL MAJOR CREDIT CARDS*

This posh little number smack dab in the deadest and bar-free part of town is always a good pick for a cocktail. Clumsy bartenders mix decently overpriced drinks to a crowd that is young, trendy, and looking to score. The warm art deco feel of the space may remind you of the bar from "The Shining" with its dark wood, illuminated glass bar and burnt orange lighting. When all is said and done, Clementine makes for a romantic spot good for classic drinks and sumptuous appetizers...especially during the weekend when the Jersey folk stay, um, home.

## CLOISTER CAFÉ
**238 E. 9th St. (bet. 2nd & 3rd Aves.)**
**777-9128**

*CASH ONLY*

Just around the corner from the din and bustle of the East Village is a little piece of serenity. The outdoor garden is complete with a ceiling of grapevines and tables surrounding a fountain trickling into a narrow ten-foot-long goldfish pond. If you're a student, this is a gentle place to bring your parents so they'll know "everything's okay." The crowd here is mixed and most importantly, relaxed. The high-calorie food also helps to slow everything down. It's the closest thing to Zen garden (or nature for that matter) in the area.

## THE CLUB CAR
**1696 2nd Ave. (bet. 87th & 88th Sts.)**
**348-4368**

*ALL MAJOR CREDIT CARDS*

Open for about one year now, The Club Car is a tiny bar shaped as an old-fashioned steam train car. With black and white photos of old diesel trains adorning the walls, a large oak bar and a piano, one is transported back in time. Catering to an older, more mellow crowd of Upper East Siders, The Club Car hosts a daily happy hour Monday through Friday from 4pm –7pm with discount drink prices. With eight beers on tap and 7 bottled beers, drinks are reasonably priced. Besides the large bar, a couple of tables and chairs are aimlessly scattered about. Play darts, a video game or choose from an eclectic mix of jukebox tunes ranging from Bette Midler to Neil Diamond to "Dance Mix USA." It's very quiet and a bit on the dull side so don't expect anybody to actually dance to "Dance Mix USA"!

## CLUB MACANUDO
**26 E. 63rd St. (bet. Park & Mad. Aves.)**
**752-8200**

*ALL MAJOR CREDIT CARDS*

When The Club opened in 1996 during the start of the cigar craze, it instantly became an exclusive hit on the East Side. Boasting one of the finest selections of cigars in the city, this humidor-haven also has a full menu restaurant and bar. The prices are surprisingly reasonable with appetizers ranging from $8-$14, and entrées from $18-$28. There's also a very respectable wine and liquor list starting at around $7 and shooting up to $150. They offer almost every wine by the glass affording you the option to sip on something new and different. For all the Italian leather and maple trim, The Club remains inviting and comfortable. You don't have to spend a fortune to enjoy your stay, but you'll probably have a better time if you have cash—this is a crowd with money to burn. Even Denzel Washington rents one of the humidor lockers for $800 a year! Although they claim to have a relaxed dress code, leave your jeans at home and break out a blazer.

**THE COCK**
**188 Avenue A (At 12<sup>th</sup> St.)**
**777-6254**

*CASH ONLY*

Sorry boys, the Frolic Room is officially defunct, but it's time to embrace something new and it's called The Cock! Here's a place to *not* bring mom but *definitely* bring an open mind. The raw and minimal decor sets the scene for those who come to lounge on couches, listen to music and gaze at beautiful boys. Drinks are cheap and strong just like the sexy bartenders. On Saturday night, say "goodbye" to mellow and say "hello" to "Foxy"— the flagship night at The Cock when you pay a $5 cover to watch drag performances, male waiters in g-strings and, if you're lucky, sexually deviant behavior. Witness the drama enfold as contestants perform "foxy deeds" such as popping Ping-Pong balls out of their butt or shoving beer bottles up their ass. Saturday night at The Cock is not for the weak-kneed but according to many, it's the best show in NYC. You can't miss this place— just look for the red, florescent cock illuminated in the window.

**COCO BAR**
**155 Ave. B (At 10th St.)**
**253-6333**

*CASH ONLY*

This tiny coffee shop turned bar attracts an artsy and tattooed neighborhood crowd as well as Soho wannabes in the neighborhood for the evening. A shiny brass bar leaves room for a couple of tables and chairs to lounge on. Make sure to take advantage of the warm weather and sit in front of open French doors that look out onto Thompkins Square Park. Theatrically lit in dim, red lighting and lightly flowing jazz music, this place would be a great visit if it wasn't for the less than friendly attitude of the staff. Other than that, drinks are reasonably priced—"special" drinks served from

7pm-4am daily. It's comfortable but definitely not the best vibe in the city.

## COCO CAFE
**7 E. 59th St. (bet. 5th & Mad. Aves.)**
**935-3535**

*ALL MAJOR CREDIT CARDS*

Coco Pazzo's laid back cousin, Coco Café, is an upscale restaurant and bar attempting to attract a more casual crowd. The bar is small yet elegant, with more attention paid to the dining room. Originally the old Playboy Club, you need to take a swanky elevator downstairs to get to the bathroom. While you're there visit the private lounge/bar which offers cigars and top-shelf liquor only. A stereo plays good jazz in the background to a very quiet crowd. The drinks are pricey: $10-$25 for cocktails and $7-$15 for a glass of wine. Try the tasty "Martini 2000" or a "Perfect Margarita." A traditional Tuscan-style menu with an extended desert and herbal tea section draws an old money crowd with a couple of celebrities mixed in. Come by for a cocktail or stay for dinner.

## CODY'S
**282 Hudson St. (At Dominick St.)**
**924-5853**

*ALL MAJOR CREDIT CARDS*

This local hangout in the lower West Village is the kind of place you go to simply grab a beer, hangout with a good friend and not worry about being part of a the scene. Despite the smoky atmosphere, the space is warm and friendly and filled with a pleasant local vibe. The reasonable drink prices don't hurt.

## COFFEE SHOP
**29 Union Square West (At 16th St.)**
**243-7969**

*ALL MAJOR CREDIT CARDS*

Although "Lights! Camera! Action!" are probably the words that the staff would rather hear than "Uh, I'll have a Martini," Coffee Shop packs them in. This trendy Brazilian-inspired eatery is open 23 hours a day (what the hell are they doing during that hour?), with the bulk of the place turning into a happening bar scene after dinner hours. The newly refurbished World Room, a trendy '50s-style tiki lounge, is a little more laid back than the counter area in the front. Great looking guys and gals convene here for excellent appetizers and moderately price drinks especially in the summertime when the outdoor tables make way for great people watching. It's a better spot during the weeknights when it's less of a scene. All in all, Coffee Shop is a good standby for last minute outings and after-work dinners.

## COMEDY CELLAR
**117 MacDougal Street
(bet. W. 3rd & Bleecker Sts.)
254-3480**

### *ALL MAJOR CREDIT CARDS*

At this subterranean old school comedy club you're likely to see a bunch of not very funny comics who are just starting their careers. Interspersed amongst these torturous acts you'll see some seasoned comics who are usually testing out their new material with some of the most difficult audiences in the country. The familiar faces you see drop by usually do some very dirty material they can't get away with on Letterman or Comedy Central. The club is a very intimate environment which makes you feel as though the comics are performing just for you...which is not always a good thing. Quite a few famous comics started their early careers here like Ray Romano, Dave Chapelle, and Dave Attell, and it's not uncommon for them to stop by. Mediocre Mediterranean food will fill you up if you're hungry, but it's nothing to write home about. You're best bet is sticking to the primary objective: laughing. Cover charge: Sun-Thurs, $5; Fri-Sat, $12. There's always a 2 drink minimum.

## THE COMFORT ZONE (AKA DAKOTA)
**405 3rd Ave. (At 29th St.)
684-8376**

### *CASH ONLY*

A gay bar in the middle of Gramercy? Who knew? This place is the "Cheers" of the gay crowd. When you walk in, nobody knows your name. By the time you leave, everyone is in your business. This typical gay bar with a rainbow flag, penis candles and diva house music draws in a local crowd of mid-20s to 30s. Monday nights host an open mike night for comedians while Wednesday nights offer you transvestite admirers watching colorful drag acts. The biggest draw of the Comfort Zone is the great pool table and the pool tournaments on Sundays. And for those who like their drinks and their men stiff, try Tuesday nights on for size. Open daily from 4pm-4am, the Comfort Zone offers a 2-for-1 happy hour from 4pm to 8pm. Open for one year, the Comfort Zone has a little bit of everything for everyone. So get out of Chelsea and step into the Comfort Zone.

## COMMONWEALTH BREWERY
**35 West 48th St. (bet. 5th & 6th Aves.)**
**977-2269**

*ALL MAJOR CREDIT CARDS*

A modern, deco-styled restaurant and brewery right in the heart of Rockefeller Center. Sure, this place looks cool, with big silver kegs of beer behind that long wall of glass, shining silver taps and polished hardwood floors, but unless you are a Rockefeller, you'll have a hard time getting fully loaded. Mainly a tourist trap and after work hangout for those midtown dwellers who fear the subway, the Commonwealth Brewery is clean and comfortable yet strangely fabricated. It's almost *too* clean and comfortable. You get the feeling the beer ain't real and the bartenders are animatronic. It does offer a place for those who savor beer and want to try one of the distinctive drafts brewed on site, but if you are looking for a pure Manhattan drinking experience that won't lighten your wallet as much, try somewhere else.

## COMMUNITY BAR AND GRILL
**216 7th Ave. (bet. 22nd & 23rd Sts.)**
**242-7900**

*ALL MAJOR CREDIT CARDS*

This gay, friendly Chelsea restaurant/bar serves up a wonderful menu filled with eclectic, tasty dishes. The handsome bar area is lit by soft modern fixtures that bring a mood of calm relaxation to the space. Community caters to this upscale gay neighborhood, but friendly service is extended to everyone.

## COMMUTER CAFÉ
**World Trade Center- Path Station**
**No phone**

*ALL MAJOR CREDIT CARDS*

If you have three teeth, wear a hairpiece, and your wardrobe is made up primarily of flammable poly-acetate blends, Commuter Café is your home away from home. Located in the breathtaking Path Station, the ambiance here is, quite simply, terrifying. Padded leather walls, Vegas carpeting and a sense of human waste reign. It's the type of place you might find Neil Diamond having a Scotch on the rocks in his darkest hour. The bartenders, however, are some of the most friendly guys you will ever meet in your life. If you need a drink before getting on the path train (and who doesn't?), look no further.

## CONEY ISLAND HIGH – (CLOSED)
**15 St. Mark's Place (bet. 2nd & 3rd Aves.)**

## CONTINENTAL
**25 3rd Ave. (At St. Mark's Pl.)**
**529-6924**

*CASH ONLY*

A staple among the East Village music scene, Continental has been entertaining audiences with legendary punk bands for years. Like CBGB's, the Continental is small, dark, cheap and loud. Pay a small cover to witness local not-for-grandma bands like "Stab City" and "Catfight." Mohawks, safety pins and carefully pierced faces dominate the scene so leave the conservative ware at home. During the warm weather, sit at tables and chairs by the open doors and indulge in the freakdom that St. Mark's Place is famous for. Cheap drinks get cheaper during Continental's happy hour from 4pm to 8pm. Enjoy some of the hardest of the hardcore music out there at this genuine old-school East Village venue.

## COOLER
**416 W. 14<sup>th</sup> St. (bet. 9th Ave. & Wash. St.)**
**229-0785**

### *ALL MAJOR CREDIT CARDS*

Formerly a meat cooler, this bar tucked underground in the meat packing district boasts a lot of memorabilia from its past. Meat hooks hang from the ceiling, and a large scale used for weighing carcasses stands in the center of the bar. There's no sign out front— just ominous-looking metal doors and a staircase leading down to a basement. Live music is featured every night so be sure to call ahead for the lineup and the cover charge. If you can't push your way to the front for a close-up view of the performance, take a seat at one of the two bars and watch the act on TV screens. Unfortunately, Cooler isn't cooler in the summer due to its lack of air conditioning.

## COPACABANA
**617 W. 57th St. (bet. 11<sup>th</sup> & 12th Aves.)**
**582-COPA**

### *ALL MAJOR CREDIT CARDS*

This large and super-cheesy dance club on the West Side is the perfect place to bust your dance moves in a setting that would fit Barry Manilow like a second skin. Live bands in matching sequin outfits and big hair sing everything from disco classics to the Lambada to a crowd of 30-year-olds from out of town. Like all clubs, there is a cover to get in and drinks are expensive. If you're looking for a place that looks and feels like a conference room in a Miami Hilton hotel, this huge space is for you. Don't get too excited, this isn't the Copacabana that inspired Barry to write his song.

## CORNELIA STREET CAFÉ
**29 Cornelia St. (bet. W. 4th St. & Bleecker Sts.)**
**989-9319**

***ALL MAJOR CREDIT CARDS***

This charming cafe/bar nestled right in the heart of the West Village attracts artsy, pleasant patrons who come to take in readings and art exhibits with a glass of wine. A mural of children's paintings landscape the walls, while French doors open onto the small sidewalk in the front of the cafe. The menu offers an array of inexpensive dishes like grilled portabello mushrooms with goat cheese and mussels. Along with the food, champagne, beer, and wine is available at very reasonable prices. The crowd is local and family-oriented.

## THE CORNER
**133 Ludlow St. (At Rivington St.)**
**473-4100**

Conveniently located on "the corner" of Ludlow and Stanton, this 8-month-old baby is dying for some excitement. A very non-specific crowd sip on martinis, beer, wine and sake while listening to Dj'd lounge music. Every Saturday, The Corner hosts a comedy night with a cover charge of $5, while Wednesday nights host "Bite Me," a full-on lesbian night with no cover before 11pm. With $3 drafts all night, sex toy prizes, erotic poetry readings and topless pool games, this night attracts girls and more girls. Typical bar food is served till closing while a happy hour serves up $2 pints and $8 pitchers with a plate of buffalo wings from 7pm – 10pm daily. The cold, dank, stinky basement has a pool table and gray plastic couches to lounge on. With a little thought, creativity and pizzazz, this space could be amazing.

**CORNER BISTRO**
**331 W. 4th St. (At Jane St.)**
**242-9502**

*CASH ONLY*

All good things come to those who wait. Keep this in mind when you (hopefully) snag a table at the very popular Corner Bistro. The burgers are the best in NYC and the ambiance is New York and eclectic. Unfortunately, you could get better service at your great-grandmother's house. Avoid going on the weekends unless you have a camaraderie with Jersey folk.

**COWBOY BAR**
**1495 1st Ave. (At 77th St.)**
**288-6636**

*ALL MAJOR CREDIT CARDS*

As you well know, the Upper East Side is notorious for harboring a male population that is raw, rustic, and in touch with nature—true "cowboys" if you will. That being the biggest boldfaced lie ever told, it's time to get to the bottom of this "Cowboy Bar" that sits right at the pulse of America's most homogenous, pansy-ass neighborhood in the free world. Though the buffalo head, saddle-style seats and chaps-clad host almost gives you the feeling of being out in the Old West, the Monday night football being cheered at by a group of young fraternity meatheads ruins the rustic mood. In all fairness, the service is great, the drinks are cheap, and there's a full, yet fattening, menu. If you live nearby, stop in, otherwise it's not really worth the trip.

**COWGIRL HALL OF FAME**
**519 Hudson St. (At 10th St.)**
**633-1133**

*ALL MAJOR CREDIT CARDS*

This large bar/restaurant has the best white trash eats on

the East Coast. The bar area, usually jammed with an odd looking but peaceful bunch of local yokels and stray suburbanites, proudly serves Pabst Blue Ribbon and assorted trailer trash drink concoctions. The late 20s-30s crowd comes here for dependable eats, the entertaining waiters and the hokey country music. The chicken fried chicken will literally make your soul quiver. Make sure to try the Frito pie—chili, sour cream and cheese served in a bag of Fritos. If you're looking for a kitschy place for a great meal and good drinks, look no further.

## COYOTE UGLY
**153 1st Ave. (bet. 9th & 10th Sts.)**
**477-4431**

*ALL MAJOR CREDIT CARDS*

Alert! Trailer park activity right in the heart of the East Village! Imagine an even trashier version of Hogs and Heifers. This dingy, male dominated, parolee-type hole in the wall offers free shots to women who are willing to hand over their bra to the bartender. Pabst Blue Ribbon flows steadily here, as does the beer and hard liquor. That's it. Don't even *think* about asking for a mixed fruity drink unless you want to be berated, squirted with water or subjected to your own personal, sleazy bar dance by one of the intoxicated bartenders. Drunkenness is encouraged here at the Coyote Ugly. In fact, buying yourself and the bartender a shot is a must if you want to "bond" with the locals. A jukebox screams out Rock & Roll with a touch of Country Western. Drinks are as dirt cheap as the atmosphere. It's scary, it's trashy and it's *very, very* ugly.

## CREAM
**246 Columbus Ave (bet. 71st & 72nd Sts.)**
**712-1666**

*ALL MAJOR CREDIT CARDS*

Is "cream" not one of the more offensive words in the English language? Brought to you by the owners of the mega-club, Life, Cream might be the best dance club on the Upper West Side. The large space is modern and sleek and caters to an eclectic crowd of aging yuppies and jappy girls toting Kate Spade bags. If you want to dance in this part of town, this is really one of your only choices. There's a velvet rope so dress to impress.

## CROSSROADS
**300 E. 77th St. (bet. 1st & 2nd Aves.)**
**988-8737**

Don't let the cheesy Whitesnake-type banner out front send you running: Crossroads is one of the few places on the Upper East Side with live entertainment. It's loud and smoky, and the cramped quarters are not really suited for live bands. For those of you who are starved for blues and burn a candle in memory of Manny's Car Wash, try this spot. There's a cover charge most nights.

## CUB ROOM
**131 Sullivan St. (At Prince St.)**
**677-4100**

*ALL MAJOR CREDIT CARDS*

The Cub Room hosts a bevy of aging yuppies on a nightly basis. A favorite among the thirtysomething crowd, the Cub Room is an impressive, rustic space that serves pricey drinks in a cozy lounge setting. Although the current crowd consists primarily of Wall Streeters in black turtlenecks, there are also a smattering of European tourists and Hoboken dwellers. The friendly bartenders will serve you almost any drink you request, including ice cold milk. Nice place to stop for an afternoon lunch and cocktail or a first date.

## CUBBYHOLE
**281 W. 12th St.**
**243-9041**

*CASH ONLY*

This is not a lipstick lesbian bar. The Cubbyhole is a serious dyke stomping ground with just enough kitschy décor to make you feel like you might have wandered into butch Disneyland. The barstools and walls are covered in Warner Brothers characters and although you may not have a problem sitting on a Bugs Bunny decorated stool, you might have issues when it falls over from disrepair. The crowd is a consistent mix of older women who are far more likely to order a Coors than the Mimosas the bar serves up special for its Sunday morning liquid brunches. Let's put it this way: The Cubbyhole, despite the cheerful flowers pasted in the window, is not a pretty place. Expect to leave depressed and pessimistic about the gay woman's Manhattan scene.

## CUCKOO CARIBE (CLOSED)
**81 Ave. A (bet. 5ᵗʰ & 6ᵗʰ Aves.)**

## CULTURE CLUB
**179 Varick St. (bet. King & Charlton Sts.)**
**243-1999**

### ALL MAJOR CREDIT CARDS

After staring with disbelief at the awning with a Pac Man on it, enter Culture Club, the dance club created in the '90s but made to feel like it's from the '80s. Do we really need to relive big hair and blue eye shadow? Located on the outskirts of SoHo, it's all about the B&T crowd. Cheesy painted murals of such 80s icons as Adam Ant, Milli Vanilli and the cast from "The Breakfast Club" adorn the walls while a real Delorian straight out of "Back to the Future" sits next to the dance floor. Like the décor, the music selection is (yawn) boring. Dance to "The Safety Dance" or "Angel is a Centerfold" as you choose from an array of specialty cocktails named after 1980s legends or the $4 bottled beer and $5 well drinks. It's definitely not the hippest place in town, but if you're craving Duran Duran and A Flock of Seagulls, the shoe fits.

**THE D LOUNGE (IN THE DELMONICO HOTEL)**
**502 Park Ave. (At 59th St.)**
**355-2500**

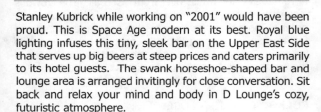

*ALL MAJOR CREDIT CARDS*

Stanley Kubrick while working on "2001" would have been proud. This is Space Age modern at its best. Royal blue lighting infuses this tiny, sleek bar on the Upper East Side that serves up big beers at steep prices and caters primarily to its hotel guests. The swank horseshoe-shaped bar and lounge area is arranged invitingly for close conversation. Sit back and relax your mind and body in D Lounge's cozy, futuristic atmosphere.

**DAKOTA BAR AND GRILL**
**1576 3rd Ave. (bet. 88th & 89th Sts.)**
**427-8889**

*ALL MAJOR CREDIT CARDS*

This Upper East Side restaurant/bar is still the "I just landed an analyst position at Morgan Stanley" hangout. The decor is boring and dated with animal skulls on the walls, hotel-like upholstered furniture and top 40 pumping on the stereo. Bartenders serve overpriced beer and mixed drinks to a preppie, immature crowd of recent college grads. The real downside is that Dakota has recently been invaded by a Bridge & Tunnel crowd whose mission is to score. This makes for good people watching if you're tired of Marlin Perkins' "Animal Kingdom."

**DANGERFIELD'S**
**1118 1st Ave. (bet. 61st & 62nd Sts.)**
**593-1650**

*ALL MAJOR CREDIT CARDS*

If you're on the Upper East Side and you have a hankering for comedy, but you're not with any funny friends, and the wind is blowing your hair into your eyes, you may stumble into Dangerfield's . If you find yourself in this unfortunate locale don't get too upset, there's always Merchants across the street. Relax and enjoy the very dated 1970s wood paneled walls, dimly lit red hued room, and bask in the depressing humorlessness of it all. Or you can slide back in your red banquette and order some very overpriced fried food from your half-in-the-grave waiter. Dangerfield's is celebrating its 25th anniversary. It seems the only reason they've survived this long is because of the celebrity name on the front door.

## D.B.A.
**41 1st Ave. (bet. 2nd & 3rd Aves.)**
**475-5097**

*ALL MAJOR CREDIT CARDS*

Stands for "Doing Business As." What that means, couldn't tell ya. This mini microbrewery has become quite popular over the past few years, and though it is in the East Village, it caters to a predominately yuppie uptown crowd. D.B.A. is a comfortable place with nice big tables, a huge beer selection and friendly service. With its special drink events such as bourbon, cognac and malt tasting nights, the drink aficionado is sure to remain occupied. Beer "flights" are available if you can't decide on a beer and you want to sample several specialty brews at a time. In the spring there's a large garden out back that's a definite plus.

## DEADLINE (CLOSED)
**1649 3rd Ave. (At 92nd St.)**

## DECADE
**1117 1st Ave. (At 61st St.)**
**835-5979**

*ALL MAJOR CREDIT CARDS*

Finally, a place where the 30s-50s crowd can let loose! Decade, a large and upscale baby boomer's supper club, packs a dance floor with hits from the `60s, `70s and `80s. The

83

outer borough crowd is dressed up and primped to the max (jackets are required). Upstairs, a VIP dining room sits within the confines of a 4,000 bottle wine vault. There's also a glass-encased private humidor room for members. The service is impeccable, down to the coat check, making it a truly adult experience. There's even an ATM machine at the end of the bar! Cover is $20 on the weekend, and it gets crowded so get there early.

## DECIBEL
**240 E. 9th St. (bet. 2nd & 3rd Aves.)**
**979-2733**

*ALL MAJOR CREDIT CARDS*

Descend the stairs into the dark and cramped basement entryway and enter what could be mistaken as a Japanese brothel with lights dark enough to protect the anonymity of its patrons. Round the corner and you'll find a room large and comfortable enough to put you at ease but with ceilings low enough and tables small enough to make you feel like you're in an authentic Japanese bar. The Japanese decor, Japanese bartenders, and largely Japanese clientele only further this authenticity. Even the menu, which features an extensive list of sake, is in Japanese with English subtitles. There's a selection of reasonably priced, yet unreasonably small appetizers. A great place for those who like something different.

## DELIA'S SUPPER CLUB
**197 E. 3rd St. (bet. Aves. A & B)**
**254-9184**

*ALL MAJOR CREDIT CARDS*

Open since 1988, Delia's used to attract more of a downtown scene but has since turned its tiny dance floor over to the Euro and Upper East Side crowds. Nonetheless, a four course prix fixe dinner for around $35 makes this a great place to spend the evening eating, lounging, dancing, etc. The dance floor is tiny, so be brave and claim your spot before it gets packed. If you're just looking to dance, aim to go after midnight when the cover is a mere $10.

## DELMONICO'S
**56 Beaver St. (At South Williams St.)**
**509-1144**

*ALL MAJOR CREDIT CARDS*

Originally serving the New York City big wigs from 1838, Delmonico's reopened its doors to the dark suited, well established Wall St. crowd in May 1998. The well dressed, older and predominately male clientele cluster around a large octagonal bar sipping Scotch and talking shop. Some highlights of this old school bar are the 13 single malts and 14 whiskies ranging from $7-30. The bar menu varies from steak sandwiches to oysters on the half shell ($6-$15). The atmosphere is dark, quiet and noticeably smoky with soft, indescribable easy listening music filling the air. Females entering Delmonico's alone and not clad in conservative business attire may find themselves being gawked at as if they are high priced call girls. Delmonico's best serves those who are on a "the sky's the limit" expense account M-F, 12-1am and Sat. 4-12am.

## DELTA GRILL
**700 9th Ave. (At 48th St.)**
**956-0934**

*ALL MAJOR CREDIT CARDS*

The facade is that of a Bourbon Street pub—somewhat tacky for New York and certainly out of place for Hell's Kitchen. The kitschy Louisiana theme continues inside where a homogeneous crowd seems to be seeking refuge here because it feels "more like home." A bright neon beer sign above the bar makes the lighting bright and awkward and will reveal any facial flaws...not good for dates! Nonetheless, it's a lively place that offers a good selection of beers and some Cajun specialty eats. If you want a real non-New York experience, come here.

**DENIAL**
**46 Grand St. (bet. W. B'way & Thompson Sts.)**
**925-9449**

*ALL MAJOR CREDIT CARDS*

Along the trendy, loud streets of SoHo lies a small comfortable retreat called Denial. This sake bar/lounge serves 15 high-end sakes and finger food. The décor is simple, modern and comfortable with very peaceful music playing in the background. This isn't the place to come rage with your frat buddies, but it's not a bad spot to take your date and show that you have evolved from dragging your knuckles on the ground.

**DENIM & DIAMONDS (CLOSED)**
**511 Lexington Ave. (47th/48th St.)**

**DENNISON'S**
**137 Franklin St.**
**226-9000**

*ALL MAJOR CREDIT CARDS*

If not for the great live music, at least stop by to meet the owner—a hysterical, energy-filled, throwback from the '70s, equipped with a Scooby Doo tie and a wardrobe that puts "Welcome Back Kotter" to shame. No-frills trashy restaurant by day/club by night, Dennison's is open till the crowd leaves. Thursday, catch the Joy Riders River Club Band playing soulful blues. Friday, Carlos Cervantes' Latin Jazz Funk holds court in the intimate lounge upstairs. Late night on Fridays, the DJ from the club "Mother" spins tunes to draw the NY freaks to Tribeca. All in all, it's a great little music spot for the 30s+ crowd and worthy of a visit if you happen to be in the neighborhood.

## DETOUR
**349 E. 13th St. (bet. 1st & 2nd Aves.)**
**533-6212**

*ALL MAJOR CREDIT CARDS*

Jazz, jazz, and more jazz. This cozy club, which has been around for three years, is a pleasant get away from the surrounding East Village bars. People come here for the free music seven nights a week. Friendly bartenders serve strong and reasonably priced drinks in a comfortable space with air that is surprisingly not soup-thick with cigarette smoke. For a fun, easy going and relaxed evening, this is a great little spot. Happy hour is Monday-Friday 4pm-7pm.

## DHARMA
**174 Orchard St. (bet. Houston & Stanton)**
**780-0313**

*ALL MAJOR CREDIT CARDS*

Who knew that an old shoe store could look so swank? If you're looking for that perfect little jazz spot on a creepy block to bring your date, this is it. Dharma, opened in 1998, has ambiance and class. On a balcony at the end of this long narrow space, top-notch salsa and jazz groups groove like superstars. Seating, though somewhat limited, is simple and cozy. Catering to an array of well-behaved yuppie bohemians, Dharma is unique and definitely worth the trip. An exceptionally friendly staff and beautiful space make Dharma one of a kind. Great spot for that after dinner drink.

## DICK'S
**192 2nd Ave. (At 12th St.)**
**475-2071**

*CASH ONLY*

Although an appropriate name for this sleazy East Village bar, don't let it scare you away. At first glance, Dick's is a seedy, darkly lit and minimally decorated bar filled with oglers past their prime. On second glance, it's basically the same. It takes until about three or four glances to realize that the bar is actually a pretty relaxed and friendly neighborhood dive where the drinks are as cheap and strong as the clientele. The geriatric locals play pool or pinball while surreptitiously glancing at the porn flicks that sometimes play on the overhead television sets. Meanwhile, those bored with the other East Village bars revel in the excellent jukebox that features alternative rock and semi-rarities from the 70s and 80s. Dick's is a fine place to start the night and a sad place to end it.

## DIVA
**341 W. B'way (bet. Broome & Grand Sts.)**
**941-9024**

*ALL MAJOR CREDIT CARDS*

This elegant and romantic little hot spot is known more for its eye candy than its food. High ceilings, deep red walls, and small candle-lit tables set the stage for a romantic Euro-trash evening. Rife with model wannabes and men in black turtlenecks, the crowd is certainly easy on the eye. Come for dinner and drinks, hang out at the bar, and flex your ego. If the "Gypsy Kings" are your band of choice, you'll love it here. Late night, Diva and its neighboring bar Novecento turn lower SoHo into "Euro-Trash Drive."

## DIVE 75
**101 W. 75th St. (bet. Columbus & Amsterdam)**
**362-7518**

*ALL MAJOR CREDIT CARDS*

Formerly a scuba diving shop, Dive 75 now features cigars priced from $2.50-$10 in addition to an international beer list. There's an awesome modern jukebox with tunes from John Cougar Mellencamp to Ella Fitzgerald and a center stage fish tank filled with exotic, aquatic creatures. Sit on one of the stools that line the street window or on the red velvet couch and relax with a Belgian beer and a cigar.

**DIVINE BAR**
**244 E. 51st St. (bet. 2nd and 3rd aves)**
**319-9463**

*ALL MAJOR CREDIT CARDS*

This two-story midtown bar has a mixed crowd ranging from in-the-know twenty and thirtysomethings to the older and more established. The first floor has a restaurant feel with large terra-cotta tiles and large vintage posters of wine and Bacchanalia. The second floor lounge area, with its couches and fireplaces, is a cozy retreat from the noisy and cigar friendly first floor. Tapas are Divine's specialty, as are the 60 wines they offer on tap and the extensive foreign beer menu. A popular after-work spot for the chic midtown suits. Open for business Mon.–Wed., 5pm-2am; Thu.–Fri., 5pm-3am; Sat., 7pm-3am and Sun., 7pm-1am.

**DIVINE BAR**
**55 Liberty St. (bet. B'way and Nassau)**
**791-WINE**

*ALL MAJOR CREDIT CARDS*

Chic velvet couches, marble tables, funky lighting, art deco posters and zebra print bar stools lure the new generation of Wall St. hipsters into the financial district's most unorthodox lounge. While a selection of 45 imported and domestic beers, 65 wines by the glass, 8 single malt scotches, 14 flights of wine, and a list of specialty martinis may be daunting, the friendly waiters and funky colorful décor make it next to impossible to have a bad time. The upstairs to this large bi-level lounge has enough sofas and chairs to seat a small nation comfortably. Since the music is set at a volume pleasing to most ears, engaging in a conversation with friends isn't a harrowing experience. The tapas menu is extensive and offers a wide range of items suiting even the most finicky palate. Every hour at Divine Bar has the potential to be a happy hour.

### DOC HOLIDAY'S
**141 Ave. A (At 9th St.)**
**979-0312**

*CASH ONLY*

To call this place a dive would be a complement. At Doc Holiday's, the drinks are cheap and so is the atmosphere. A lot of thought went into the décor. Neon beer signs, a string of Christmas lights over the bar, and a couple posters of half-naked women scotch taped to the walls screams, "class." The only reason to go here is to play pool or hook up with an ex-con on a pinball machine.

### DOC WATSON'S
**1490 2nd Ave. (bet. 77th & 78th Sts.)**
**988-5300**

*ALL MAJOR CREDIT CARDS*

This narrow Irish bar is cozy and laid back and is a breath of fresh air in this frat-infested area. The bartenders are attentive and friendly, and there is a definite fuzziness about it that keeps a regular crowd coming back for more. A full bar and decent beer selection makes this a great pit stop for a quick one.

### DON HILL'S
**511 Greenwich St. (At Spring St.)**
**334-1390**

*CASH ONLY*

Don Hill's defines the down and dirty club scene that NYC is known for. The space is minimally decorated with graffiti art and an urban old-school style, bringing a streetwise realness for the freaks to party in. The huge space provides plenty of room at the bar for drinking and a great space for dancing, Pay $10 to join "Thursday Night Fever" at "BeavHer" and dance your ass off to early '80s pop wave. Friday's "Squeezebox" rocks on with a punky, queer crowd with a fair helping of straights, celebrities and freaks. Miss Guy spins freaky funk and punk rock while Sherry Vine plays hostess to drag acts and bands. Live rock n' roll acts including the well known punk band called "The Toilet Boys" are well worth the $10 cover charge. Drinks are strong and reasonable while admission differs per night. Climb out of the mainstream and join the psychotic funkiness of downtown's Don Hill's.

## DOCK'S OYSTER BAR
**633 3rd Ave. (At 40th St.), 986-8080**
**2427 B'way (bet. 89th & 90th Sts.), 724-5588**

*ALL MAJOR CREDIT CARDS*

Packed with an eclectic older crowd, Dock's offers a lively scene. If you can find a seat, it's a great place for an after-work drink and appetizer. Though Dock's is mostly known for being one of New York's finest seafood restaurants, a large bar in the center attracts the "drinks only" crowd making it a tight squeeze during happy hour.

## DONALD SACKS
**220 Vesey St. (World Financial Center)**
**619-4600**

*ALL MAJOR CREDIT CARDS*

This unremarkable and overpriced Wall Street bar, like many of its nearby nemeses (Moran's, Johnny's Fish Grill and Minters), caters to a captive audience of suits and draws a crowd simply because there is nowhere else to go. What it lacks in ambiance, it does not make up for in food and drink. After-work 2-for-1 Bud Light specials and free stale pretzels are about the only reason to come here.

## DON'T TELL MAMA
**343 W. 46th St. (bet. 8th & 9th Aves.)**
**757-0788**

*ALL MAJOR CREDIT CARDS*

This is one of Manhattan's greatest bars open daily from 4 pm till 2 am and Friday and Saturday till 4 am. With live jazz music nightly, this cabaret/piano bar and nightclub is free! There's a daily half-price happy hour from 4-7 pm and drinks prices range from $4-$6. For those of you who like Karaoke the good old fashioned way—impromptu and loud—there's a piano player following the live jazz. Even though it tends to be a tourist trap, it's a great place to practice your Broadway show tunes.

## DORIAN'S
**1616 2nd Ave. (At 84th St.)**
**772-6660**

*ALL MAJOR CREDIT CARDS*

This is the bar that you go to when you come home from college because you think it's *really* cool. After realizing the error of your ways you then spend the rest of your life denying that you ever went there and bashing it for being a bastion of fratheads and airheads looking to get lucky. Dorian's has been around forever, everyone has heard of it, and everyone knows exactly what to expect. It's your basic bar that is chock full of young Upper East Siders armed with great fake IDs. Picnic-style tables with good eats in the back has kept this place a popular pit-stop to eat, fill up on booze and pick up a date for the walk home.

## DOUBLE HAPPINESS
**173 Mott St. (At Broome St.)**
**941-1282**

*ALL MAJOR CREDIT CARDS*

Hidden in the heart of Little Italy, this cavernous, basement lounge is extremely trendy. A renovated mob restaurant, it's simply decorated with a Chinese/Mediterranean feel and lots of original brickwork in the archways and behind the bar. With white tile lining the walls and dim candle light, the scene is comfortable and relaxing. Expect to lounge around with an artsy crowd listening to the sounds of a live DJ who spins 7 nights a week from 7pm - 4am. Owned by the people who own the Orchard Bar, "Double Happiness" represents

92

the Chinese character for marriage. Good luck finding this place. It is very hidden with no sign and there's no hint of life in the area. But seek and ye shall find...Double Happiness.

## DOWN THE HATCH
**179 W. 4th St. (bet. 6th & 7th Aves.)**
**627-9747**

*ALL MAJOR CREDIT CARDS*

Relive your glorious fraternity days at this all-you-can-eat, all-you-can-drink, best-bang-for-your-buck underground dive. Wash down plate after plate of the best chicken wings in town with pitcher after pitcher of watery beer. The crowd is predominately made up of young, post-college guys and gals looking to do what it takes to get some lovin'. This is a wing and beer lovers delight where people don't call it quits until what goes "down the hatch," comes back up.

## DOWNTIME
**251 W, 30th St. (bet. 7th & 8th Aves.)**
**695-2747**

*ALL MAJOR CREDIT CARDS*

A hangout for musicians, rockers and clubers, Downtime's three-tiered space hosts various events nightly. The bottom level showcases bands on a decently sized stage surrounded by candlelit tables. The balcony has a smaller bar and a pool table that overlooks the stage. The top floor is a comfortable dance space with yet another bar and pool table that's open Fridays and Saturdays at 11pm. The crowd changes nightly but expect plenty of "bridge and tunnelers." Mondays hosts a blues jam, Tuesdays through Thursdays are rock nights, and the weekend is reserved for R & B and hip-hop. Beer starts at $5 and drinks range from $6-$10. Prepare to yield at the velvet rope and pay a small cover charge. Call ahead for event listings.

**DRINKLAND**
**339 E. 10th St. (bet. Aves. A & B)**
**228-2435**

*CASH ONLY*

Though the popularity of this hot spot has died down significantly, Drinkland remains one of the cooler looking downtown bars. If you're in need of a dark funky place to find a seat and talk, you can actually do it here. Eclectic, fashionable and young sophisticates cluster in one of three separate drinking areas. There's a long slick bar in the main room that leads into a nook of glowing, spiral tables among velvet-draped walls. But the piece de resistance is the notorious White Room, a wall-to-wall vinyl den right out of "Clockwork Orange." Drinks could be bigger, better, and stronger but no one seems to be complaining. A cool meet-for-a-drink date spot.

**DRIP**
**489 Amsterdam Ave. (bet. 83rd & 84th Sts.)**
**875-1032**

*ALL MAJOR CREDIT CARDS*

Matchmaker, matchmaker, make me a match! Waiting for the person of your dreams? Cindy Crawford is unavailable, but why not mull over your other 13,000 options with a spiked Milky Way Latte. This Upper West Side rendition of Chuck Woollery meets Starbucks has been a hot spot since it opened over two years ago. They have already matched two marriages and four couples are on their way to the altar. This coffee bar and drink lounge provides a dating service free of charge. Simply fill out a Drip dating form and voila! You're in the database. Drip is complete with a full bar and special liquor-laced drinks.

**DROVER'S TAP ROOM**
**9 Jones Street (bet. Bleecker & W. 4th Sts.)**
**627-1233**

*ALL MAJOR CREDIT CARDS*

With only 11 seats at the bar, DTR seems like a quaint, homey neighborhood place, but in fact patrons travel crosstown and downtown for a taste of classic American comfort food. Named after the bootlegging grandparents of the owner, Drover's is more a restaurant (offshoot of "Home" on Cornelia St.) than a bar, but it sure is great. They only serve New York beers on tap—how's that for being hometown proud? Come here with a few friends and bask in the ambience of simplicity.

## DRUIDS
**736 10th Ave. (bet. 50th & 51st Sts.)**
**307-6410**

### ALL MAJOR CREDIT CARDS

For all those non-Hell's Kitchen denizens looking for a quiet beer garden in the summer, or a change of pace for an after work cocktail, Druids should be your destination from this point forward. A wonderful mix of locals, friends, and workers, the mood is always festive. The mahogany bar beckons the Ireland of yore and the modern paintings don't really fit in, but somehow they go perfectly. Drink prices are much less expensive than most watering holes—$4 bottled beer and most well drinks are $4. American cuisine with a flair is sold if you work up an appetite.

## DT/UT
**1626 2nd Ave. (bet. 84th & 85th Sts.)**
**327-1327**

### CASH ONLY

Not so much a bar per say, but definitely worth mentioning, this downtown-meets-uptown spot is a combo coffee bar/drink bar that's very popular among the young and hip Upper East Siders (yes, there are a few). It's a comfy place to sit, read, write, hang, have a coffee, have a beer...whatever! It's the only place like this that you'll find in this neck of the woods. The crowd is young, healthy looking and intellectual. A snack bar offers a slew of yummy treats.

## THE DUGOUT
**185 Christopher St. (bet. West & Wash. Sts.)**
**242-9113**

Good summer hangout for the pier cruising set. Hairy older guys with large bellies enjoy the drink specials, large TV, pool table and pinball machine. All in all, it's a very laid back bar with an older and friendly crowd who have seen it all. Stop in on roller blades for a Bloody Mary or beer and then navigate the piers afterwards.

## DUKE'S
**99 E. 19th St. (bet. Irving Pl. & Park Ave. S.)**
**260-2922**

*ALL MAJOR CREDIT CARDS*

Names and locations can be deceiving. This ain't no Park Avenue martini bar, it could possibly be the Bennigan's of New York City. With lots of neon signs, wood furniture and assorted rummage sale items pinned to the walls, this bar/grill draws the after work crowd and delights them with inexpensive margaritas, nachos and chicken wings. While classic rock wails from the stereo, young urban professionals tie one on until the doors close at 11 pm. (On the weekends they close at 1 am.) Hearty portions of ribs and chicken are served at the bar as well as in the large restaurant area in the back. Tread carefully down the steps to the bathroom—the grease-laden steps could cause you to plummet into a license plate nailed into the wall. Don't dress to impress at Duke's—a drunken co-worker is bound to spill some high-octane margarita all over you.

## DUPLEX
**61 Christopher St. (At 7th Ave.)**
**255-5438**

*CASH ONLY*

This popular, lively West Village bar dishes up the kind of vibe and energy that makes you want to jump up on the bar and burst into song...and that's exactly what some people do. Like a duplex, there are two levels: An upstairs which is a tiny, nondescript room with a bar, pool table and jukebox, and a main floor where you'll find the happy-go-lucky, I'm-okay-you're-okay songbirds singing along to the tunes banged out by the eccentric pianist. There's Karaoke on some nights, but they warn ahead that you can take the mike only if you can *actually* sing. The crowd is 30-ish and predominantly gay.

## DUSK
**147 W. 24th St. (bet. 6th & 7th Aves.)**
**924-4490**

*ALL MAJOR CREDIT CARDS*

Dusk of London conveys the feeling of a private club. The lounge is grand with its long flowing bar and a vibe that is pretentious, tranquil and cushy. With exposed brick walls, dim lighting and old-fashioned, library-type tables and chairs, you get the feeling of being in some underground lounge in the outskirts of London. While your average mixed drink is about $5.50, beers are $4 and the bar offers a selection of cigars. House wines range from $11 to $28 a glass, while Johnny Walker Blue goes for about $20 a shot. For regulars, you can expect your own private bottle of liquor waiting for you on the top shelf of the bar. The sound system leaves something to be desired, and the energy of this bar is nonexistent.

## E&O (THE SUZY WONG ROOM) (CLOSED)
**100 Houston St. (Laguardia Pl./Thomp.)**

## THE EAGLE
**142 11th Ave. (At 21st St.)**
**691-8451**

*ALL MAJOR CREDIT CARDS*

This is a serious leather/Levi's spot open for the 30+ crowd only! This one pick-up spot where the proceeds on every drink benefit the PWA Coalition. Here real men participate in Wet Jock Strap contests every Wednesday night. Thursday you can put on your best leather and smoke cigars with the bad boys while licking someone's boots. Cigars are only $1! Come play pool, relax, kick up your boots, and experience classic leather at its best.

**EAR INN**
**326 Spring St.**
**(bet. Greenwich & Wash. Sts.)**
**226-9060**

*ALL MAJOR CREDIT CARDS*

An absolute charmer of a place, it's hard to imagine that this once was a riverside bar before the landfills extended the shoreline of Manhattan. Since the 1870s, Ear Inn , NYC's 2$^{nd}$ oldest bar, has been catering to the many thirsty souls of the city. It's amazing that the very down-to-earth, no frills crowd has not gotten pushed aside by the new wave of SoHo/TriBeCa locals, or the uptown hipsters that cram into Don Hill's around the corner. Ear has a fine selection of beer on tap and the food is quite good. For added entertainment you can color on your paper tablecloth while experiencing a piece of history.

**EAST OF EIGHTH**
**254 W. 23rd St. (bet. 7$^{th}$ & 8th Aves.)**
**352-0075**

*ALL MAJOR CREDIT CARDS*

Downstairs, off the not-so-happening 23$^{rd}$ street strip, you'll find this cozy Chelsea semi-lounge. It's a warm, friendly place that stands on its own as a bar, even though it's really part of a restaurant that caters to a sophisticated, predominately gay crowd. Far from a pick-up scene, East of Eighth is a neighborhood place where anyone is welcome. The beer selection is good and moderately priced, and the hip tunes keep the vibe alive. If you're lucky enough to grab one of the few tables, plant yourself there for the evening. Otherwise it's standing room only, and it gets crowded!

## EAST SIDE ALE HOUSE — CLOSED
**961 2nd Ave. (51st St.)**

## THE EDGE
**95 E. 3rd (bet. 1st & 2nd Aves.)**
**477-2940**

*CASH ONLY*

What looks like an East Village bar from the outside is just a facade for a scary neighborhood bar gone frat. Covered in lots of masonry, this two-room bar has a pool table and a dart board and attracts lots of trashy clientele wearing sneakers and shorts. Cozy up to the bar with frat boys who want everyone to know they're loving life. The jukebox is this dive's only saving grace and plays the likes of "The Boomtown Rats," "Adam Ant" and "Prince." Open for 12 years, this is definitely not a pickup bar.

## EIGHTY EIGHT'S
**228 W. 10th St. (bet. Bleecker & Hudson Sts.)**
**924-0088**

*ALL MAJOR CREDIT CARDS*

Upstairs, this swinging Cabaret Room hosts acts from the famous to the infamous for a varied cover charge and a two-drink minimum. Downstairs, the newly refurbished piano bar plays fabulous show tunes with a humorous twist. Talented staff will sing you some soulful solos or, if you're feeling Julie Andrews-ish, get up and sing one of your own!

## EL FLAMINGO
**547 W. 21st. St. (bet. 10th & 11th Aves.)**
**243-2121**

*ALL MAJOR CREDIT CARDS*

A very Latin crowd heads down to El Flamingo for their amazing "Latin Night" every Sunday. Different, and usually well-known live acts give you Manhattan's best salsa and merengue. Cover is $5 for ladies all night and $10 for men. The club's serious 1940s deco interior brings out the best in Latin fashion and the dress code is serious. No jeans or sneakers and if you're not decked out in your best, it might be difficult to get inside. They have theme nights during the week (call ahead for details) but generally expect music that caters to a Latin crowd. Have a cocktail ($5-6) and witness some amazing dancing.

## EL TEDDY'S
**219 W. B'way (bet. Franklin & White Sts.)**
**941-7070**

*ALL MAJOR CREDIT CARDS*

This swanky and ultra-popular upscale Mexican restaurant is a good spot for doing the after work dinner/drink thing. The small bar in the front is always crowded with young, professional singles *trying* to keep a low profile as they subtly check each other out. The enormous bi-level space is a work of art (literally) with its intricate ceilings and walls of mosaic and broken glass. Serving close to 30 different margaritas (one will do the job), El Teddy's mixes a great drink that's well worth the extra cash. Outdoor tables in the summer make for a great weekend afternoon date spot.

## ELAINE'S
**1703 2nd Ave. (bet. 88th & 89th Sts.)**
**534-8103**

*ALL MAJOR CREDIT CARDS*

Woody Allen and Geraldo Rivera are just a few of the celebrities who pay homage to this historical and unpretentious bar/restaurant. The nightly presence of Elaine herself makes this standby authentic, and her love of the arts is obvious when you see the many playbills and movie posters hanging from the walls. The menu is expensive and so are the drinks. Have a seat at the small bar next to some faintly familiar looking people since the tables and chairs are reserved for certain "important" guests. Take this place for what it is—a place to people watch and collect stories to tell. A definite 30s-40s+ crowd.

## ELBOW ROOM
**144 Bleecker St. (bet. Thompson & LaGuardia Pl.)**
**979-8434**

*ALL MAJOR CREDIT CARDS*

It's standing room only in this remarkably huge, musical showcase bar. Funk, blues, rock and hardcore bands perform nightly on a concert-like stage that is illuminated by amazing theatrical lighting and backed by a kick-ass sound system. Between bands, loud techno and house music fill the hall. Although there is a small cover on the weekends, drinks are cheap. Be prepared to fight to get a drink with a young, bridge-and-tunnel crowd made up mostly of men on the prowl.

## ELEMENT ZERO
**215 E. 10th St. (bet. 1st & 2nd Aves.)**
**780-9855**

*CASH ONLY*

A funky, London underground scene situated right in the heart of the East Village, Element Zero is reminiscent of a high school rave. With a very friendly and young crowd, it's a great bar to take your out-of-town friend. Only one friend though; maximum capacity in this place is about 10 people! The low ceilings and trippy lighting will lead you straight to the bar for a Schlitz beer or Vodka Cool-aid.

## ELEVENTH STREET BAR
**510 E. 11th St. (bet. Aves. A & B)**
**982-3929**

*ALL MAJOR CREDIT CARDS*

Golly Gee! It's the official John Tesh bar of the East Village! With its wide-planked wooden floors, long simple bar, and corn husks on the wall, Eleventh Street Bar feels more like a place out of DC or Boston, and leaves you with a "clean" feeling. Beer, wine and coffee are served to an older, more conservative crowd that seeks refuge from the artsy-fartsy Avenue A scene. Ample seating at the bar and candlelit tables in the back make it a great place to chat or bring a date. Note: There's no sign outside so have patience.

## ELLEN O'DEES
**130 E. 40th St. (bet. Lex. And 3rd Aves.)**
**213-3998**

*ALL MAJOR CREDIT CARDS*

The first thing you will want to do when you walk in is march up to the owner and tell him to update the sign outside. We're talking 1960s bubble writing...yikes! This brightly lit bar offers the local clientele inexpensive drinks, beer by the pitcher, and other assorted specials. A jukebox, pool table and array of video games help keep everyone entertained. Bartenders have little or no interest in new-comers, and the locals will throw you a glance as you stroll past them on your way to the dark restrooms downstairs. Come by if you're interested in establishing a presence, but otherwise stick to some of the better places in the area.

## EL RIO GRANDE
**160 E. 38th St. (bet. Lex. & 3rd Aves.)**
**867-0922**

*ALL MAJOR CREDIT CARDS*

Made up of two separate spaces—an indoor restaurant and an outdoor terrace—this spot is strictly for the after-work crowd. It's one of the few large outdoor terraces in the area besides the Penn Top and the drinks are actually affordable. However, it is so crowded on nice summer days that it becomes painfully hard to reach the small bar for one of the great margaritas. The crowd here is typical of any popular midtown after-work spot—it has a little bit of everything and is predominantly made up of twentysomethings.

**ELSIE'S**
**304 E. 84 St. (bet. 1st & 2nd Aves.)**
**No Phone**

*CASH ONLY*

Elsie's is an institution on the Upper East Side. There is no sign outside—only a few burned-out neon lights. After a quick knock on the door, Elsie will buzz you in because, well, it's her apartment. You will instantly feel like you're in your grandmother's living room as you sit at the short wooden bar and listen to a jukebox that plays recordings from the '30s. Once you see Elsie throw back a shot of Jaeger, you'll realize that your grandmother was never quite like this! If you're looking for an exciting, earth shattering experience, this place is not for you.

**EMERALD PUB**
**308 Spring St. (At Hudson St.)**
**226-8512**

*ALL MAJOR CREDIT CARDS*

A tad too blue collar for this part of town, Emerald Pub has been open for 27 years and could easily be found in any suburban town on the East Coast. With very bright lighting, sports playing on TV and a working fireplace, there is not much happening at the Emerald. With seven beers on tap, mixed drinks will run you between $4-$6 while beers go for $3.50 - $4. A reasonably priced menu serves up burgers, salads and pasta while a dull jukebox plays anything from Journey to the Pogues. An open mic night on Wed. night is about it for entertainment. Open daily from 10:30am – 4:00am.

**EMERALD SALOON**
**618 Amsterdam Ave. (At 90th St.)**
**787-9628**

*ALL MAJOR CREDIT CARDS*

This Irish, neighborhood saloon is what you would expect to find after getting a flat tire in the middle of nowhere. The wood paneling is a small hint that not much has changed in the last 20 years, including the weathered clientele. Everyone knows everyone else here, and they look out for each other. A handwritten sign stating "Resuscitator Behind Bar" sums up the vibe where the bartender has a striking resemblance to Moe from "The Simpsons." Drinks are cheap—$2.75 beers; $3 well drinks; $3.75 pints—and there's free food on Sundays and holidays.

## THE EVELYN
**380 Columbus Ave. (bet. 78th & 79th Sts.)**
**724-2363**

*ALL MAJOR CREDIT CARDS*

A larger-than-expected series of rooms are filled with a very good-looking crowd made up of mostly tall men and spunky girls in cute outfits. There are two full bars and four separate rooms for hard-core lounging. Come to The Evelyn to hang out, maybe get a few digits or just people watch. If you get hungry, the restaurant upstairs—formerly Phebes—offers American fare at reasonable prices. Evelyn tries to be a sleek downtown scene for uptown yuppies but the cool yuppies are already south of Houston, so don't expect to meet any Renaissance men and women. The bar service is of good quality but the mediocre drinks and presentation do not warrant the $25+ you'll drop for three of them. The times that we visited we were happily surprised with the quality of live music. Two excellent jazz acts far exceeded our expectations. Never a cover!

## EXILE
**117 W. 70th St. (bet. Columbus & B'way)**
**496-3272**

*ALL MAJOR CREDIT CARDS*

Dark enough to hide all of your sins, yet light enough to establish whether or not you are willing to commit them with your neighbor, this new West Side establishment has a unique split-level bar and lounge area that conveys a bigger, yet more secluded feel to most of the seating. The additional outdoor garden is a huge draw in the warmer months. There is much posturing going on here, but the crowd seems to require that attitude to have fun. This feel is new for the Upper West Side, but the downtown brethren would be bored by it. To be fair, you are likely to run into an old college buddy here, but just as likely to have an uptight, Prada-toting poser trip on you as she stumbles for the bar.

**40 Flavors**
**40 W. 8th St.**
**(bet. MacDougall St. & 6th Ave.)**
**995-5767**

If hip-hop is what you want, then hip-hop is what you get at this small but cutting edge bar/club on the middle of the sleaziest block in Greenwich Village The crowd is young and urban hip with dance moves that would make James Brown jealous. The music is loud, the drinks are pretty cheap, and the mood screams party. This is as close to an LA rave as you're going to get in NYC. If the white man's over bite is your usual dance step, don't embarrass yourself, there is nobody here named Biff or Skippy. However, the crowd is a mult-cultural mix.

**44 @ THE ROYALTON HOTEL**
**44 W. 44th St. (bet. 5th & 6th Aves.)**
**944-8844**

*ALL MAJOR CREDIT CARDS*

Though somewhat past its glory days, 44 remains one of the better looking lounges in the city. The lobby of this un-marked Ian Schraeger hotel (the man behind Miami's Delano Hotel and NY's Asia de Cuba) is definitely where those who are in-the-know come to strike a pose. An ultra-thin staff in black mini-dresses wait on you hand and foot as you lounge on one of the many stark white cotton couches in the spacious lobby, or in the intimate leather-padded round room in the back. Pricey appetizers are served if you need a fix. For a super sleek and almost futuristic experience, check out the bathrooms. Men aim at a chrome wall—don't worry, a sensor picks up your presence and triggers a waterfall to wash over the mess.

## 420 BAR & LOUNGE
**420 Amsterdam Ave. (At 80th St.)**
**579-8450**

*ALL MAJOR CREDIT CARDS*

As bridge-and-tunnel as this crowd looks and acts, they're willing to spend the extra dollars (saved on Hoboken vs. NY rent) to pose at this SoHo-meets-Upper West Side lounge. Girls carry matching pocketbooks, while guys sporting black turtlenecks and sport coats lay rap. The upstairs bar is sleek and art deco with small tables filled with cliquey after work groups. The lower level is a bit more laid back with couches, a mini-bar, a pool table and 3 TV's. There is a private party room available, and a DJ spins booty-shaking tunes on Friday and Saturday nights. Good after-work spot.

## FANELLI'S
**94 Prince St. (At Mercer St.)**
**226-9412**

*ALL MAJOR CREDIT CARDS*

Built in 1862, this old style saloon has retained its Old World charm while the rest of SoHo has transformed into a strip mall. The mood inside is jovial and heavy. Like the black and white photo of Jake LaMotta on the wall, the clientele and staff are tough and down to earth. If it's a beer and burger that you crave, you've come to the right spot. The crowd ranges from 25 to almost pushing up daisies, but they all seem to enjoy the primitive and raucous neighborhood bar that was here long before SoHo was. Good place for afternoon lunch with the parents.

**FASHION CAFÉ (CLOSED)**
**51 Rockefeller Plaza**


**FEZ**
**380 Lafayette St. (At Great Jones St.)**
**533-2680**

***ALL MAJOR CREDIT CARDS***

Morocco meets a 1950s hair salon at this cozy and comfortable lounge with cushy couches, chairs and tiled tables. Colorful tiles line the walls as candlelit lanterns hang from the ceiling. Sadly, this interesting setting is one of the only worthwhile things about this place. The non-existent soul in conjunction with roped off couches on reserve and barely audible music makes the Moroccan Room of Fez not worth the time or the money. The bitchy hostess and waiters don't boost your moral either. Fez's saving grace is its basement lounge. Venture downstairs and pay $5 to see live reggae, swing and jazz bands. But don't get too excited about this musical oasis, the drinks are unbearably over priced. A Guinness is $5.75 while the "Fez" drink made of Absolut Citron, cranberry and lime juice is $7. Not only does Fez leave you with a bruised ego and an empty wallet—it may actually suck the life right out of you.


**55**
**55 Christopher St. (bet. 6th & 7th Aves.)**
**929-9883**

This West Village jazz/blues club is only slightly larger than your living room, with about 10 times more tables and chairs. Just imagine your normal neighborhood bar shrunk by 50%. Don't expect to have a conversation once the first set starts at 10:15 pm; just busy yourself with the tunes and the two-drink minimum per set. (Drinks are sold at the usual bar rate, but what you get is a little stingy.) The performers are on a rotating schedule of unknowns with the odd gem thrown in—hence the occasional inexpensive cover. Hey, you get free popcorn!

**5757 (AT THE FOUR SEASONS HOTEL)**
**57 E. 57th St. (bet. Park & Mad. Aves.)**
**758-5757**

*ALL MAJOR CREDIT CARDS*

Located in the lobby of the Four Seasons Hotel, this chic and stunning bar/restaurant is large, elegant and just what you'd expect from the people behind the Four Seasons. With live jazz nightly, the deco-styled room with its 18-foot windows, 33-foot ceilings and bronze chandeliers, is a perfect setting for a romantic after dinner drink. Dress to impress!

**FILM CENTER CAFÉ**
**635 9th Ave. (bet. 44th & 45th Sts.)**
**262-2525**

*ALL MAJOR CREDIT CARDS*

Though somewhat uninviting from the outside, this deco-style bar, opened in 1937, is a regular place, serving regular beers, to a regular crowd. TV's anchored in the corner of the mirrored bar play old movies to lounge/hipster music. Most people come here for the food, not the bar. Happy hour: ½ price drinks, Monday – Sunday from 4-6pm.

**FINNEGAN'S WAKE**
**1361 1st Ave (At 73rd St.)**
**737-3664**

*ALL MAJOR CREDIT CARDS*

Overshadowed by its popular neighbor, Yorkville Brewery, this intimate setting has a tendency to be a little sparse. Its heavy tables, pub menu, and dark décor remind one of an old Welsh pub, lending a charming atmosphere. Drinks are reasonably priced and if you're in the mood to chat with friends and stretch your legs, bring the gang here. The owners will *love* you for it.

**FIREHOUSE**
**522 Columbus Ave. (At 85ᵗʰ St.)**
**787-FIRE**

*ALL MAJOR CREDIT CARDS*

This is the place to go to watch football, get a beer (or three), and eat great wings. A favorite of the Upper West Side, the Firehouse has TVs at every angle and a satellite hook-up so you can't miss a play. During the NCAA's, they manage to show every game at once to satisfy its sports-obsessed clientele. A friendly, funny, down to earth wait staff serves some of the best bar food you can find. The inside of the bar is covered in antique firehouse paraphernalia giving it a really comfortable neighborhood feel. Of course, if you want to skip the sports and just go for the food, you can always opt for a table outside.

**FITZPATRICK'S**
**1641 2nd Ave. (At 85th St.)**
**988-7141**

*ALL MAJOR CREDIT CARDS*

If good clean drinkin' and sports watchin' is what you're lookin' for, your search ends here at Fitzpatrick's. Despite its seen-one-seen-'em-all décor, it's more upscale than most. The crowd at least appears to shower on a daily basis. The plethora of neon beer signs and sports TV's anchored in every corner definitely secures this as a guy's bar. However, the nightly drink special, the "Wu Wu," is somewhat out of its macho character.

**FLAMINGO EAST**
**219 2nd Ave. (bet. 13ᵗʰ & 14th Sts.)**
**533-2860**

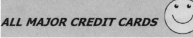

*ALL MAJOR CREDIT CARDS*

With its two floors of cool, modern, lounge furniture, this swanky East Village bar really hits the mark. Downstairs there's a sleek dining area with modern light fixtures and a small bar. Upstairs there's a much larger space with a second bar packed with a trendy, twentysomething crowd. If it gets too smoky, get some fresh air on the outdoor terrace. By far one of the better East Village venues, Flamingo East is a fun, cool place to lounge and meet people.

## FLIGHT 151
**151 8th Ave. (bet. 17th & 18th Sts.)**
**229-1868**

*ALL MAJOR CREDIT CARDS*

A great bar to start the night with a few friends, Flight 151 features good food and drinks, at great prices. Have a hamburger and a beer while you draw on the paper tablecloths with crayons to the beat of your favorite songs. In any Midwestern city, Flight 151 would really, well, take off! But in trendy Chelsea, a bar whose motif is airplane kitsch and weekday specials includes "Flip Night" (if you call the coin flip correctly, you can drink free), flight 151 gives the impression of trying too hard. By employing all of the tools of the trade on how to entertain customers, it makes for a hokey and entertaining evening. It's also one of the only straight bars in this neck of the woods.

## FLIGHT 1668
**1668 3rd Ave. (bet. 93rd & 94th Sts.)**
**426-1416**

*ALL MAJOR CREDIT CARDS*

If you're a "Wings" fan, you'll love Flight 1668. This Upper East Side bar is replete with vintage airplane paraphernalia, and although on first impression you'll think it's cheesy, this theme bar is a nice break from the three-Irish-pub-per-city-block quota in this part of town.

## FLOAT
**240 W. 52nd St. (bet. 8th Ave. & B'way)**
**581-0055**

*ALL MAJOR CREDIT CARDS*

The badly behaved offspring of a cutting-edge club *and* a country club, this is Float, people, and it needs to sink. Never mind that Jennifer Lopez celebrated her 30th birthday here, let's start at the beginning, shall we? If you're bitchy and fabulous enough to make it past the velvet rope without choking someone with it, and can live with yourself after coughing up the offensive cover charge ($20, wed. and thurs.; $25, fri. and sat.), you enter the *pretend* privileged world of this night haunt, wandering down a dark hall to the thundering vibrations of progressive house music. Sound original? Well, it's not. With fake attitudes firmly in place and all the trimmings included, Float feels like a cheesy, TV version of a night club set brought to you by the FOX Network. The producers and set decorators thought of everything: The sexy, futuristic, glowing bar, the attractive, modern furniture right out of a Calvin Klein ad, the lit-from-within, icy blue, dancing platforms...it's all there, but with no sense of glamour, no soul. Once you're "in," it's "Blade Runner" all the way. Without explanation, a very "Men In Black" guy silently grabs your arm and stamps your inside wrist twice with an invisible something. Later, as you ascend a random staircase, another Corey Hart, "I Wear My Sunglasses At Night" dude cuts you off at the pass, reads your unseen tattoo with an infrared light saber "thingy," and up you go. Only after you wind up at the door to the VIP lounge does the mystery unfold, and another weirdo decodes you again. Want some advice? Don't go to Float unless you're prepared to go down with the rest of the crew.

## FLUTE
**205 W. 54th St. (bet. B'way & 7th Ave.)**
**265-5169**

*ALL MAJOR CREDIT CARDS*

Built into the floor of this small, ultra-chic former speakeasy, you'll find a bottle of '28 Vintage Krug in an air sealed, climate controlled encasement. Despite an initial temptation to smash it open with your foot, one must remain poised in this ultra-swanky champagne-lovers paradise (developed by the same mind behind Tribeca's Bubble Lounge). The thick blue velvet couches, small golden tables, and dim candlelight takes you away from the hectic midtown scene and causes you to momentarily forget the concrete jungle outside. The small, beautiful space serves more than 105 champagnes including 15 by the glass. (A flute of Dom is $26.) Complete with an impeccable staff, Flute is romantic, simple, elegant and calming. It's a perfect place for an after-theatre drink, or as an impress-your-date spot.

## FRAUNCES TAVERN RESTAURANT
**54 Pearl St. (Off Broad St.)**
**269-0144**

### *ALL MAJOR CREDIT CARDS*

Welcome to a little slice of history on Wall Street. Constructed in the 18th century and supposedly a favorite of George Washington's, this colonial tavern has a comforting lodge appeal. Looming taxidermy, from rhinos to lions to antelope, greet you at the door while genuine revolutionary muskets, flags, and etchings hang from the walls. Suits whoop it up while watching the game on TV and settling down into millionaire-style leather chairs with their stogies. For less noise, head to the spacious back room where you'll find a restaurant that serves a menu reminiscent of Maryland's Eastern Shore. Drink specials are offered nightly, Monday through Thursday. You don't have to be a Revolutionary War buff to truly appreciate this place—Fraunces is a real find.

## FRED'S BEAUTY
**4 W. 22nd St. (bet. 5th & 6th Aves.)**
**463-0888**

### *ALL MAJOR CREDIT CARDS*

Easily confused with Beauty Bar, a theme bar that looks like a beaty salon, Fred's Beauty is less concerned with manicures and more interested in packing the party in. This long and narrow bi-level space is huge and filled on the weekends with good-looking, young singles with style. The music is excellent and so are the drinks, provided you can get to the bar. A huge glass chandelier in the back hangs heavily over the crowd and forces one to wonder throughout the night, "how many people would it kill if it came crashing down?" Sick, but true. The glass theme is carried over to the brickwork where swirls of blue and green are soothing on the eye. Brutus-like bouncers stand inside and outside the bar to keep the masses in order. We suggest snagging a seat in the upstairs lounge to get some air.

**FREDERICK'S (CLOSED)**
**26 E. 64th St. (Madison/5th Ave.)**

**FRESSON**
**421 W. 13th St. (bet. 9th Ave. & Washington)**
**645-7775**

*ALL MAJOR CREDIT CARDS*

Deep in the heart of the meat packing district lies a diamond in the rough called Fresson. This swanky restaurant/ bar has a large dining area with cork-covered tables, extremely spacious booths and the most romantic lighting this side of Paris. Fresson does everything right. The drinks may be a bit pricey but they're strong and large. They serve basic American cuisine (grilled tuna, chicken, oysters), but do it better than most. Fresson seems to have put a lot of time and care into this lofty, beautiful space, and it shows by the throngs of beautiful people who keep coming back time and again for the food and the great bar scene. This is a definite recommendation for your next date or night out with your friends. Dress to impress.

**FROLIC ROOM (CLOSED)**
**188 Ave. A (12th St.)**

**FUJIYAMA MAMA**
**467 Columbus Ave. (bet. 82nd & 83rd Sts.)**
**769-1144**

***ALL MAJOR CREDIT CARDS***

A consistently smooth bar crowd and killer atmosphere can be found at Fujiyama Mama. With its soothing blue lights and zen-inspired decor, the Upper West Side should be thanking its lucky stars that it actually has a restaurant with character. An extremely serious staff whips up delectable sushi as the disco music blares and the after–work crew unwind.

**G**
**223 W. 19th St. (At 7th Ave.)**
**929-1085**

***ALL MAJOR CREDIT CARDS***

G is a super swanky, ultra trendy gay bar with awesome frozen cosmopolitans. Expect long lines every night of the week to enter the gay world of fashion and attitude. Banquettes and huge ottomans offer comfortable lounging and a good place to check out some of Manhattan's hottest men. The service is quick and friendly, and in addition to a top-notch martini, G also sports an incredible juice bar. Happy hour: Mon.- Fri. from 4-9pm.

**THE GAF**
**251 E. 85th St. (bet. 2nd & 3rd Aves.)**
**288-0966**

***CASH ONLY***

Formerly Pedros, The Gaf, which loosely translates into the "Meeting Place," is a miniscule Irish bar with original brick floors dating back to the 1890s. Attracting a recent college grad crowd, The Gaf is open seven days a week from 3:30pm – 4am. With cheap drink prices—$2 domestic beers, $3 drafts, and $4 shelf drinks—The Gaf hosts a daily happy hour from 4pm-7pm. With top forties hits on the jukebox, a bowling pin arcade, multiple sports banners and sports playing on television sets, the regulars say that The Gaf, "feels like home."

## THE GAF
**401 W. 48th St. (bet. 9th & 10th Aves.)**
**262-2883**

*CASH ONLY*

For those who are moving on up and feel nostalgia for Normandy Court days, this is the place to come. A satellite of the well-known Upper East side's Gaf, this brand new hangout is the perfect alternative for frat party revivalists, and new neighborhood yuppies from Wall Street and nearby ad agencies. Regulars crowd the place on Wednesday, Thursday and Saturday evenings. Entertainment abounds here— from the jukebox, to the TVs and mini bowling alley. A velvet lounge downstairs is safe for the more crowded nights, harking favorite college basement parties. Stop by to try the house special—the Bobby Socks cocktail.

## GALAXY
**15 Irving Place (At 15th St.)**
**777-3631**

*ALL MAJOR CREDIT CARDS*

This dark, crowded and loud restaurant/bar leaves you smelling like fried food. Carl Sagan's presence is strong as you sit in Galaxy's version of a planetarium equipped with black walls and teeny flashing stars on the ceiling and walls. To complete the mood, there are several astronomy-related drink specials to make you to feel like a total space cadet. As the techno music plays, bridge-and-tunnelers sardine themselves into booths on the weekend for very affordable food that many say is "from another world." (Interpret that how you like.) Come here for a bite after catching a show at its neighbor, Irving Plaza.

## GARAGE
**99 7th Ave. S. (bet. Barrow & Grove Sts.)**
**645-0600**

*ALL MAJOR CREDIT CARDS*

Like any good garage that stores a collection of many different things, this bar/restaurant, with its central location, draws an eclectic crowd. The warm, casual and relaxed atmosphere offers free live jazz. Date hit a plateau? Sit at one of the tables or booths upstairs, grab a beer and you'll be overcome by the romantic atmosphere (fireplaces have that effect) in no time! If that doesn't put you in the mood, the large island bar filled with 20- to 40-somethings serves raw bar specialties like oysters.  At times the bar gets cozy, but fear not, there's plenty of room to cruise. It's also tame enough to take the folks for a friendly and reasonably priced drink/brunch/dinner.

## GASLIGHT
**400 W. 14th St. (At 9th Ave.)**
**807-8444**

*ALL MAJOR CREDIT CARDS*

Check your coat at the door, sit in the main room on wrought-iron patio furniture or at one of the tall tables and soak in the great view through the floor to ceiling French doors. Reminiscent of a Victorian parlor with its antique couches, metal ceilings, hardwood floors and large mirrors, this open, loft-like bar is pleasing to the eye.  Dark velvet drapes separate the front from a smaller and more intimate back nook where live (though not great) music can be heard almost any night of the week.  Crowd ranges from age 25 to 40-years-old.

## GEMINI LOUNGE
**221 2nd Ave. (bet. 13th & 14th Sts.)**
**254-5260**

*ALL MAJOR CREDIT CARDS*

**SHIT LOUNGE!!! AVOID THIS PLACE UNLESS YOU WANT TO BE TREATED LIKE CATTLE. RUDEST BOUNCERS/ DOOR THUGS IN NYC. DON'T BOTHER WITH THIS SPOT.**

## GIN MILL
**442 Amsterdam Ave. (bet. 81st & 82nd Sts.)**
**580-9080**

### *ALL MAJOR CREDIT CARDS*

The Gin Mill, with its two floors of fun, really packs it in on the weekends. While a serious game of fooze-ball takes place in one corner, girls in overalls dance near the bar while goofy frat boys impress the babes with their funnel sucking capabilities. It's a get-drunk-and-have-fun place that will remind you of a Saturday night basement frat party after a big rugby game. A series of booths occupy the back area where you can order wings from Pluck-U. And speaking of chicken, the weekend Wing-a-thon offers patrons an all-you-can-eat deal for $12. The lower level is an inconspicuous private party room where additional drinking stupidity takes place. Happy hour: 4pm-7pm daily offers half price drinks. Ladies night: Tues. with $1 margaritas and free drafts from 7pm till closing. Outdoor seating in the Spring is always a plus.

## GINGER MAN
**11 E. 36th St. (bet. 5th & Mad. Aves.)**
**532-3740**

### *ALL MAJOR CREDIT CARDS*

Soft lights, high ceilings, and a rich decor lend ambiance to this popular bar that caters to a young and talkative after-work crowd. With a wide selection of over 100 inexpensive beers, helpful bartenders provide a few taste tests if you can't pick an ale on your own. This perfect after-work venue has a kick-ass jukebox that seems to please everyone's tastes. If you're not in the mood to deal with the meatmarket crowd in the front, escape to some of the couches tucked away in the back. Cigar-friendly.

**GLOBAL 33**
**93 2nd Ave. (bet. 5ᵗʰ & 6th Sts.)**
**477-8427**

*ALL MAJOR CREDIT CARDS*

This tapas bar located below street level hosts an array of cool lounge drinks, great snack food and a chic good-looking crowd. The bar area, with its lit-up wall of slide photos is modeled after an airport lounge from the 1960s. The drinks are a little pricey and the bar can get crowded, but it's great for people watching and definitely a pick-up spot for the ultra-hip.

**THE GLOBE**
**373 Park Ave. S. (bet. 26ᵗʰ & 27ᵗʰ Sts.)**
**545-8800**

*ALL MAJOR CREDIT CARDS*

This large, sterile bar located in the back of a '50s art deco restaurant is probably one of the most inviting lounges you'll find in Gramercy. In the front is a restaurant bustling with a lively mix of people who are enthusiastic about the predictably delicious cuisine and extensive wine list. Head to the back bar and you're greeted by comfortable booths and a friendly staff. The Globe is a great place to head after work or to bring a date.

**GLOCCAMORA**
**304 3rd Ave. (bet. 23ʳᵈ & 24st Sts.)**
**473-9638**

*ALL MAJOR CREDIT CARDS*

Gloccamora, a name taken from the movie "Finnians' Rainbow," represents a Shangri-La where everyone forgets their troubles...not! This neighborhood pub is coarse and draws a rough white trash clientele that enjoys shooting pool and eating shepherd's pie. With a jukebox playing rock-and-roll, it's a good place to drink cheap beer and hard, brand-x liquor in an attempt to temporarily forget the fact that your entire life is coming apart. With a couple of TVs showing sports highlights, the bar's only saving grace is the fact that Brad Pitt's cute little tush graced a bar stool or two—yes ladies, "Devil's Own" was shot here.

## GOLD BAR
**345 E. 9th St. (bet. 1st & 2nd Aves.)**
**505-8270**

### CASH ONLY

Around for 10 years, this tiny East Village bar draws in a local artsy crowd. Designed by German architect Thomas Leeser, the perfect combination of minimalism and industrialism transplants you into a modern day, Sprockets-like Germany. A lot of concrete, steel and granite add to the cool feel of this small bar.  You'll never see more than a handful here during the week making it a good place for quiet conversation.  The weekend however gets crowded as a DJ spins acid-jazz, hip-hop, reggae and bass. Although this joint is small and a bit cold and uncomfortable, the Gold Bar is a good space to view some art and interesting architecture.

## GONZALES Y GONZALES
**625 B'way (bet. Bleecker & Houston)**
**473-8787**

### ALL MAJOR CREDIT CARDS

Offensively large and crowded, this huge restaurant has been a fixture in the Village for about 10 years now. A flashy neon sombrero outside reel in tourists, neighborhood dwellers and Staten Island folk for its weekend salsa fests. Live bands perform nightly starting at 10pm from Wed. to Sat. turning the relatively calm restaurant into the Tijuana of New York City. Lots of hootchies and their men bust out their Latin moves among an overwhelming young and scantily dressed crowd. The bar is the longest bar in Manhattan serving up freezing margaritas, flavorable daiquiris and an array of Tequila. Open from 11am till 3am, this place is good for dinner with a large crowd. Just make sure you get there early and avoid it on the weekends.

## GOOD WORLD BAR & GRILL
**3 Orchard St. (At Division St.)**
**925-9975**

*ALL MAJOR CREDIT CARDS*

Yea! Another brand-new addition to the Lower East Side bar family! Good World's vibe is casual and so is the crowd. It's dark and probably for a good reason—the décor is nothing to write home about. But thank god for the French doors that open onto the street, keeping the place comfortable and airy. Locals and their dogs gravitate to the back patio where they can hang at picnic tables. Expect a different DJ every night. The mixed Scandinavian menu and selection of imported beers is a nice change.

## GOTHAM BAR & GRILL
**12 East 12th St.**
**(bet. 5th Ave. & University Pl.)**
**620-4020**

*ALL MAJOR CREDIT CARDS*

If you're looking for a way to impress a client, a date, or just looking for a way to spend a spectacular evening, look no further than Greenwich Village's quintessential dining experience. Gotham has cornered the market on flawless service, a superb wine list and providing tran-scendental experiences to those select few who can afford its sky-high prices. If you can only afford to indulge yourself, try ordering a meal served at the bar on a specially engineered tray, and choose a half bottle of wine from the extensive list.

## GOTHAM COMEDY CLUB
**34 West 22nd St. (bet. 5th & 6th Aves.)**
**367-9000**
*ALL MAJOR CREDIT CARDS*

Definitely one of the newest and nicest comedy clubs to hit New York in recent years, Gotham serves the typical fare of young and up-and-coming acts. Depending on the night you go, you may see some real bombs or catch an ingenious new talent. It's very unpredictable. Call ahead to find out the evening's lineup, lest you be caught in a comedy conundrum. Private party space is available downstairs. You won't find any wedding receptions here, but maybe a birthday or bachelorette party. Cover charges are: Sunday-Thursday @ 8:30pm, $8 and Friday-Saturday @ 8:30 and 10:30pm, $12. There is always a 2 drink minimum.

## GRAMERCY PARK HOTEL BAR
**2 Lexington Ave. (At 21st St.)**
**475-4320**

*ALL MAJOR CREDIT CARDS*

Ah, welcome to New York's answer to Hollywood's Dresden Room! Off of the lobby of this well-worn hotel sits a diamond in the rough. Its candlelit piano bar serves as a perfect spot for a midnight tryst for an older, fortyish crowd. The kitchy female piano player admits that she sounds like she is in pain and happily accepts requests such as obscure Billy Joel songs and the old Don McClain favorite, "American Pie." This fifty-year-old bar, open daily until 12:30am, serves mixed drinks, wine and beer. Although the drinks prices are a bit steep, this romantic hotel bar has charm and character.

## GRAND BAR (AT THE SOHO GRAND HOTEL)
**310 W. B'way (bet. Canal & Broome Sts.)**
**965-3000**

*ALL MAJOR CREDIT CARDS*

This Ian Schrager-esque hotel bar, located on the second floor of the SoHo Grand Hotel, looks like Andre the Giant's old living room. Decorated with oversized lamps, large couches, and floor-to-ceiling windows, the smoky space is filled with an artistic melange of the hip, shallow and predominantly foreign. The bar area is crammed and smoky but the long lounge area outside the bar is what makes the Grand a memorable experience. It's a perfect place for meeting large groups of friends in a comfortable and elegant setting where there are great views of SoHo.

## THE GRANGE HALL
**50 Commerce St. (At Barrow St.)**
**924-5246**

### ALL MAJOR CREDIT CARDS

Ah, the Grange Hall. Where else can you find regulars like Uma Thurman and Ethan Hawke puffing away in a smoking booth on a given Sunday? This West Village institution serves delicious comfort food that would put your Grandma's cooking to absolute shame. Excellent Bloody Mary's, a good selection of beers on tap, and an impressive wine list, make up just part of the libations that are served here daily. A Diego Rivera-esque mural hangs on one wall in the main dining area, and there are several booths for the smokers in the front across from the bar. Recently the Grange has been offering free wine tasting and special dining events. When all is said and done, the Grange Hall's got it all—great food, great neighborhood and great ambiance.

## GRANVILLE LOUNGE (CLOSED)
**40 E. 20th St. (bet. Park Ave. S. & B'way)**

## GRASSROOTS
**20 St. Marks Pl. (bet. 2nd & 3rd Aves.)**
**475-9443**

### CASH ONLY

Conveniently located across the street from a drug and alcohol rehabilitation center, is Grassroots. Opened since 1975, this wood-paneled saloon attracts tourists, NYU students, old locals and AA dropouts who are here to drink heavily and play darts. Come watch patrons slur rock-and-roll lyrics out of time with the old jukebox. The bartender, who has been pouring drinks at Grassroots for close to 10 years, serves 12 inexpensive beers on tap. If you're looking for a no-frills joint to get bombed, this might be a good place for you. A pitcher of beer is priced under $10, while a cocktail will run you about 4 bucks.

## THE GREATEST BAR ON EARTH
**1 World Trade Center, 107th floor**
**524-7105**

*ALL MAJOR CREDIT CARDS*

If not for the spectacular views of New York, The Greatest Bar on Earth feels more like a wannabe American bar found in Prague. This is a tourist trap, plain and simple. Chances are that it's listed in all the major European tour guides as one of the cooler NY spots next to the Hard Rock and the Harley Davidson Café. Once your ears pop from the ride up, you'll find the decor to look much like a hotel lobby (circa 1982 designed by Little Richard). Drinks are expensive and not worth the wait. Wednesday night is boasted as the big club night where a middle aged DJ spins the modern lyrics of Jerry Lee Lewis and Patsy Cline to a crowd that unfortunately knows all the lyrics, word for word. All in all, if you are looking for New York culture at its best, this is not a recommendation. If you are looking for a taste of that American style bar that you hung out at during your college study semester abroad, you might dig this scene.

## GREAT HALL BALCONY - METROPOLITAN MUSEUM OF ART
**1000 5th Ave. (At 81st St.)**
**535-7710**

*ALL MAJOR CREDIT CARDS*

Amazing views and well-dressed clientele make up for the very limited hours. When up on the roof of the Met, you suddenly understand why many New Yorkers are convinced that this is the center of the universe. On the roof, you sip wine and look out on Central Park and think about the centuries of artwork beneath your feet. The alcohol and view combined cause you to reach a level of sublime happiness— a joie de vivre that can only come from the heady combination of culture and activity that personify New York. The view alone is worth it, but the trip through the artwork of the Met caps it. There could not possibly be a more romantic, beautiful spot to spend some time.

## GREENWICH BREWING COMPANY
**418 6th Ave. (At 9th St.)**
**477-8744**

*ALL MAJOR CREDIT CARDS*

There was more action and excitement happening at this location when it was a Pizzeria Uno. Other than the obtrusively large circular bar planted smack in the middle of this restaurant/bar, the place looks exactly like its predecessor. With bright lights, some tables and chairs and Led Zeppelin softly streaming out of the jukebox, this place is as depressing as it gets. A handful of guests in their mid-thirties quietly convene at the bar patiently waiting for "Deputy Quickdraw" to (hopefully) pour them a drink. Don't worry, you won't be bored waiting for the slow-handed bartender, you'll have *plenty* of sports to watch on the TV. While the food is run-of-the-mill American, this joint's saving grace is its massive selection of beers, microbrews, champagne and wine. Happy hour draws in the after work crowd daily from 4:40pm - 6:30pm when 2 for 1 home brews are served. There is simply a whole lot of nothing going on at the Greenwich Brewing Company. Kind of makes you long for the days of screaming teenagers stopping for a slice on their way to the 8th Street PATH station.

## THE GROOVE
**125 MacDougal Street**
**673-5576**

Look up the word "pushy" in the dictionary and you'll find The Groove as its definition. From the moment you walk in it's like a saleman's convention gone terribly wrong. Outside, a greasy dude is practically screaming for you to come inside. Once inside, the bartenders harass you to buy drinks and do shots before you've even taken a seat! The crowd is mostly young collegiate types who are so ripped they don't even notice the one good thing about this place—the music. There is live music nightly and for you NYU kids with a college ID, you can get in free. Open till 4am daily, the Groove is sadly, out of the groove.

## H2K
**219 9th Ave. (At 23rd St.)**
**727-2616**

*ALL MAJOR CREDIT CARDS*

Created by two brothers (H + H) and their friend (K) from Dublin, H2K is a new kind of Irish pub. The floors ain't covered with sawdust, there's no green in sight, and everything on the menu isn't preceded by "O'" or "Mc." Instead, the décor is modern and hip, with a strange, almost Asian feel. More of a lounge than a bar, there's plenty of comfortable seating and room to relax. H2K is brand spanking new, and is quickly picking up a loyal following. This is the best addition to the Chelsea bar scene in quite along time. No attitude, great space and a great crowd. Note... if it's a taste of true Ireland you desire, try the Oysters and Guinness special...it will get you just drunk and horny enough to make you think that Leprechauns are kinda sexy.

## HALO
**49 Grove St. (At Bleecker St.)**
**367-9390**

*ALL MAJOR CREDIT CARDS*

The West Village has got a new rich kid on the block, and his name is Halo. If you can manage to squeeze by the velvet ropes, you'll be treated to the most opulent, posh interior this side of SoHo's Spy bar. Halo makes it very clear what kind of a crowd it is looking for—pouty models who won't eat anything on their select menu, muscle-bound moneybags who demand bottle-service, and anyone who has never bought an article of clothing at the Gap. Dark, atmospheric, wonderfully moody and filled with plush couches that scream, "Get your freak on but keep your flu-

125

ids off," Halo is one of those places you see in the movies, read about in magazines, and get turned away from because your socks don't match.

## HANGER
**115 Christopher St. (bet. Bleecker & Hudson)**
**627-2044**

It's either a hit or miss. When it's good it's amazing. When it's bad it sucks. Most of the action centers around the pool table in the back where "interesting" videos play overhead. Designed to look like an airplane hanger, Hanger is the epicenter of gay pride. Happy hour, cheap drinks and different entertainment nightly reels them in.

## HARD ROCK CAFÉ
**221 W. 57th St. (bet. 7th Ave. & B'way)**
**459-9320**

*ALL MAJOR CREDIT CARDS*

We all know what to expect from the mother of cheesy theme restaurants—clueless tourists with fanny packs. Europeans and families from Ohio flock to this rock-and-roll memorabilia haven to gawk at its framed photos, hanging guitars, and clothing worn by famous musicians. Patrons cram into tables looking way too excited to be shelling out $12 for a hamburger and up to $11 for a drink. (Well, at least you get to keep the glass as a souvenir.) Watch out for the huge line in front of the Hard Rock Cafe's merchandise store where tourists sprint after their meal to buy ugly tee-shirts to bring back home and show off at the local Friendly's.

## HARGLO'S CAFE
**974 2nd Ave. (bet. 51st & 52nd Sts.)**
**759-9820**

*ALL MAJOR CREDIT CARDS*

With $2 Jell-O shots and spicy jambalaya, this Southwestern Cajun bar tries its hardest to make you forget that you are in a lame part of town. Red and neon on the outside, jazzy and Cajun on the inside, this mock Mardi Gras bar offers a happy hour from 12pm-7pm daily serving beers for a measly buck! Ladies score the best deal with ½ price drinks, Monday-Wednesday. And if you feel a little up on your luck, play the lottery!

## HARLEY DAVIDSON CAFE
**1370 6th Ave. (At 56th St.)**
**245-6000**

*ALL MAJOR CREDIT CARDS*

Yes, it's one of those awful midtown theme bar/restaurants that on average attracts anywhere from two to four thousand customers a day and is full of tourists. Normally we would recommend that you run for your life. But believe it or not, the bar aint that bad! Their novelty drinks like the "Flat Tracker" or "Hill Climber" for $10.25, will leave you buzzing for hours considering they are served in a 20oz. take home glass and taste like fruit juice. Specialty shooters like the "Shock absorber" and "Wheelie" go for $6.25 a pop. If you're not up for getting looped, try the "Easy Rider" made with grape soda, whipped cream, and a cherry. Or you can wind down with a tea or coffee (coined on the menu as "Standard Lubricants"). Sports fans will dig this place with its big mama TV screens over the bar. And who, I ask you, can resist the Elvis impersonator who appears on Saturday nights from 7:30pm-midnight?

## HARMONY
**100 W. Houston St.**
**(bet. LaGuardia Pl. & Thompson St.)**
**254-7000**

*ALL MAJOR CREDIT CARDS*

This place feels exactly like where it is located—not SoHo, but almost. Bright, breezy and sleek, Harmony is a quiet bar/lounge that wishes it was located a few blocks farther south. Colorful bottles pressed into the large glass picture window create one of the coolest exteriors on Houston, and the silver and white interior is equally as pleasing. While not quite as hip as it would like to be, Harmony does offer a comfortable atmosphere, lots of plush couches and booths, and a downstairs lounge open on the weekends. The food menu is expensive, but does offer some interesting selections: Caviar, salmon, gazpacho. Probably due to its location, this place seems to have a hard time finding its crowd, so when the bouncers in SoHo give you that "not a chance in hell" look, head north a few blocks for a little Harmony.

## HEADLINERS BAR AND LOUNGE
**1678 1st Ave.**
**426-6309**

Even after two years, Headliners is definitely not making any headlines, but it will pass as your average, neighborhood bar. Sadly, décor is not their strong suit. Walls covered in ratty headlines and a skanky lounge area is strictly for 23- to 25-year-olds who are looking to party but not looking for ambiance. Headliners offers 10 beers on tap, 9 bottled beers, 10 single malt scotches and 5 different types of cigars. A Tuesday night Ladies' Night gets the women loose with free Bud Light and drafts at the bar. With a $2 drink happy hour, drinks are pretty inexpensive. Along with a typical top forties jukebox, a 10" big screen TV, and 6 other satellite televisions, a weekend DJ gets down with Hip-Hop, R&B and '80s music. Open daily from 2pm - 4am.

## HEARTLAND BREWERY
**35 Union Sq. W. (bet. 16th & 17th Sts.), 645-3400**
**1285 6th Ave. (At 51st St.), 582-8244**

### *ALL MAJOR CREDIT CARDS*

This enormously popular bar/restaurant offers seven delicious home-brews as well as seasonal beer specials. We recommend ordering one of their beer "flights" which gives you a sample of each. The decor of dark wood and old-fashioned lights gives off a warm feeling, though one can

128

not escape the ever-present Houlihan's and TGIF cheesiness that reigns. Despite the out-of-town clientele that the bar attracts, the beer is exceptional, making it a great place to come after work with a group of friends. Try to get a table upstairs to get away from the noise.

## HELENA'S
**432 Lafayette St. (At Astor Pl.)**
**677-5151**

***ALL MAJOR CREDIT CARDS***

Opened for two years, Sag Harbor was the original home of Helena's. This beautifully decorated tapas bar serves great tapas and potent drinks in a simply lovely atmosphere. Decorated with bright fresh flowers, red walls, Spanish-styled tiles and tiny balconies, Helena's is definitely a great date spot. Thursday nights draws in Flamenco musicians and dancers while throughout the week, unobtrusive Latin Jazz fills the atmosphere. The liquor selection is vast with drink specials like the delicious "Helenita" which will keep you coming back for more. Most people are drawn to Helena's mammoth back garden, covered by a large tent and perfect for large parties. Attracting locals and theatre goers, Helena's hours are: Thursday, Friday and Saturday, 12pm-1am (kitchen open); Sunday from 2pm - 3am (bar open); Wednesday, kitchen closes at 12am while bar remains open till 2am. Definitely a Shecky's pick!

## HELL
**59 Gansevoort St.**
**(bet. Greenwich & Washington)**
**727-1666**

***ALL MAJOR CREDIT CARDS***

If this is Hell, then by all means lets all be really, really bad. With red velvet drapery and an elaborate chandelier, this vaulted space in the meat-packing district makes you feel like you are indulging in the good life somewhere in Satan's mansion. Catering to a predominantly gay crowd, Hell serves up an unusual selection of cocktails like Lucifer Take Manhattan, Devil's Punch and the French Martini (all $6.50). Drink specials change daily as does nightly festivities, so be sure to call ahead for more info.

## HENRIETTA HUDSON
**438 Hudson (bet. Morton & Barrow St.)**
**924-3347**

*ALL MAJOR CREDIT CARDS*

Thumbs up for Henrietta's almost exclusively lesbian nightspot. With décor that feels like a smoky roadhouse on a highway to nowhere, Henrietta's has established itself as a comfortable, easy-to-get-to-know-ya kind of place. The crowd is a diverse group of gay women from cowgirls to seven sisters-type lesbians to dykes on bikes. Happily, Henrietta's feels less like a pickup joint, and more like a gritty (and gay) version of your corner watering hole. Patrons listen to a great jukebox with standards like Janis and Melissa while they shoot pool in the backroom or sip drinks at the long and adequately stocked bar. Bartenders earn points for the quick and generous alcohol service. Mixed drinks start at a reasonable $4 and you can carry them to the outside tables to sit and chat during the warmer months. Gay or straight, any woman can walk in, sit at the bar, order a drink and carry on a conversation with the woman next to her without sexual tension. You may or may not get some lady's phone number on a cocktail napkin, but you will definitely make a couple of friends and enjoy some intelligent conversation.

## HI-LIFE
**1340 1st Ave. (At 72nd St.)**
**249-3600**

*ALL MAJOR CREDIT CARDS*

This cool 60s martini bar with padded black leather booths and aluminum walls is a great place to take your "babe du jour" for a cocktail and some foolish affection. It's best if you manage to snag one of the two booths where you can enjoy the 1940s nude photos above and around the bar. The DJ isn't top-notch, but he's hip enough to keep you entertained. If you're hungry they've got everything from Sushi to potato skins.

## THE HOG PIT
**22 9th Ave. (At 13th St.)**
**604-0092**

Strap on your feedbag, hop on a Harley, and get your ass down to The Hog Pit for some good ol' country cookin', beer and a game of pool. This large restaurant/bar nestled within the meat packing district serves up fried chicken, black eye peas, macaroni and cheese, ribs and collared greens to a mixed clientele. If it wasn't for so many of the regulars being covered in tattoos, the setting would transport you to a hillbilly town. Hog riders and their women, yuppies and locals listen to a mixed jukebox while playing pool or foozeball. Friendly and warm with great food, service and decent drink prices, The Hog Pit is more tame and less skanky than its neighbor, Hogs and Heifers.

## HOGS & HEIFERS
**589 Washington (At W. 13th St.)**
**929-0655**

### *CASH ONLY*

What's scarier? Walking the dark streets of the meat-packing district to find this place, or mingling among the regulars once you've found it? You're not a fan of Pabst Blue Ribbon beer, are you? In that case, you're better off ordering your drinks quietly. Mangy lingerie hanging behind the bar and the topless patron dancing on the bar offend you? Keep your eyes shut. This must-go-there-once-to-say-you've-been establishment is certainly an experience. With an odd mix of bikers and Wall Street suits, it's like West Side Story meets Deliverence. The tension is high and someone is bound to get strangled by their own tie. So dress down, avoid eye contact, and stay off the pool table unless you are a pro.

**HOLIDAY LOUNGE**
**75 St. Marks Pl. (bet. 1ˢᵗ & 2nd Aves.)**
**777-9637**

*CASH ONLY*

Home of the cheapest drinks in New York City! Be prepared to wait a while for service— this family-owned bar is well known for its perpetually drunk, elderly bartender. After much slurring, staggering, and a few attempts at singing a song, the bartender *might* remember the drink you ordered about a half hour ago. But what do you expect? It's a dive! And they have a great jukebox, a television, deer antlers on the wall and a video game machine! Do you really need more? Holiday opens early in the morning and closes every night at 1am. With $2.50 mixed drinks and $2.50 beers, every day at Holiday Lounge is happy hour.

**HOUSTON'S**
**153 E. 53ʳᵈ St. (At 3ʳᵈ Ave)**
**888-3828**

*ALL MAJOR CREDIT CARDS*

Opened in 1997, this southern chain based in Atlanta (not Texas), was surprised to see their upscale "Friday's" transformed into an over-stuffed yuppie hangout. Known for their large portions of unhealthy food and their "no-problem" attitude, you're guaranteed to be nauseous by the end of your visit. Houston's gets a huge lunch crowd and is a sardine-packed after-work scene. Enjoy pricey $10 martinis while dodging hot plates of cheese-and-artichoke dip. All the drinks are steep, and the bartenders are usually too busy to make eye contact, let alone get your drink correct. There are no soda guns (for quality control), and only one sink for the five bartenders who are crammed into the space. The clientele consist of local suits and obnoxious ex-frat boys who scored good jobs in midtown. The women, probably ex-sorority girls, have traded in their lettered sweatshirts for Ally McBeal power suits. A musician plays easy-listening show tunes on a baby grand in the corner, but don't expect to hear it over the roar of this midtown meat-market.

## HOWARD JOHNSON'S
**1551 Broadway (At 46th St)**
**354-1445**

*ALL MAJOR CREDIT CARDS*

On reviewing HoJo's Bar, the manager initially refused to relinquish his liquor prices, but after a little sweet talking with the waitress, the prized information was ours to publish. In the middle of the newly refurbished Times Square, HoJo's, with its unchanged 50s décor, sticks out like a sore thumb. But who cares? It's a landmark! Sit in a booth and have a bottle of beer for $3.95, or a top-shelf drnk for $5.50. Happy hour is from 11am to 7pm, which includes free hors d'oeuvres and $2.95 for all well drinks. The bar opens at 8am with the restaurant, but the crowd of tourists and foreigners probably won't shuffle in until the evening. HoJo's is an amusing novelty if you're already drunk, or if you want to enjoy pancakes with your Tom Collins.

## HUDSON BAR & BOOKS
**636 Hudson St. (bet. Horatio & Jane Sts.)**
**229-2642**

*ALL MAJOR CREDIT CARDS*

English gentile meets the West Village in this wonderfully ingenious bar. With a theatrically lit ensemble of couches and books, the decor is definitely set out of a James Joyce novel. Although the midtown location requires a jacket, the West Village bar is casual. With quiet jazz music and a beautiful brass bar, there is plenty of seating and the extensive liquor menu includes a top-notch selection of Scotch, Cognac, Port, and Wine. For those of you with sophisticated tastes (or a corporate credit card), enjoy a $125 shot of Remy Martin Louis XIV or a Civil War aged port. For those without the corporate credit card, a glass of wine will run you between $6-$22. For the cigar lover, this upscale cocktail lounge offers quite a selection. This English study-like hangout attracts an older crowd of writers, film industry types and neighborhood locals. This warmly lit bar is a perfect place for a date.

133

## ICE BAR
**528 Canal St.**
**(bet. Washington St. & West Side Hwy.)**
**226-2602**

*ALL MAJOR CREDIT CARDS*

The term "Don't Wear White After Labor Day" definitely does not apply at Ice Bar. The all white interior, the modern design, the cool blue lit bar, and the hip music being spun by the DJ are only some of the reasons to travel to this out-of-the-way hot spot. The friendly staff, great mixed drinks and good-looking, attitude-free crowd are the rest. Open since the first week of August, Ice Bar has quickly picked up a loyal following that's willing to make the trek downtown. Once the crowd settles in, they're in for the night. Try the Blue Mandarin martini; it's to die for. Shecky Prediction: One of 2000's top spots.

## IDLEWILD
**145 E. Houston St. (bet. 1ˢᵗ & 2ⁿᵈ Aves.)**
**477-5005**

*ALL MAJOR CREDIT CARDS*

Historical fact: Before JFK airport was named JFK it was called Idlewild. And you thought Shecky's wasn't educational. And hey, what do you know, Idlewild looks exactly like the inside of an airplane—even the bathrooms are as tight and annoying as the real thing. The space itself is quite impressive and is equipped with cocktail waitresses and busboys dressed as stewardesses and cargo boys. There is a strict dress code that insists the clientele refrain from wearing sneakers, grunge and bridge-and-tunnel ware. So if you're a fashion victim, re-think the clothes unless you want the fashion police (bouncers) to turn you away. Bring your friends from out of town—they'll think it's da bomb! A good mix of gay and straight makes this one of the more interesting bars in the city.

*ALL MAJOR CREDIT CARDS*

This long thin dive bar feels like an East Village watering hole on the Upper East Side. There's ample seating, a drink-accessible bar and a pool table in the back. The crowd is a little grungier than the usual frat boy found in this 'hood and the drinks are pretty cheap. A nice fish tank up front adds some charm, otherwise, call it what it is—a dive.

**IGUANA**
**240 W. 54th St. (bet. 8th Ave. & B'way)**
**765-5454**

*ALL MAJOR CREDIT CARDS*

Can you say queso? That's Spanish for cheese, you grin-gos. Yes, the cheese factor here is high, but it feels good. It's a one-stop evening at this all encompassing bar *and* club *and* restaurant owned by the same people who brought you Le Bar Bat years ago. *You too* can feel just like a cast member from "Ally McBeal" as you stop in to boogie at 6 pm on your way home from the office. That's when the DJ starts spinning downstairs on Thurs., Fri., Sat., so happy hour becomes "White Man's Overbite Hour." It's actually a fun idea and a fun place where you can groove your work stress away with the help of 35 different tequilas, 15 beers (5 on tap) or an "Iguanarita," their specialty margarita. You'll need food after that—they call it "Border Cuisine," we call it "Tex Mex." They have it all—TVs at the bar for the sports fans, and imported terracotta tile for those who care. The good news is there's no cover, drinks are $6-$8, and that aforementioned D. (who *is* accessible and who *does* take requests) plays everything from progressive house to disco till 4 am. Make sure you're over 21 and not wearing jeans or sneakers. For the midtown, mainstream, 25-40s after work crowd, it's *all that* and a bag of Doritos.

**INDIGO BAR**
**487 Amsterdam Ave. (bet. 83rd & 84th Sts.)**
**362-0373**

*ALL MAJOR CREDIT CARDS*

Your spirits will be lifted by the indigo walls where live bands play on Wednesday, Thursday, and Friday nights. Though the crowd tends to be a mish mosh of well-dressed pseudo-intellectuals, you can tell that these folk were a hash-smoking barrel of bad asses in their college days. Be sure to wear your finest L.L. Bean threads. If you're looking for a quick basic bar to dip into, this one might work.

**'INO**
**21 Bedford St. (bet. 6th Ave. & Downing St.)**
**989-5769**

*ALL MAJOR CREDIT CARDS*

This place is exactly like its name—small and Italian. Reminiscent of a true side street café you would find in Rome or Venice, 'ino offers a solid wine list, a couple of beer choices, and some of the best damn sandwiches this side of the Mediterranean. Intimate and cozy, the seating is limited but the prices are right. 'Ino is not a place to get drunk and loud with a bunch of co-workers, but perfect for a quiet conversation with a lover or best friend. Just make sure you bring a tin of Altoids—a table for two brings you closer than the missionary position.

**INTERNET CAFÉ**
**82 E. 3rd St. (bet. 1st & 2nd Ave.)**
**614-0747**

*ALL MAJOR CREDIT CARDS*

"Surf and Ye Shall Find" is the mantra of this off-the-wall, slightly bizarre bar/café/music venue/computer geek establishment. Open Monday through Saturday from 11am - 2am, and Sunday from 11am - 12am, don't expect to have a rowdy, beer chugging time in this quiet, candlelit cavern of hush. Below street level, the Internet Café offers an array of beers from the USA, Canada, UK, Germany and Belgium. In place of a bar is an industrial sized refrigerator that is well stocked with beer, coffee and edible goodies. The low ceilings and the papers and junk shoved into cabinets kind of remind one of Grandpa's litter-filled basement. A happy hour offers $1 beers Monday - Saturday from 5pm to 8pm. Open since 1995, weekly jazz bands perform with a $5 cover charge. With a $2.50 usage charge every 15 minutes you can use one of the computer terminals sitting on...candlelit tables? If the low ceiling makes you claustrophobic, step outside to the back garden where internet gurus very quietly (yes, quietly) sit on plastic deck furniture and talk shop in dulcet tones. While it's a great place to surf the net and drink foreign beer, don't expect to be hanging from the chandeliers.

## IRIDIUM ROOM
**48 W. 63rd St. (Columbus Ave.)**
**582-2121**

*ALL MAJOR CREDIT CARDS*

Iridium, which means"to bring forth light," has catered to an older, more mature uptown crowd for the past four years. With dinner served nightly, this jazz/blues club features top acts such as Les Paul, Wynton Marsalis, and John Abercrombie. With a $20 cover and a $10 drink minimum per table, this upscale music venue is perfect for the mellow 30+ crowd. The club is open Monday through Sunday from 7pm to 1am and reservations here are a must.

## IVY NIGHT CLUB & CIGAR LOUNGE
**2130 B'way (At 75th St.)**
**579-1000**

*ALL MAJOR CREDIT CARDS*

If you're in the mood to shake that booty to some salsa or merengue this place is probably you're best bet without having to board a plane headed to Miami. This 5 room club gets jam-packed with guys and gals looking to dance the night away. Once you feel like you've sweated enough, grab a seat on one of the velvet couches that line the entire place with your drink and cigar. Specialty nights are hosted by promoters, so call ahead to be sure of the evening's theme. There is usually a $10 cover charge at the door and the bouncers look very intimidating, but are actually quite friendly.

## IZZY BAR
**166 1st Ave. (bet. 10<sup>th</sup> & 11th Sts.)**
**228-0444**

*ALL MAJOR CREDIT CARDS*

This great little bi-level party spot has an excellent DJ up-stairs and live music downstairs. On any given night you can expect to hear a group of people yelling out, "Oh my god, remember this song!" and then erupting into full scale lip syncing and matching dance moves. Downstairs, a larger than expected space showcases excellent live music within an arms reach. It gets crowded on the weekends but great during the week when you can grab a seat in the back and lounge. The crowd that it draws is diverse, funky, and appreciates the finer things in life, like good quality disco.

## JA
**84 7<sup>th</sup> Ave.**
**243-7888**

*ALL MAJOR CREDIT CARDS*

This unassuming lounge is the nicest and least offensive place you'll find in this area. Tucked discretely away on a strip known affectionately as "Little Jersey," Ja is a tiny oasis catty corner from the epicenter of hell, otherwise known as The Caliente Cab Co. Although it may look like like your run-of-the-mill lounge, inside the vibe is inviting and comfortable. What's even more impressive is the crowd Ja attracts—these 20 to 30-year-olds are more interested in good conversation than getting a date. The bartenders are good-looking *and* friendly...Ja!

## JL SULLIVANS
**1715 1st Ave. (Bet. 88th & 89th Sts.)**
**831-7419**

You know it's a bad sign if a bar is playing Chumbawumba's "Tubthumping" and people are actually dancing to it. The decor is white trash and boring but strangely enough the place is always packed. There is a $5 cover on the weekend just to get into this skanky college scene comprised of 90% dorky men and 10% women looking for an ego boost. The inexpensive drinks are poured by underage looking guys all wearing shirts and ties. There are six televisions playing typical sports highlights to a jukebox that plays bad pop music. The bar sells a selection of 65 micro-brewed beers and cigars of the month.

## JACK DEMPSEY
**61 2nd Ave (bet. 3rd and 4th Sts.)**
**475-2729**

*ALL MAJOR CREDIT CARDS*

Jack Dempsey is basically an Irish sports bar with a pool table, darts, a decent jukebox and live musical acts. With little regard for décor, this large space is all about Irish motifs and really bright lighting. It's ladies' night on Thursday with ½ price drinks from 9pm -12pm. With eight beers on tap, drink prices are pretty cheap. A mid-twenties to forties crowd convene here nightly to shoot some pool or listen to anything from Led Zeppelin to Patsy Cline on the jukebox. Wednesday nights hosts live bluegrass bands without a cover charge. A daily happy hour offers $1 shot specials from 10pm - 2am. It's just your run-of-the-mill bar with not much going on.

## JACK THE RIPPER
**228 W. 4th St. (bet. 10th St. & 7th Ave.)**
**691-3631**

Another one of those theme bars that got off the Times Square track and landed in the village. Tourists flock here to witness the kitschy paintings drip with blood or drink beer out of a yard glass served in 50 flavors. It's worth checking out for one beer if you're in the mood to see kitchen utensils and skeletons hanging from the walls.

### JAKE'S DILEMMA
**430 Amsterdam Ave. (bet. 80th & 81st Sts.)**
**580-0556**

*ALL MAJOR CREDIT CARDS*

Plaid to the left, plaid to the right...good god it looks like L.L. Bean exploded in here! This place is packed at all times with the young and restless boys of the Upper West Side. Weekends are a testosterone mob scene where men are on the hunt, making for a somewhat dangerous environment for women to be mingling alone. So, if the occasional bar brawl and men in fraternity plaid curls your toes, you'll like this frat stop.

### JAMESON'S
**975 2nd Ave. (bet. 51st & 52nd Sts.)**
**980-4465**

*ALL MAJOR CREDIT CARDS*

The assortment of beer-labelled mirrors, tacky dog paintings and trashy faux-stained glass lamp shades plummets you right into the middle of a Middle America trailer park bar. With nine beers on tap and a jukebox, this ten-year-old establishment attracts an older local crowd who stop by after work for a drink and a helping of shepherd's pie. There is plenty of seating with cheap drinks and food that's served until midnight during the week. The bartenders are friendly and always happy to see a new face walk into the bar.

### THE JAZZ STANDARD
**116 E. 27th St.**
**(bet. Park & Lex. Aves.)**
**576-2232**

*ALL MAJOR CREDIT CARDS*

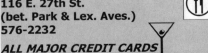

Since October of 1997, The Jazz Standard has been presenting mainstream jazz acts to young and up-and-coming musicians to an older crowd who like martinis and a first-rate American-style cuisine. Upstairs serves as a bar/dining room, while downstairs looks like a turn of the century jazz club. With dim lighting, the atmosphere is unobtrusive and very avant-garde in its simplicity. Tables are proportionately spaced giving the audience plenty of room to relax and enjoy the show while candles complete the romantic atmosphere. Unfortunately, the inattentive wait service and the terrible acoustics dampen the comfortable ambiance.

## JEKYLL AND HYDE
**1409 6th Ave. (bet. 57th & 58th Sts.), 541-9517**
**91 7th Ave. So. (bet. Bleecker & Christopher Sts.), 989-7701**

### *ALL MAJOR CREDIT CARDS*

This ghoulish theme bar draws in a huge crowd of tourists nightly. If you are looking to experience a Walt Disney version of a haunted mansion with your burger and beer, this is your place. There are ceilings and walls that collapse, enchanting haunted characters, talking paintings, and gargoyles that poke fun at nearby eaters. There is also an hourly awakening of Frankenstein who drops slowly from the ceiling accompanied with the drone of a heavy organ. A word of caution, do not wait until the last minute to use the bathroom; it's nearly impossible to find. Owned by the same mind behind The Slaughtered Lamb and The Night Gallery, Jekyll and Hyde is a gold mine. Since 1985, Jekyll and Hyde has served 250 types of beer in everything from bottles to yard length glasses. This is a great place to bring your out-of-town cousins and their kids but keep in mind that it's a theme bar and you know what that means—fromage.

## JEREMY'S ALE HOUSE
**254 Front St. (At Dover St.)**
**964-3537**

### *ALL MAJOR CREDIT CARDS*

It's as if you never left the frat house: Pinball, fake moosehead, street signs, lifesavers, something-for-every-one jukebox, neon bar logos, and bras everywhere you look. On Thursdays and Fridays, it's five guys to every gal, and the clientele is a Wall Street/blue collar mix. They're not kidding about the 8-10 am happy hour ($1.50 Miller Draft and 1/2 off everything else)—it's for the Seaport fishermen and cops coming off the late shift. Originally a pushcart at the South Street Seaport 28 years ago, Jeremy's then settled

It's as if you never left the frat house: Pinball, fake moosehead, street signs, lifesavers, something-for-every-one jukebox, neon bar logos, and bras everywhere you look. On Thursdays and Fridays, it's five guys to every gal, and the clientele is a Wall Street/blue collar mix. They're not kidding about the 8-10 am happy hour ($1.50 Miller Draft and 1/2 off everything else)—it's for the Seaport fishermen and cops coming off the late shift. Originally a pushcart at the South Street Seaport 28 years ago, Jeremy's then settled into its current location in the '80s—a former garage for city buses. When you first enter, let your eyes roam upward and around the massive single room to see the hundreds of bras and ties left by forgetful (or impatient) patrons. Behind the battle-scarred, rangy bar is a full grill cooking up cheap food, as well as clams and calamari voted the best in the city since 1982. Grab a 32 oz. "bucket" beer—equivalent to four bottles—for $4 to $7 and don't miss out on their summer parties; $10 gets you all you can eat and drink. There's no air-conditioning, so it gets sticky in summer, but there's a fine beer garden with a lovely view of the underside of the Brooklyn Bridge. The official alehouse motto is, "If it ain't fun, it ain't worth it."

## JET 19
**19 Cleveland Pl. (At Spring St.)**
**343-8907**

*ALL MAJOR CREDIT CARDS*

As if the first few Jets to pop up in Miami and New York did not offer enough attitude overkill, Jet had to grace Little Italy with yet another trendoid hell. On initial entrance to the space, provided you are cool enough to get past the mammoth bouncers and their clipboards, Jet appears to be impressive. Upon closer inspection however, you'll soon realize that the bar is small, smoky, loud and packed with wayward Upper East Siders and Jerseyites. With its Pier One attempt at a Moroccan, Indian, and Chinese decor, Jet plays host to poser girls with pierced belly buttons and men in poor quality shoes. For a Jet, we were disappointed with this one. If you must go, try the one across town instead.

## JET LOUNGE
**286 Spring St. (bet. Hudson & Varick)**
**929-4780**

### ALL MAJOR CREDIT CARDS

The Jet Lounge makes you feel like you could strut in with a Siberian Husky, dressed in a white furry seal hat (faux, of course) and a pink velour cat-suit. With mirrored cut glass in various sizes and shapes covering every inch of the domain, designer Paul Andre, better known as Rosie, has created a bar that looks like an ice castle. It's a bit obnoxious and bridge-and-tunnel on the weekends, but worth seeing during the week. There's no dancing, but heck, there's a DJ spinning from Thursday-Saturday and the crowd can't help but shake. Be sure to check out the downstairs lounge area that is filled with mirrors, making it easy to re-apply your lip gloss. For all you beautiful people, the friendly staff will usher you in without a bat of an eyelash, but to everyone else it's considered the door policy from hell.

## JIMMIE'S CORNER
**140 W. 44th St. (bet. B'way & 6th Aves.)**
**944-7819**

### CASH ONLY

This 24-year-old bar is a Times Square fixture with a jukebox that plays the likes of Barry White, Frank Sinatra, and Prince. Decorated with tons of boxing photos ("Raging Bull" was filmed here), Jimmies stretches back into a long narrow corridor with just enough room for several tables and a pinball machine. It's a no-frills dive bar that definitely has its regulars.

## JIMMY WALKERS ALE HOUSE
**245 E. 55th St. (bet. 2nd & 3rd Aves.)**
**319-6650**

Large sports bar in a TGI Friday's setting. Ya gotcha pool table, ya gotcha neon signs, ya gotcha American flare, ya gotcha sports TV, ya gotcha homogeneous beer loving crowd.

## JL SULLIVANS
**1715 1st Ave. (bet. 88th & 89th St.)**
**831-7419**

With chug contests, karaoke and a "spin the wheel for drinks" game, you know you have entered the depths of frat hell. The décor is white trash and boring yet this place is always packed with testosterone-filled beer chuggers who like to dance to tacky top forties jukebox songs. There is a DJ on the weekend and 6 televisions for entertainment. Get ready to drink up cause there's a $10 unlimited draft cover charge on Thursdays and Fridays from 6pm till 10pm and a $15 unlimited drafts and well drinks cover charge from 8pm - 11pm on Saturday nights. The clientele who actually pay to get in this pre-pubescent, skanky hell hole is comprised of 90% dorky boys and 10% women looking for an ego boost. With 10 beers on tap, drinks are relatively inexpensive. The bar sells a selection of 65 microbrewed beers and cigars of the month.

## JOE'S BAR
**520 E. 6th St. (bet. Aves. A & B)**
**473-9093**

*CASH ONLY*

Just another hole-in-the-wall in the East Village, Joe's mostly attracts regulars who come to play pool, listen to loud jukebox music, and drink cheap beer. Lots of pool trophies garnish the seedy walls along with kitschy Elvis posters and red Christmas lights.  The bar dwellers, who are not fully acquainted with the process of showering, add to the seediness and smell of this dive bar. Drinks are strong and cheap, just like the bartenders pouring them.

## JOHNNY'S BAR
**90 Greenwich  Ave. (bet. 12ᵗʰ & 13ᵗʰ Sts.)**
**741-5279**

***CASH ONLY***

Back in the day, an older Greek man who lived on Greenwich Avenue would religiously sweep the sidewalk and befriend most of his West Village neighbors. He didn't speak much English, but his name was Johnny. Hence, Johnny's bar was named. Seven years later, his namesake is still going strong serving a mixed crowd of locals, construction workers, models and even a couple of celebs here and there. This tiny bar is very friendly and welcoming and serves super cheap drinks 365 days a year from noon to 4am daily. Along with $2.75 Bud Ices there are 4 beers on tap, 11 kinds of bottled beers, wine and liquor. A daily happy hour from 12-3pm serves up ½ price drinks while from 4pm - 7pm you can get a $3.25 deal on Jack, Jagermeister and Quervo. Owned by the proprietor of Alchemy, the atmosphere is warm, friendly and very neighborly. It's a very tiny bar with lots of beer signs and wood walls. Along with a couple of TVs and a video game, the jukebox has an amazing selection. From Bowie, The Stooges and The New York Dolls, to Pearl Jam, The Sex Pistols, Madonna and Lyle Lovett, you sure get a cross section of music. If the cheap drinks, friendly bartenders and the great music don't grab you, check out Johnny's on Monday and Tuesday nights. From 10pm - 2am pay $5 for an all-you-can-drink Bud Ice-athon. It's definitely a warm and friendly escape from the expensive, trendy bars popping up all over the West Village.

## JOHNNEY'S FISH GRILL
**4 World Financial Center (Vesey St. bet. West St. & the Hudson River)**
**385-0333**

***ALL MAJOR CREDIT CARDS***

It seems as if the sole purpose of this bar is to serve as a stopover point for employees of the exchange and the Financial Center before they hit the public transportation systems and head home. Yes, the beers are cold, and perhaps that's reason enough to keep the white shirt clad gentlemen pouring in here. If it weren't for the sheer convenience of this location (smack in the middle of the Financial Center's atrium) it's hard to imagine folks would continue flocking to this faux decorated fishing boat. Johnney's is closed on weekends and only open till 10pm on weeknights. If you need to curb your appetite, try sticking to the basics like fried calamari—more complicated items tend to be as bland as hospital food.

**JOLLY ROGER**
**155 2nd Ave. (bet. 9ᵗʰ & 10th Sts.)**
**777-6514**

This pirate-inspired bar should have stayed on the high seas. It tries too hard with every gimmick to get you to come in and drink. Beer specials, shot specials...nothing special. This place offers pool, darts, and two floors of lousy music. The crowd is nondescript and as dull as a roof shingle. We're not sure who this bar is trying to cater to.

**JUDSON GRILL**
**152 W. 52ⁿᵈ (bet. 6ᵗʰ & 7ᵗʰ Aves.)**
**582-5252**

*ALL MAJOR CREDIT CARDS*

Do you *really* want to have a drink in a restaurant/bar that looks like a bank? If you work in midtown, the answer is yes. This large and overwhelming space is one of the few good after-work spots in this barren part of town. The crowd is yuppy and looking to score some action with the secretarial pool, so watch out.

**JULIE'S**
**204 E. 58th St. (bet. 2nd & 3rd Aves.)**
**688-1294**

*ALL MAJOR CREDIT CARDS*

If you're a 30-year-old lesbian in a suit, you'll fit right in. Loud music and a dim decor attract a crowd that on the weekends can spill onto the front stoop—quite a gauntlet to swim through if you're a first-timer. Come on by for a raucous alternative pickup scene.

**JULIUS**
**159 W. 10th St. (At Waverly Pl.)**
**929-9672**

*ALL MAJOR CREDIT CARDS*

This must be the longest standing gay bar in the West Village, hands down. Formally a hangout for celebrities and jockeys, Julius now caters to a mature, loud neighborhood crowd with their younger admirers. The hamburgers and french fries are excellent, especially at 4 am when you're bombed.

**JUNIPER CAFÉ & BAR**
**185 Duane St. (bet. Hudson & Greenwich Sts.)**
**965-1201**
*ALL MAJOR CREDIT CARDS*

This little, out-of-the-way spot is a great start to a fun evening in TrBeCa. If the cozy, warm feeling and the friendly staff aren't enough to get you in the right mood, maybe the creative American food with a French flair will. The mushroom pate, grilled shrimp and the marinated beets are only a few of the wonderful choices you have in this attitude-free date spot. If beer or wine is your thing, you're in luck. They offer 25 beers from around the globe and an extensive wine list. This is not the kind of spot to come with your frat buds to chow down, unless of course your frat pal is Audrey Hepburn.

## JUNNO'S
**64 Downing St. (At Varick St.)**
**627-7995**

***ALL MAJOR CREDIT CARDS***

Tucked away on an adorable and very un-New York street you'll find a cozy, ultra-Americanized Japanese restaurant/bar/lounge. The proprietor, Junno, used to run an illegal lounge out of his apartment above McBell's on 6th Ave. His "speakeasy's" popularity eventually led to its downfall. Luckily, the entrepreneurial owner didn't give up; instead he opened a hip bar bearing his name. The staff is personable, young and accommodating and the food is so inexpensive and delicious you may be tempted to do a sampling of everything. The music is young and hip like the crowd. Open till 4am on the weekends, it's a great place to hang out all night.

## JUSTIN'S
**31 W. 21st St. (bet. 5th & 6th Aves.)**
**352-0599**

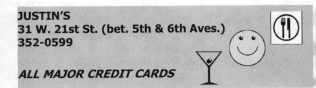

***ALL MAJOR CREDIT CARDS***

Let's be honest—does anyone really care about Puff Daddy anymore? Probably not, but at least he has a spacious and super swanky restaurant in Chelsea. Justin's, not Sean "Puff Daddy" Combs, draws a fashionable urban crowd who come for the excellent food, soothing décor, and top-notch music. A perfect date spot to linger well into the night for the movers and shakers, this is a perfect combination of excellent food, excellent vibe and a fun thirties-plus crowd.

### KARAVAS TAVERN
**162 W. 4th St. (bet. 6th & 7th Aves.)**
**243-8007**

*CASH ONLY*

Open for eight years, this West Village bar caters to a crowd of rowdy bridge-and-tunnel types with a couple of old-timglam rockers thrown in for color. This ugly bar with wooden beams, ceiling fans, and booths offers nothing pleasing to the eye. Bartenders pour inexpensive mixed drinks and a good choice of 12 beers on tap. Hot, stuffy and smoky, this place is very boring. Open daily till 4am.

### KASTRO LOUNGE
**237 E. 5th St. (bet. 2nd & 3rd Aves.)**
**475-4949**

A small bar with moderately priced drinks, Christmas lights, and lots of smoke. Local NYU students and neighborhood stragglers like this non-trendy escape to drink good beer and listen to surprisingly good music. Nothing special to travel to if you're not in the neighborhood, but a nice simple place to sit and chat.

### KAVA LOUNGE
**605 Hudson St. (At W.12th St.)**
**989-7504**

Named after a popular drink in New Zealand, Kava looks like a coffee house, turned bar. The long thin layout has a bar in the front and comfy seating in the back that draws a downtown crowd in their twenties. With an extensive wine collection and super friendly bartenders, Kava guarantees an enjoyable time. If you're looking for a mellow spot to catch up with friends or take your date, stop by this relaxing and at times romantic spot.

## KAVEHAZ
**123 Mercer St. (bet. Prince & Spring)**
**343-0612**

*ALL MAJOR CREDIT CARDS*

Open for 3 years, this roomy café-cum-gallery attracts a SoHo evening crowd who can't decide between a light late gourmet dinner, early jazz or liquored coffee. If you can, grab a seat on one of the tasteful, cushy sofas and read the extensive wine list by the soothing art deco lights. This small, live jazz club is sure to impress the dilettantes and placate the music experts. Live jazz bands perform on the weekends with no cover. Hours are 9pm-12am during the week and 8pm-3am on the weekends. Also a good place to come if you're just in the mood for a coffee and desert.

## KELLY'S CORNER (CLOSED)
**1725 2nd Ave. (89th/90th St.)**

## KENNEDY'S
**327 W. 57th St. (bet. 8th & 9th Aves.)**
**489-8335**

*ALL MAJOR CREDIT CARDS*

Irish eyes are smiling at Kennedy's. This comfortable bar/restaurant has lived on for the past 30 years where a loyal crowd gathers nightly to chat, watch the game on one of seven TVs, or have arguably one of the best pints of Guinness in New York. Named after, you guessed it, that infamous Irish, Catholic family, Kennedy's plays host to an eclectic mix of monsignors and cops, neighborhood couples, and young singles. The staff is authentic, with their appealing Irish accents and no-fuss professionalism. But the man to see when you're at Kennedy's is Morris, king of the back bar. This classic Irish gentleman looks straight out of Central Casting with his adorable grin and eyebrows to match. He's been there for 25 years and is a real gem, so give him the respect he deserves. Even if you're not part of his loyal following, he'll make you feel so at home you won't want to leave. With 12 beers on tap, tasty Irish continental food (chicken pot pie to die), and piano in the back six nights a week, we hope Kennedy's (and Morris) will live on forever.

## KENNY'S CASTAWAYS
**157 Bleecker St. (bet. Thompson & Sullivan)**
**473-9870**

*ALL MAJOR CREDIT CARDS*

"Through these portals walk the famous" is posted inside this miniature version of LA's House of Blues. With a history of famous musicians performing here such as Bruce Springsteen, Blues Travelers and Social Distortion, this blues club rocks the house nightly. For a small cover charge, the spacious club showcases an eclectic variety of live music. Follow the red carpeting leading up to the balcony lounge to watch the bands from above. In between acts, a jukebox spits out rock-and-roll while television sets present sports highlights. The Elvis lamp, tree trunk extending from the bar, rock-and-roll memorabilia make this bar unique in comparison to its neighbors.

## KENN'S BROOME STREET BAR
**363 W. B'way (At Broome St.)**
**925-2086**

*ALL MAJOR CREDIT CARDS*

This rustic little tavern out of place on the trendy SoHo strip serves a very good beer selection at moderate prices. The locals who frequent this semi-dive range from lost Euro-tourists and after-work Wall Streeters, to blue collar workers and NYU students. The food is your typical bar fare, ranging from burgers to cheese fries. All in all, it's a solid laid back place that's a nice escape from the ultra-hip, over-priced venues that surround it.

## KETTLE OF FISH
**130 W. 3rd St (At Macdougal St.)**
**533-4790**

*ALL MAJOR CREDIT CARDS*

Alive and kicking since 1950, Kettle of Fish has been a staple amongst the West Village hippies, frat boys, and tourists in search of a crowd. In desperate need of a theme, Kettle of Fish is a designer's nightmare. Covered in sports memorabilia, posters, license plates and street signs which read, "Yankee's Fan Parking Only," this look screams TGIF. Bartenders who look they've been working here since the bar's inception serve up cheap drinks daily with no happy hour ($12 pitchers of Bass; $3.75 well drinks) as a jukebox plays old favorites from U2, Crosby, Stills and Nash and Tom Petty. This two-room bar has a spacious back room with wooden tables and chairs, video games and the most prestigious dart team in the city. Don't come dressed to impress—1980s Levis and t-shirts seem to be all the rage.

## KEVIN ST. JAMES
**741 8th Ave. (bet. 46th & 47th Sts.)**
**977-5984**

### ALL MAJOR CREDIT CARDS

A pleasant addition to an otherwise barren stretch of 8th Avenue, Kevin St. James is a warm and friendly Irish pub and restaurant serving cold pints and a full Irish/American menu. Another good after work spot for all the midtown professionals looking for a change of pace. Take off your tie, bask in the unpretentious atmosphere and strike up a conversation with the very friendly staff.

## THE KEY CLUB
**76 East 13th St. (bet. B'way & 4th Ave.)**
**388-1060**

This quasi-chic, trying-too-hard-to-be-cool club plays host to the weekend throngs of the bridge-and-tunnel crowd. Key Club considers itself an "upscale night club" with panache. This is why they can demand a $20 cover charge per person. The only thing you receive for this sick price is a wait in a tremendously long line, crappy dance music, drinks in plastic cups, and totally cheesed out Guido guys.

It's really a meat market in disguise. Don't be fooled into thinking this is the "in" place by the long line outside—just move right along.

## KGB BAR
**85 E. 4th St. (bet. Bowery & 2nd Ave.)**
**505-3360**

*CASH ONLY*

On the second floor of what looks like an apartment building, KGB has the potential to be a lot more interesting than it is. The bar is small, smoky and dirty with bartenders that are not very eager to serve. The beat crowd evokes an annoying art-snob aura that takes you back to those annoying "theater people" that you hated during high school. Painted red walls are covered with a slew of cheesy Russian propaganda posters in cheap K-Mart frames. You would expect the drinks to be reasonably priced in a place like this, but they're not. This bar is not worth the trip.

## KING COLE BAR (@ THE ST. REGIS HOTEL)
**2 E. 55th St. (bet. 5th & Madison)**
**339-6721**

*ALL MAJOR CREDIT CARDS*

This beautiful hotel lounge in the heart of midtown is gently lit with elegant chandeliers. Established in 1949, this lounge only allowed men into its masculine room until the late 1950s. Comfy seating surrounds the beautiful cherry oak bar where a huge mural (painted in 1906 and now worth $4 million) was painted by Maxfield Parrish. The painting, called "Flatulence," depicts a king who just farted and his loyal subjects reacting to his deed. King Cole looks down on NY's high society happily drinking an array of cognacs, ports, champagnes, and brandies. Dress to the hilt to blend into this posh hotel scene. Good place for meeting up for a drink before a black tie event.

## KING NYC
**579 6th Ave. (bet. 16th & 17th Sts.)**
**366-5464**

*CASH ONLY*

The vault-like doors that stand between the outside world and this borderline Chelsea boy bar could be your saving grace if it weren't your intention on going to one of the biggest gay pickup joints this side of the Mississippi. This place "rocks out with its cock out," literally. Open every night from 4pm-4am, the real fun begins at 10:45pm when the live, almost nude and gyrating like there's no tomorrow dancer/models strut their stuff on the stage upstairs. If you stop by early, there's not much action, but you can occupy your time watching the gay soft porn on the TV monitors by the 1st floor bar.

## KINSALE TAVERN
**1672 3rd Ave. (bet. 93rd & 94th Sts.)**
**348-4370**

*ALL MAJOR CREDIT CARDS*

This is the real McCoy. A traditional Irish pub with traditional Irish fare showing televised soccer and rugby matches on several TVs above the bar. The satellite hookup allows them to show the sports you can't see at the other Upper East Side bars. Although they recently revamped the interior, it's the same solid pub that has existed in this spot for over 15 years and down on 86th street for years before that. The clientele here are truly locals in the fact that they are loyal regulars, but certainly are not natives to this country. Patrons range in age from barely 21 to too old to even guess. The popularity of this bar crosses over to the typical East Siders as well, probably because of the unbelievable 32 beers offered on tap and the solid "shepard's pie" and "bangers and mash."

## KIT KAT CLUB
### 124 W. 43rd St.
### 819-0377

*ALL MAJOR CREDIT CARDS*

The Kit Kat Club is a high voltage, youthful and happening scene. When this multi-level club opens its doors at 10pm you'll find yourself waiting outside until the door people deem you "rad" enough to enter the heart-pounding, bass-pumping, hip-hoppin' space. If sweat and adventurous dance moves are not your thing, move upstairs to the balcony lounge for a great view of the club. Cover is $20.

## KNICKERBOCKER BAR & GRILL
### 33 University Place (At 9th St.)
### 228-8490

*ALL MAJOR CREDIT CARDS*

This upscale and excellent steakhouse makes for an all around fun evening, especially if you need a good setting to rehash "the good ole' days" with your pals. The front of the restaurant has an old-style bar of heavy dark wood, and caters to a sophisticated, upscale, 40s+ crowd. There's a definitive good-ole-boys feel to the place. Maybe it's the prevalence of red meat, heavy jazz tunes and cigar smoke.

## KNITTING FACTORY
### 75 Leonard St. (bet. Church & B'way)
### 219-3055

*ALL MAJOR CREDIT CARDS*

It's worth a trip to Tribeca to check out the Knitting Factory. The top floors of this tri-level space features live music with a cover charge while the downstairs lounge offers free live jazz seven nights a week. Its long, narrow bar, both comfortable and somehow familiar, is filled with people who are really interested in music. Enjoy one of the nightly drink specials like $3 pints. Grab a seat on the sofa in the back or get a better view of the jazz at one of the tables up front. It will be closing time at 4am before you know it.

**KORI**
**253 Church St.**
**(bet. Franklin & Leonard Sts.)**
**334-0908**

    ***ALL MAJOR CREDIT CARDS***

TriBeCa's newest and brightest spot is a Korean restaurant/
bar with a lofty feel and an eclectic drink menu. Serving up
originals such as the "Lolita," "Disco Queen," and "Crystal
Ball" (made with Soji white sangria), Kori has quickly become a favorite among TriBeCa's artsy and in-the-know.
The scene is mellow, the food is creative and full of flavor,
and the staff is very friendly. This is a great date spot and
an unusual start to a night out on the town.

**KOROVA MILK BAR**
**200 Ave. A (bet. 12th & 13th Sts.)**
**254-8838**

***ALL MAJOR CREDIT CARDS***

Despite its quasi-futuristic "Clockwork Orange" setting,
the Milk Bar rarely attracts a sizable crowd. Naked
mannequins with wind-blown hair, television art hanging
from the walls and kooky psychedelic writing transport
you into a 1960s trippy haze. The crowd seems to consist
of primarily out-of-towners and youths who had the
misfortune of watching (and studying) Riki Lake's "Gothic
Makeover" show. The Milk Bar boasts a bunch of drink
specials such as 1/2 price drinks for ladies on Wednesdays and Cuervo shots with Corona chasers for $5. So
forget about Stanley Kubrick's recent flop and remember
the good ole' days when movies were actually good and
bars were actually groovy, baby.

**KUSH**
**183 Orchard St.**
**(bet. Houston & Stanton Sts.)**
**677-7328**

This Moroccan-themed bar on the Lower East Side is a nice change from the hipster lounges that have been popping up every 10 feet in this area. With white washed grotto walls and wall hangings, the décor is authentic and beautiful. Another draw is the olives at the bar instead of pretzels and the reasonably priced drinks. Except for the asthma-inducing incense burning, this space is a nice retreat from the dark, smoke-filled, overplayed lounge thing.

## LAKESIDE LOUNGE
**162 Ave. B (bet. 10th & 11th Sts.)**
**529-8463**

*CASH ONLY*

Open since April 1996, this large, dark, and grungy bar plays host to live bands five to six nights a week with no cover charge. The crowd is local, young, and loud. The bar area itself is small, but there is a separate room with many candle-lit tables where you can sit and listen to extremely loud music. The owner, Roscoe, who also owns the Avenue B Social Club, gets a kick out of the unique scraps of pictures found on the floor at the end of the night. (The drunk and disorderly like to indulge in the $3 photo machine.) Open from 4pm till 4am, this loud collegiate bar will leave your ears ringing and your clothes smelling like cigarettes for days.

## LA LINEA
**15 1st Ave. (bet. 1st & 2nd Sts.)**
**777-1571**

*ALL MAJOR CREDIT CARDS*

Reminiscent of a pot-head's dorm room, this lounge-like bar hosts an array of mismatched 1980s styled chairs and couches that are illuminated by a few red and green lights. Cool photography hangs in the front bar area and the ceiling looks like a giant black mattress. Soothing acid jazz is spun in back by the DJ while a very capable sound system enhances the euphoric feeling. The drinks are moderately priced and the artsy, relaxed crowd makes it a great after dinner hang.

## LA NOUVELLE JUSTINE
**24 First Ave. (bet. 1st & 2nd Sts.)**
**673-8908**

***ALL MAJOR CREDIT CARDS***

Drinks, food and a bit of S&M? Sure, why not? Don't be alarmed by the drunk Wall Street yuppie bound and swinging from chains as the crack of leather on skin echoes throughout the room. For $20 you can be whipped and burned with hot wax while chained up in front of tourists, local drag queens, leather daddies and screaming bachelorettes. Recently moved from 23rd Street to the cavernous back room of Lucky Cheng's, this restaurant/bar exudes gothic torture and mischievous fun. Open seven nights a week with no cover charge, a kitchen serves up American/French cuisine nightly from 7pm to 1am. With dark, blood red walls, gothic crosses, medieval lighting and burning votives, get ready for a bit of abuse. Crawl up to the glass bar which encases various sex toys and torture devices and be served by your mistress or servant of the night. If all of this S&M doesn't do it for you, catch the nightly drag acts in the ghostly back room. The menu is a bit pricey as are the drinks, but hey, how many legal places in the city can you be served by staff wearing miniscule leather Speedos with chains that connect nipples to lip piercings? This is a perfect spot for all you voyeurs, the curious, and tourists who are into something a little different. Definitely not a first date spot or a place to take your parents, unless you thoroughly want to freak the hell out of them!

## LANSKY LOUNGE
**104 Norfolk St.**
**(bet. Delancey & Rivington St.)**
**677-9489**

***ALL MAJOR CREDIT CARDS***

Down a dark staircase and through a creepy alleyway is one of the coolest bars that you'll find in the city. The Lansky Lounge is swanky with a capital S. Come here and order some late night potato pancakes and other kosher fare with a martini. The kitchen is connected to Ratners Restaurant, one of the most famous Jewish restaurants in NYC. The bar truly captures a 1920s speakeasy feel with its wood-paneled walls, cool music of the era, and a bouncer dressed in a zoot suit. Saturday night is a mob scene, but during the week it's a little more laid back with a local artist crowd and a few stragglers from the Upper East Side. Try one of their special martinis except for the one that tastes like Stridex. Closed on Fridays to observe the Sabbath.

## LA NUEVA ESQUELITA
**301 W. 39th St. (At 8th Ave.)**
**631-0588**

*CASH ONLY*

The long-running and consistently popular Escuelita is set in an underground ballroom in New York's new heart of sleaze. The large one-room space with a wide square dance floor in the front and plenty of seating in the back has none of the glitz and glam of New York's more well-known nightclubs. But what it lacks in style, it surely makes up for with nightly drag performances where pre- and post-op beauties lip-sync their hearts out. Five wildly popular in-house drag queens churn through the current standards and very often get the crowd in a frenzy. The clientele is mostly Latin, young and old, and a minority of them are women (especially on Fridays). Thursday is the most popular night (only $2) and the packed dance floor literally throbs to the beat of salsa and merengue. Friday has more hip-hop and far less energy while Saturday features more house music. A great club for the more adventurous who dare to trek to midtown.

## L'ATTITUDE
**470 6th Ave. (bet. 11th & 12th Sts.)**
**243-2222**

Formerly Orienta Downtown—an Asian bar/lounge/restaurant with French influences— L'Attitude is now a French bar/lounge/restaurant with Asian influences. What's the difference? No friggin' idea, Monsignor Wang. Wicker chairs and dangling red lights fight with red vinyl booths and surreal Parisian paintings for a singular theme. The menu is French, but what's with the big curtain covered with Chinese elephants? Catering to the West Village college crowd—NYU and The New School—L'Attitude offers a quiet, airy and mellow environment, 10 special martinis to choose from, and a cozy dining room. Prices are reasonable, and they plan to have bands three to four nights a week in the fall.

**LAVA**
**28 West 20th Street (bet. 5ᵗʰ & 6ᵗʰ Aves.)**
**627-7867**

*ALL MAJOR CREDIT CARDS*

The "volcanic lava" theme and the steroid-induced musclemen at the door who grunt, "Can I see some ID" should give you a pretty good idea of what to expect inside this bar/lounge. Try to stifle a laugh as you step into the glowing red lava light and see a giant picture of an erupting volcano over the bar. After a pumped bartender asks, "Whaddya ya want?" in broken English, make your way to the beautifully decorated lounge with its high ceilings, antique couches, and cool art. There you'll find a greasy Tapas menu to order from, but don't expect anyone to wait on you, it's just not happening. Lava has serious potential but it needs renovation in more ways than one. Expect a long wait to get inside, unless of course you read this review, then you won't have to wait at all!

**LE COLONIAL**
**149 57th St. (at Lex. Ave.)**
**752-0808**

*ALL MAJOR CREDIT CARDS*

This hip, sophisticated Vietnamese restaurant/bar is a breath of fresh air among the throngs of sterile midtown eating and drinking establishments. The upstairs lounge and bar area, is the kind of romantic hideaway you would expect to see in a 1940s movie starring Humphrey Bogart. The bamboo décor and comfortable couches provide a backdrop for the perfect date. The drinks are expensive, the food is to die for and the crowd is easy on the eye. This is worth the trip.

## LEMON
**230 Park Ave. S. (bet. 18th & 19th Sts.)**
**614-1200**

### ALL MAJOR CREDIT CARDS

Lemon, plain and simple, *is* a lemon. Like every other bar downtown, this very spacious bar and restaurant was once a firehouse.  With the exception of the cement floor, which could cause a flashback to your parent's basement, fine details such as a beautiful art deco pine wood bar and a scrim-muted poppy mural make Lemon a spectacular site. The first floor bar, tucked behind a short glass wall, allows for a view of those partaking in Lemon's mediocre cuisine and ridiculously overpriced drinks.  The second level, a horseshoe-shaped lounge area, provides a good perch for voyeurs. Go during the week, the Lemon sours on the weekend when busloads of the bridge-and-tunnel crowd invade the Park Avenue South drinking establishments.

## LET'S MAKE A DAIQUIRI
**89 South St., Pier 17, 3rd Floor**
**406-1486**

### CASH ONLY

How about let's hightail it out of here as quickly as possible before this suburban "hanging out in the mall on a beautiful sunny day" mentality gets the best of us. This crappy, dilapidated daiquiri stand in the middle of the South Street Seaport food court serves pineapple, strawberry, and banana daiquiris at $5.75 a pop. I guess if you're really hankering for a frozen delight in the middle of a shopping spree you won't have much of a choice. Cheers!

## LEXINGTON BAR AND BOOKS
**1020 Lex. Ave. (At 72nd St.)**
**717-3902**

### ALL MAJOR CREDIT CARDS

Walk inside and find what looks like a well-appointed library from a 5th Avenue mansion, complete with antique books and leather wing chairs. Feel free to settle in and enjoy a cigar and an extremely rare aged cognac like the Remy Martin Louis XIII or the Hennessy Richard. (If you're willing to shell out the cash.) Of course, they have an excellent array of brandies and martinis for those who actually work for a living. The clientele, consisting of 30-somethings and up, are treated to live jazz on Friday and Saturday nights.

## THE LIBRARY
**7 Avenue A (bet. Houston & 2nd St.)**
**375-1352**

### CASH ONLY

For cheap drinks and a great jukebox, stop by The Library where an energetic and thankfully non-tourist crowd hang. Decorated in deep red and shelves stocked with stolen library books, the atmosphere will remind you of what you loved and hated most about being young. Sit at the bar or head to the back where old Kung Fu movies are shown on a giant screen. The dim lighting and dark walls provide the perfect setting for the Sunday matinee—B-movies from 2pm - 7pm. The main attraction is the jukebox loaded with your favorites like Adam Ant, The Stooges, MC5, Television, Jimi Hendrix and Corner Shop. Very friendly bartenders not only welcome you and treat you like a friend but are in the habit of buying back drinks. Open 7 days a week from 12pm - 4am, the Library offers a 2 for 1 happy hour from 5pm to 8pm.

## LIFE / THE KI CLUB
**158 Bleecker St.**
**(bet. Sullivan & Thompson Sts.)**
**420-1999**
### ALL MAJOR CREDIT CARDS

One of NYC's more popular, Miami-esque dance clubs, Life is the saving grace of Bleecker street. The decor is early 80s and John Hughes to the core. A spacious main room with its wraparound neon bar, DJ sky box and sweeping dance floor keeps the "not cool enough to be in the VIP lounge" crowd moving to the loud, throbbing, house music. This room plays host to many live performances by '80s icons such as Siouxsie and the Creatures, Nina Hagen, and Skid Row. If you're deemed "money" enough to deserve VIP status, you can lounge downstairs with models and their Calvin Klein clad studs. The weekends tend to attract a host of out-of-towners and scantily dressed twentysomethings posing around hoping to get a glance at someone famous. Unless you're on "the list," expect to pay a $ 20 cover for weak and expensive drinks served in plastic cups. Life is a good place to see and be seen but if you're looking for substance, it ain't here.

**LIFE CAFÉ**
**343 E. 10th St. (bet. Aves. A & B)**
**477-8791**

***ALL MAJOR CREDIT CARDS***

This funky, old, East Village haunt has miraculously survived the gentrification of the East Village. The same cool, heart-filled hangout continues to attract an old school neighborhood crowd. Open daily from 11am till 1am, the bar is small and draws in a very native, artsy crowd. Hang out at the bar and chill with the friendly, tattooed bartender or take a seat in the cafe area for some healthy and cheap food. (Weekend brunch is the best deal in the house.) A daily happy hour from 5pm till 9pm offers a "buy one, get one free" discount on the already cheap drinks. Life Café is especially popular in the summer when the back garden opens up and there's sidewalk seating.

**LIMELIGHT**
**47 6th Ave. (At 20th St.)**
**807-7790**

***ALL MAJOR CREDIT CARDS***

The Limelight's heyday is definitely over. The club kids and ravers have moved on to more exciting locations and now this former cathedral is a haven for Upper East Side girls, boys and B-list models. If you can make it inside the heavily roped VIP rooms, you'll notice the revamped local isn't very glamorous at all. In fact the choosy bouncers seem to need bigger glasses than muscles. If you stillwant to pay too much($5-$8) for a watered down drink after you've paid $15 (reduced list) to $20 admission fee, make sure to have that drink in the newly opened Giger room.Once inside this little and very packed meat-market,you'll be pleasantly pleasedby the astounding furniture and wall candy all courtesy of the very talented artist, H.R. Giger.

## LION'S DEN
### 214 Sullivan St.
### (bet. Bleecker & W. 3rd Sts.)
### 477-2782

Smack in the middle of Greenwich Village, this dive bar plays hosts to NYU students as well as a vast array of New York music lovers. They offer live music every night of the week ranging from rock to reggae to rap. A few years ago it was much grungier, but a recent renovation has certainly brightened and cleaned things up. You need to call in advance for the lineup and the cover charge usually ranges from $7-$10. In the summertime it gets like a boiler room in there, so wear a lot of deodorant and loose clothes.

## LIQUIDS
### 266 E. 10th St. (bet. 1st & 2nd Aves.)
### 677-1717

### ALL MAJOR CREDIT CARDS

Once you get past the doorman, you'll enter a decadent, dark, candlelit cavern filled with great DJ'd music and a dorky but hip heterosexual mid-twenties crowd. While the drinks are way over priced, Liquids is famous for its "Liquid Martini" which is potent and worth the cash. You won't find a happy hour or drink specials at this classier than most East Village hot spot. The sound system and funky music is a definite draw. Good early-in-the-eve date spot.

## LIQUOR STORE BAR
**235 W. B'way (At White St.)**
**226-7121**

*CASH ONLY*

Set in what appears to be a quaint house from the 1700s is an old-style, no-frills beer tavern in TriBeCa. When the warm weather rolls around, there are tables outside where people-watching becomes the sport of choice. Innocent passersby are inevitably checked out and often undressed to the bare bones by some of the Wall Street types that go there after work. Aside from that, it's a great little place to grab a drink and a perfect place to bring your pooch.

## LIVE BAIT
**14 E. 23rd St. (bet. Park & 5th Aves.)**
**353-2400**

*ALL MAJOR CREDIT CARDS*

This funky Cajun/Bait-and-Tackle theme bar used to be the talk of the town but has since lost its luster. Nonetheless, it remains a popular venue among the younger horny generation that flocks here after work for a cold one. Pencil-thin bartenders keep the women in a constant state of butt size insecurity. The lack of cool bars in this neck of the woods is probably what has kept it afloat after all these years. It's a definite singles scene.

## LIVE PSYCHIC
**207 E. 84th St. (At 3rd Ave.)**
**744-5003**

Who ever said, "white people can't dance"? After going to Live Psychic, you'll be saying it too. Live Psychic has been around for years and is the only real dance spot on the Upper East Side. This large, no-frills space, equipped with two bars and a decently sized dance floor, attracts a young, single crowd that is not in-the-know. The tunes, however, are excellent and range from '70s disco to '80s faves to top 40. Open Thursday through Saturday, Live Psychic offers one of the better deals around: A $10 cover on Friday and Saturday includes an open bar from 8:30pm to 10:30pm.

## LIVING ROOM
**84 Stanton St. (At Allen St.)**
**533-7235**

*CASH ONLY*

Is that Yanni doing his interpretation of the "Rebirth of the Sunflower" or is it some avant-garde, lower eastsider commenting on the cutting edge of unexplainable art? Lots of folk singers, performance artists and New Age musicians convene at this restaurant/bar/performance space. Open for only eight months, drinks are pretty cheap and food is served into the wee hours of the night. This place is just plain weird. Either you're being hushed by the bartender while a live band is playing, or the beer of your choice keeps running out. The crowd looks like casting rejects from "Reality Bites" with a severity that is painfully unnerving. For those of you into performance art, local music and perhaps a person wrapping themselves in saran wrap fighting to break out of the cocoon called life, then this is the perfect place for you.

## LOCAL 138
**138 Ludlow St.**
**(bet. Stanton & Rivington Sts.)**
**477-0280**

*CASH ONLY*

A homey addition to the Ludlow Street strip of hipster bars. The Irish lads who run the place stock a thoughtful, eclectic assortment of draft beers and put in new color tellies just for the World Cup. Oodles of warm wood paneling and little votive candels make up the décor of this modestly sized bar. Try to score one of the two commodious booths that flank the entrance and look out onto the street through large windows. Frequented by Lower East Side regulars, it's a place where outgoing types can make friends fast.

### LOLA
**30 W. 22nd St. (bet. 5th & 6th Aves.)**
**675-6700**

*ALL MAJOR CREDIT CARDS*

This longstanding romantic Chelsea restaurant offers live R&B, funk and jazz after the dinner hours on Wednesday-Saturday evenings. Catering to an upscale, older and mixed ethnic crowd, it's a perfect late night pit stop to pop into and impress a date. There is never a cover charge!

### LOOKING GLASS
**108 3rd Ave. (bet. 13th & 14th Sts.)**
**777-3363**

Was that Huggy Bear, Baretta and Starsky & Hutch at the bar, or do my eyes deceive me? This dive feels like a bar you would see in a 1970s police show. Fully equipped with what looks like the first TV set to ever roll off the assembly line, the decor is as dive-like as it gets. It's sleazy with a crowd that is part NYU student, part dregs of the earth. It must be the cheap drink specials that keep the crowd coming back time and again.

### LOUISIANA BAR AND GRILL
**622 B'way (bet. Houston & Bleecker)**
**460-9633**

*ALL MAJOR CREDIT CARDS*

This Cajun restaurant/bar plays host to different musical acts nightly. Monday is its infamous swing night. Dressed to the nines, cool cats and hip ladies show each other up on the dance floor to a live big band. The energy and the amazing music attracts New York City regulars and eager tourists interested in reliving the days of swing. Although there is no cover charge, reservations are a must if you plan to dine. The food is spicy and reasonably priced while drinks are a bit on the pricey side.

## LOT61
**550 W. 21st St. (bet. 10th & 11th Aves.)**
**243-6555**

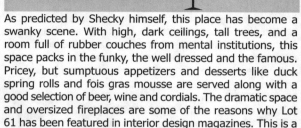

**ALL MAJOR CREDIT CARDS**

As predicted by Shecky himself, this place has become a swanky scene. With high, dark ceilings, tall trees, and a room full of rubber couches from mental institutions, this space packs in the funky, the well dressed and the famous. Pricey, but sumptuous appetizers and desserts like duck spring rolls and fois gras mousse are served along with a good selection of beer, wine and cordials. The dramatic space and oversized fireplaces are some of the reasons why Lot 61 has been featured in interior design magazines. This is a definite date place. Call ahead for reservations.

## L-RAY
**64 W. 10th St. (bet. 5th & 6th Aves.)**
**505-7777**

**ALL MAJOR CREDIT CARDS**

This very trendy and new neighborhood hot spot draws the crowd with its eclectic menu encompassing anything from Cuba to the Bayou. Come here to sample some of the best margaritas and mojitos in town while catering to a good-looking, hip Greenwich Village crowd. On any given night the downstairs bar is filled with people sipping one of the many tequilas and munching on appetizers such as taco-on-a-stick, guacamole (better than Rosa Mexicano's), and the sliced duck. This is a welcome addition to this some-what quality-starved part of town. Make reservations or the margarita wait will knock you on your butt.

## LUCA LOUNGE
**220 AVE B (bet. 13th & 14th Sts.)**
**674-9400**

Fashionably worn antique furniture, superb Italian cuisine, fair prices and a friendly atmosphere has made the family owned Luca Lounge an instant hit. Outfitted with provincial Italian decor, the Di Tomaso family has put their heart and soul into this Avenue B restaurant/lounge. With hard wood floors, antique wood furniture and warm candle light, the Italian influence is obvious. Relax to acid jazz and Portishead at the bar or lounge on old couches and chairs in the front parlor or outside in the vast back garden. Drinks are reasonably priced: tap beer, $5; glass of wine, $6 - $7; mixed drink, $5. The menu offers cheese plates, Bruscetta, the special pizettes, pasta, cappuccino and desserts. The rustic setting fuses with simple elegance to make the Luca Lounge a very welcoming experience. Hours: Tues., Wed., Sun., 7pm-1am; Thurs. – Sat., 7pm-4am.

## LUCKY CHENGS
**24 1st Ave. (bet. 1st & 2nd Sts.)**
**473-0516**

*ALL MAJOR CREDIT CARDS*

Open seven days a week until 2am, this Asian drag queen theme bar attracts anyone from the curious tourist to the businessman who wants to entertain his clients. The exquisitely dressed waitresses will keep you wondering for weeks if they are male or female. Its dark, red lounge is adorned with mirrored walls, leopard-printed tables and couches, and Chinese lanterns hanging from the ceilings. Like a scene out of an Asian gender bender, this lounge is a perfect place to have a birthday celebration. Come for the experience, not for the food.

## LUCKY STRIKE
**59 Grand St. (bet. W. B'way & Wooster)**
**941-0772**

*ALL MAJOR CREDIT CARDS*

Before Balthazar, The Odeon and Pravda made their mark as some of the trendiest places to go downtown, there was Lucky Strike. Located on Grand Street, this gem of a bar/restaurant with its hip and cozy décor is usually packed with young twentysomethings. The light fixtures are draped in vintage Russian propaganda posters and the bistro theme is played up with the dinner menu written on mirrors and chalkboards. Wooden floors, high ceilings, dim lighting and an attractive crowd make this bar a good date spot. One small drawback is that the pricey drinks are served in offensively small glasses. (It's a Parisian thing.)

## LUDLOW BAR
**165 Ludlow St. (bet. Houston & Stanton)**
**353-0536**

### ALL MAJOR CREDIT CARDS

This tiny little cave-like lounge used to host an array of live folk music but has since become a retro hangout. A young, hip, artsy crowd gathers on the weekend to dance to funky Latin acid trip-hop. There's a pool table in the back that shuts down when it gets too crowded. The drinks are moderately priced, and if you nab a couch it's a fun place to hang out with some hipsters and people watch. This is definitely a pickup spot.

## LUKE'S BAR AND GRILL
**1394 3rd Ave. (bet. 79th & 80th Sts.)**
**249-7070**

### CASH ONLY

This gently lit and beautiful oak-paneled bar/restaurant plays host to a diverse crowd of after work suits and casual Upper East Siders. Humbly put by the owner, Luigi, "This is the best bar on the Upper East Side." Well, maybe not the *best*, but it could be considered a mini oasis in an area dominated by a sea of frat bars. This is a comfortable bar where everyone has impeccable bar manners and you can actually hear yourself talk over the CD player. There has never been a fight during the seven years of operation, making it a great place to take your parents to show them that New York is not such a bad place after all.

**LUNA LOUNGE**
**171 Ludlow St. (bet. Houston & Stanton)**
**260-2323**

*ALL MAJOR CREDIT CARDS*

Don't be fooled by the name; Luna Lounge is no lounge. What lounge do you know is equipped with a video blackjack machine, a fooseball game and a stage for live music in the back? The Gen-X and NYU crowd that frequent this establishment are mostly male and are looking to score. Although the bands and sound system are pretty good, Luna Lounge is nothing more than a large dive with about as much ambiance as the interior of a tube sock.

**LUNAR PARK**
**Union Square West (bet. 16th & 17th Sts.)**

Originally a beautiful spot in an incredible location, Lunar Park had the potential to go a long way but fell painfully short. People still flock to wait in long lines to gain entry, and once inside stand like cattle crammed into a pen in order to bask in this completely outdoor lounge in Union Square Park. Once *in* Lunar Park, you are treated to the likes of ridiculously expensive drinks served in plastic cups at a tiny bar that suffers from awful service. Since there is nothing lounge-like about being a sardine and drinking from plastic, it has quickly lost its appeal to the crowd it was trying to woo. Now a predominantly B&T crowd is what you will find there. (P.S.: Watch your feet because a furry little rodent might just scurry across one.)

**THE LURE**
**409 W. 13th St.**
**(bet. 9th Ave. & Washington)**
**741-3919**

*CASH ONLY*

Wednesday night at the Lure's "Pork" is where Chelsea meets his leather daddy. Equipped with its own sex shop, this fetish club is hard-core. Barely naked bartenders in leather harnesses serve cheap but strong drinks while the predominately male crowd stares at gay porn on hanging TVs. If the lone pool table doesn't intrigue you, watch a customer in a metal cage receive a very homoerotic shoe shine by a scantily dressed go-go boy. No, that wasn't Ponch from "Chips" in police garb making an arrest and no that's not a real fireman all geared up for a fire, it's just some good old-fashioned fetish fun at "Pork." On Thursdays, for a cover of $5, the normally homo crowd welcomes a mixed crowd to its Vexx get-together. As DJ Horace spins techno and electronica, Mistress Tuesday and her boys host a weekly night of naughtiness. Side shows, floggings and dominants disciplining the well-deserved is the theme at Vexx on Thursday nights. A dress code of fetish, latex and leather is strictly enforced.

### LUSH
**110 Duane St. (bet. Church & B'way)**
**766-1295**

*ALL MAJOR CREDIT CARDS*

An ultra-swanky lounge in the heart of TriBeCa, Lush has evolved into quite a popular place. On any evening on this quiet and dark block you're bound to find a large group of people waiting to get inside. The loft-like setting includes a beautiful bar, two back rooms and a surprisingly friendly staff. Owned by SoHo Grand Hotel and China Grill alumni, it is no surprise that Lush is tasteful, romantic, sexy, comfortable, and professional. The décor is modern and chic with circular shaped back rooms where 30 different types of scotch are offered. When it opened in July of '98 our prophetic Shecky saw a velvet rope in Lush's future. Too bad these prophecies come true, eh?

### LUVBUZZ
**1438 3rd Ave. (bet. 81st & 82nd Sts.)**
**717-0100**

*ALL MAJOR CREDIT CARDS*

This retro '70s bar on the Upper East Side looks like a bar opened by Greg Brady and Keith Partridge. This fun, new lounge with a mod squad interior is actually a nice addition to the strip of frat holes that dominate this part of town. Luvbuzz serves up creative cocktails with an intersting selection of crudites. Austin Powers would jump out of his skin with ecstasy once he realized Luvbuzz is doubling as a dating service similar to that of Drip Coffee bar located on the West Side. Just like a dating agency, a customer can fill out the "likes and dislikes" and then let the process begin. Luvbuzz then compiles those forms into a binder along with a digital photo to help the "luv" process move along efficiently. Luvbuzz then acts as the match-maker by setting up that first meeting in the bar. Those in fear of the dreaded stalker are encouraged to give a Luvbuzz alias until they feel more comfortable. After that fisrt meeting, let nature take its course. A very cute spot with a nice twist to help the shy oysters come out of their shells and show their shiny pearls. Monday is Boozy Bingo night.

## M&R BAR
**264 Elizabeth St.**
**(bet. Prince & Houston Sts.)**
**226-0559**

*ALL MAJOR CREDIT CARDS*

Michael and Richard are the owners of this popular, 50s-style bar/restaurant that is typically chock-full of the young and ultra-fabulous martini generation. Girls in cool frocks and guys with sideburns and tortoise-rimmed glasses pack it in on the weekends. The bar area is teeny but these cool cats don't mind being pressed against one another—they're having a blast, man. Get here early and grab one of the few tables against the wall with your friends, otherwise it's not comfortable enough to stay for long. A small artsy dining area in the back makes for a decent little date spot on a budget.

## MAD HATTER (CLOSED)
**1485 2nd Ave. (bet. 77th & 78th Sts.)**

## MAD RIVER BAR AND GRILL
**1442 3rd Ave. (bet. 81st & 82nd Sts.)**
**988-1832**

*ALL MAJOR CREDIT CARDS*

Mad River has pretensions to be something more than a fraternity party, but never quite gets there. Crowded to the point of being immobile, this is no place for wimps—only the brave make a mad dash to the bar. There is a very small seating area with a restaurant that closes too early to be useful and waitresses who openly prefer the drunken men at the bar to the potential for tips at the tables. But who can blame them? Who wouldn't be smitten with an arrogant, condescending 27-year-old with a big old beer gut?

## MADAME X
**94 W. Houston St.**
**(bet. Laguardia & Thompson Sts.)**
**539-0808**

*ALL MAJOR CREDIT CARDS*

Despite its sex club facade, this underground lounge offers a tastefully executed, extremely comfortable drinking experience. Opened by a group of professional women, Madame X is styled in the manner of an 1800s bordello with headboards lining the walls of the small but comfortable bar in front. The larger back area consists of comfortable couches that were recovered from tag sales and flea markets. The attitude is friendly, warm and receptive and the crowd is professional and artsy. There is even a roped off no-smoking section; an extremely unusual feature for a bar.

## MADISON PUB
**1043 Madison Ave. (bet. 79th & 80th Sts.)**
**650-1809**

The burgers at this very out-of-place and grungy pub on the Upper East Side rival those of the Corner Bistro, and that's reason enough to trek up here. Neighborhood folks also come here for a quick after work drink or to watch a game. The bar is very small, but there are a few private booths. Don't expect to sing along to your favorite current music because the jukebox is filled with mostly old jazz favorites.

## MADISON'S
**1584 York Ave. (bet. 83rd & 84th Sts.)**
**570-5454**

*ALL MAJOR CREDIT CARDS*

Formerly Casey's Dance Hall and Saloon, Madison's is now the same scene but with a different name. The vibe is cheesy, B&T and anyone with any taste whatsoever wouldn't be caught dead in here. There's a stand-up bar with dancing in the back on one side, and a more relaxed cigar bar atmosphere on the other. Young twentysomethings frequent this bar during the week but on the weekends it's purely bridge-and-tunnel. Nonetheless, it's a good choice if you're in the mood to dance to top 40 hits.

## MAGNUM
**357 W. B'way (bet. Broome & Grand Sts.)**
**965-1491**

*ALL MAJOR CREDIT CARDS*

Aside from the unfortunate address in the middle of SoHo tourist hell, Magnum has a lot to offer. This large, well-decorated spot is full of seating, good background music and a well stocked bar that offers a good Belgian beer selection and many top scotches. The décor is modern with velvet everywhere and cool light fixtures. A good-looking wait staff balances it all out. The crowd tends to be a bit bridge-and-tunnel on the weekends, but during the week this is a safe bet. Beware of the annoying door guys claiming that there is a private party—there isn't.

## MALACHY'S
**103 West 72nd St. (At Columbus Ave.)**
**874-4268**

One of the Upper West Side's best dumpy Irish drunkard bars. Here at Malachy's you'll find women sporting the Jacqueline Smith collection from Kmart sitting next to unhappy balding men. This place, with its blow-up Jameson's shamrock and old sports photos would be a perfect addition to Port Authority. Perhaps its only saving grace is the jukebox which has a wide selection of tunes spanning the decades. So, if you can't walk a few more feet up the street to a more upstanding establishment, crash here and have a few shots with the "Barfly"-esque patrons.

## MANITOBA'S
**99 Ave. B (bet. 6th & 7th Sts.)**
**982-2511**

*ALL MAJOR CREDIT CARDS*

For those familiar with legend punk rock songs such as "I Live for Cars & Girls" and "Teengenerate," you will certainly feel at home at Dick Manitoba's (former frontman for the Dictators) new bar. Formerly the Avenue B Social Club, Manitoba's is a small, cozy neighborhood bar with an extension of the punk rock culture that is difficult to find in the East Village. Walls covered with punk rock icons and famous boxers create an atmosphere that is local but not as grungy as one would expect from a Dictator. With a beautiful 80-year-old Brunswick Bar and a dark lounge downstairs, this place is an escape from the plethora of yuppie-esque bars lining Avenue B. If the eclectic jukebox playing The Stooges, Manitoba's Wild Kingdom and Darelene Love doesn't get you going, come and see live bands such as Beat Rodeo. A daily happy hour serves ½ price drinks from 4pm - 8pm, otherwise drinks are reasonably priced. For those of you who long for the days of '70s punk rock and hold a place dear in your heart for the Dictators, check out Manitoba's.

176

**MARIE'S CRISIS**
**59 Grove St. (At 7th Ave.)**
**243-9323**

*CASH ONLY*

A hard-core piano bar, be prepared to know all the words to "Hello Dolly" and "Gypsy." If you don't know them, you will by the time you leave. There's limited seating, so be ready to stand on the weekends because it gets packed. The waiters are as entertaining as the performers, and it's always a good time. The music begins nightly from 9:30pm, and 5pm on Sundays. Drinks cost $4.25 and there's never a cover. Bring your mom!

**MARKT**
**401 West 14th Street (At 9th Ave.)**
**727-3314**

*ALL MAJOR CREDIT CARDS*

The Belgian food craze continues with Markt (pronounced "marked"), a large, impressive restaurant located in the heart of the meat-packing district. The restaurant's dining area reminds one of old New York with its heavy wood furniture, old-fashioned lighting, etched glass and massive bar that seems to stretch into the horizon. Not only will you not feel cramped—you won't even feel like you're in the city. In the spring the restaurant opens its windows to the street making it a breezy place to drink and nibble on mussels and frites. The bartenders are somewhat cold and mix weak drinks for a crowd made up mostly of 30-year-old hipsters. Unfortunately, the menu isn't as good as one would expect from such a handsome-looking place.

### MARION'S
**354 Bowery (bet. 3rd & 4th Sts.)**
**475-7621**

*ALL MAJOR CREDIT CARDS*

This local hang for many East Village dwellers is equipped with a large fish tank, goofy 1960s paraphernalia, and a warm, spirited feeling. The bar area is miniscule, laid back and thankfully "sans attitude." It's a nice reprieve from the Bowery Bar next door which is a complete poser fest. Pepperidge Farm goldfish crackers are served at the bar...what more could you ask for?

### MARTELL'S
**200 E. 83rd St. (At 3rd Ave.)**
**879-1717**

*ALL MAJOR CREDIT CARDS*

Martell's screams, "I just got my first job on Wall Street!" Packed to the gills with young twentysomethings in suits, there could possibly be more beer spilled here than actually consumed. This is Mecca for young yuppies on their way home from happy hour— blurry-eyed, but not ready to call it a night. During the summer it opens wide up onto Third Avenue and beckons in passersby for a surprisingly good time and good food.

### MARYLOU'S
**21 W. 9th St. (bet. 5th & 6th Aves.)**
**533-0012**

*ALL MAJOR CREDIT CARDS*

Comfortably situated on one of the nicest blocks in Greenwich Village, Marylou's exudes a wonderful charm yet at the same time a sense of oddity. It's hard to figure out exactly what happens after the dinner crowd leaves and the bar takes on a life of its own. If you don't happen to be one of the "insiders" you may be treated with curt cordiality. Take a seat, order a drink from one of the seasoned bartenders and get an eyeful of prime people watching. You never know who may be sitting next to you at this quaint underground find...perhaps Jimmy Hoffa? The continental cuisine won't rock your world, but stop by soon before you need a password to enter.

## MARS BAR
**25 E. 1st St. (At 2nd Ave.)**
**No Phone**

Looking for hell on earth? This place is about at scuzzy as it gets. This small, thin and smoky bar offers next to no space to sit and relax, and the jukebox with its large selection of loudly blaring punk and modern classics is enough to keep the roaches and vermin away. There very well might be a tattoo quota to get in, so it is certainly not worth putting on your Sunday best, let alone showering or brushing your teeth. The crowd is very scary, so beware.

**YOUR COMMENTS HERE:**

## MASON'S
**462 Amsterdam Ave.**
**(bet. 82nd & 83rd Sts.)**
**NO PHONE**

You know off the bat that if a bar is playing Journey's "Don't Stop Believing" full throttle and everyone inside is singing along that there is going to be trouble. Mason's is, quite simply, a hick dive. Its lame array of seating—a few bad couches and a mishmosh of factory-rejected stools made for midgits (which makes sense since its owner Mason Reese was a mere 5')—makes this a good place to show up if, and only if, you are already drunk.

## MATCH
**160 Mercer St. (bet. Houston & Prince)**
**343-0020**
**33 E. 60th St. (bet. Mad. & Park Aves.)**
**906-9177**

*ALL MAJOR CREDIT CARDS*

Match is a great looking bar with a great looking crowd that has about as much personality and pizzazz as a bag of plaster. In its heyday, Match was much more hip. Today it's just a tourist trap for thin Europeans. Match has live jazz on Monday and Tuesday nights in the upstairs dining area while the semi-lounge downstairs is where you'll find the bridge-and-tunnel, money-spending crowd. Wednesday and Saturday, a DJ spins hip-hop, dance and reggae. Food is modern Asian with an American flair, and there is a full sushi and sashimi bar. The staff has serious attitude...what a shock. The midtown location is not as impressive looking and draws an equally shallow and lifeless crowd.

## MATT'S GRILL
**932 8th Ave. (bet. 55th and 56th Sts.)**
**307-5109**

*ALL MAJOR CREDIT CARDS*

If it was a song instead of a bar, Matt's Grill would be a James Taylor tune. This no-fuss, low-key, classic American bar is nothing wild or crazy, just casual and comfortable. Formerly a blue collar Irish pub where Matt used to work, Matt's Grill is now owned by Matt's grandson and has been a neighborhood favorite in this quiet section of midtown for the past four years. It has an appealing, easygoing vibe, two TVs, 17 bottled beers with specials, four beers on tap, a bar menu till 1am, and is cigar friendly after dinner. The décor is *basic*—neither chic, nor divy. If you're in the 'hood and you want to down a nice cold one with no 'tude attached, this is where to be.

## MAX FISH
**178 Ludlow St. (bet. Houston & Stanton)**
**253-1922**
*CASH ONLY*

Max Fish was the first of the hip Ludlow Street bars and is still going stronger than ever. The place is always crowded with a young college crowd that's looking to score. The unflattering light, if nothing else, keeps beer goggling to a minimum. There are video games in the front of the bar to appeal to your inner child and a pool table in the back for your inner adult. The drinks are fairly cheap and the distorted Julio Iglesias sign is still there after all these years.

## MCALEERS PUB
**425 Amsterdam Ave. (bet. 80th & 81st Sts.)**
**874-8037**

*ALL MAJOR CREDIT CARDS*

Open since 1953, McAleers Pub is your old reliable Irish pub serving none other than yummy Shepherd's Pie! This watering hole attracts an unpretentious neighborhood crowd that comes to watch sports and drink. Patrons play darts while rock-and-roll tunes play on the jukebox. As expected, the drink prices are reasonable which will leave some dough in your pocket for a greasy slice of pizza at 4am.

## MCBELL'S
**359 6th Ave. (bet. Wash. Pl. & W. 4th St.)**
**675-6260**

Just a random bar on a very busy section of Sixth Avenue, McBell's serves mediocre American food and drinks. There is really nothing that stands out here. If you happen to want a beer while you're walking to Eighth Street to buy shoes, or you need a bathroom stop before heading to Washington Square Park, this is as good a place as any. Not too many people make this a destination point because it has absolutely no atmosphere or personality. It's about as boring as a piece of stale apple pie.

## MCCARTHY'S
**345 2nd Ave (At 20th St.)**
**477-6201**

### *ALL MAJOR CREDIT CARDS*

For an Irish pub, this place is extremely patriotic in an American way. Tons of plastic American flags blow in the wind of the air-conditioner while a Land of Liberty sign drapes over the beer sloaganed, mirrored walls. For the past three years, McCarthy's has been attracting a mid-twenties Irish crowd. Food is served at tables or at the bar but be prepared for quite a painful wait. With seven beers on tap, TVs, darts and cheap drinks, this neighborhood pub is simply, a neighborhood pub.

## MCCORMACK'S PUBLIC HOUSE
**365 3rd Ave. (22nd & 23rd Sts.)**
**683-0911**

### *ALL MAJOR CREDIT CARDS*

In a neighborhood that offers few choices, consider yourself lucky if you wander in here. The long wooden bar is so inviting you'll be inspired to order shots for the whole place. The friendliest Irish bartenders in the city serve well mixed, moderately priced drinks and offer friendly conversation. If you find yourself in here alone and lonely, don't fret; idle chitchat is just a barstool away. If drinking works up your appetite there is a full menu served in the back room or at the bar. Soccer buffs crowd around the multiple TVs to cheer their homeland to victory during the season. Open till 4am, this is a perfect place to grab a nightcap or just casually hang out all night long.

## MCCOY'S
**768 9th Ave. (bet. 51st & 52nd Sts.)**
**957-8055**

Don't waste your time coming here unless you want to get miserable with the choir of late night sorority crooners. This pub has that genuine dumpy feel. Torn cushions, a thick cloud of smoke, and the smell of stale beer oozing from stained pine floors makes it the kind of place you end up in when everything else in life has gone wrong. The only things that might save this dive from closing are the cheap beers and basic greasy light fare served until midnight!

## MCDOOLEY'S
**133 W. 33rd St. (bet. 6th & 7th Aves.)**
**564-7424**

*ALL MAJOR CREDIT CARDS*

This place ain't just a dive, it's a friggin' triple lindy. It's one part Irish pub and one part sports bar, and both parts suck. Dark and depressing, complete with blinking string-lights, cardboard shamrocks and a fair amount of just plain filth, McDooley's is the perfect place to get in an old-fashioned bar brawl, bust up some tables and put your head through a TV. It is not, however, a good place to do much of anything else.

## MCSORELY'S
**15 E. 7th St. (bet. 2nd & 3rd Aves.)**
**473-9148**

*CASH ONLY*

If a full scale crowd rendition of "For He's a Jolly Good Fellow" is going to break out anywhere, it's going to be here. This New York institution is the home of, you guessed it, McSorely's Ale. Sawdust on the floor, old photos on the wall, and inexpensive food and drinks draw a weekend crowd that has been known to create a line stretching down the block. You don't stand a chance of getting into this place on St. Patrick's Day. Women were not always welcome here so there remains a chauvinistic feel, but when all is said and done, it's a decent place to come and suck down 30 to 40 beers in one sitting.

**MCSWIGGINS**
**393 2nd Ave. (bet. 22nd & 23rd Sts.)**
**725-8740**

### *ALL MAJOR CREDIT CARDS*

It's possible that the Irish word for fraternities is McSwiggins. The crowd is about 90% guys who believe that if they drink enough beer, a girl (both beautiful and full of desire) will suddenly appear. While Bruce Springsteen mumbles on the jukebox, frat boys play pool, darts and video games or stare at sports specials on one of the many televisions. It's sort of like being in a bar in Albany without the band. There is a happy hour daily from 4pm till 7pm that boasts $1 off pints and Friday and Saturday drink specials of $3 pints of cider and Brooklyn Lager. If you are Irish, female, and desperately in need of some attention, this place is definitely for you.

**MENDY'S WEST**
**208 West 70th St.**
**(bet. Amsterdam & West End Aves.)**
**877-6787**
*ALL MAJOR CREDIT CARDS*

You have a craving for gefilte fish and you want to watch the Mets game...where do you go? Mendy's, of course—the perfect marriage of kosher food and sports. Whatever happens, don't take a date here, don't look too closely at the floor, the bar, or the glasses, and don't sniff too hard or you'll smell a mixture of nursing home aroma and cigarettes. This has got to be one of the most dilapidated sports bars in the city. Mendy's has single handedly cornered the market on kosher sports bars in the city, and for heaven's sake let's hope it stays that way.

**MEOW MIX**
**269 E. Houston (At Suffolk St.)**
**254-0688**

This hip, lesbian hot spot offers DJ'd music, poetry readings and live bands. Call ahead for the lineup. Lesbians claim that this is one of the better pick-up spots in the city.

## MERC BAR
**151 Mercer St. (bet. Houston & Prince)**
**966-2727**

### ALL MAJOR CREDIT CARDS

The velvet rope is smaller and frayed these days at the Merc Bar. Like all good broken-in SoHo debuts, the attitude here has finally transformed itself into a kinder, gentler bar scene. This romantic Aspen-style SoHo nook attracts the movers and shakers. You'll see some suits drinking martinis, but the bulk of the crowd is in their mid-20s to 30s and looking good. A kayak hangs from the ceiling and twisted antlers and Ansel Adams-style nature photos line the walls, setting the stage for a mellow, not-in-your-face retreat for a drink with your better half. Don't get us wrong, this is still a SoHo scene, just a little more subdued.

## THE MERCER KITCHEN
**147 Mercer St. (At Prince St.)**
**966-6060**

### ALL MAJOR CREDIT CARDS

Located in the Mercer Hotel in SoHo, this place oozes scene. The large 2-floor establishment contains some of the best looking patrons in NYC and an assortment of culture vultures along for the ride. The décor is very L.A. and Ian Schrager-esque with a simple but chic lobby and a dining and bar area consisting of modern yet comfortable furniture. The restaurant, owned by the creators of Vong, Patria and Jojo's, serves excellent fare, making this a top-notch date spot *if* you can get a reservation.

**MERCHANT'S**
**112 7th Ave. (17th/18th Sts.)**
**366-7267**
**1125 1st Ave. (At 62nd St.) 832-1551**
**521 Columbus Ave. (85th/86th Sts.) 721-3689**
*ALL MAJOR CREDIT CARDS*

These romantic, mission-style lounges are immensely popular, especially among New York's young, working elite who pack the place after work and on the weekends. One might call Merchant's an upscale meat-market with decor that is simple and sexy, complete with warm fireplaces and candlelit nooks to set the tone. It's a great place to bring or find a date for a light dinner and a bottle of wine. Remember that guy in college, the one that you thought would look a lot better if he just got some hip clothes? Well, he's here, and he finally picked up on the fact that black *is* cool! The lounges are a nice retreat, but they are definitely more fun when they are less crowded.

---

**MERCURY BAR**
**659 9ᵗʰ Ave. (bet. 45ᵗʰ & 46ᵗʰ St.)**
**262-7755**

*ALL MAJOR CREDIT CARDS*

This Irish bar meets art deco lounge has the most bustling happy hour in Hell's Kitchen. For singles in their late 20s and 30s, Mercury Bar seems to be the place to go. Different from most other pubs, the atmosphere here is wanna-be swanky, featuring burgundy velvet booths, dark walls, colorful murals and dim lighting. Until 1 am, a full bar menu offers an array of fancy fast food, such as coconut beer shrimp and chicken quesadillas. Choose from over 20 moderately priced beers on tap while watching sports on the huge corner TV screens—that is, if you can hear over the blaring jukebox tunes!

---

**MERCURY LOUNGE**
**217 E. Houston (At Ave. A)**
**260-4700**

*ALL MAJOR CREDIT CARDS*

Some of the better alternative bands can be seen here at this small venue. The front of the bar is just that, a bar, but the back hosts a medium size band area with a great sound system and some top acts. There is usually a cover charge to get into the back room, but where else can you see bands like They Might Be Giants from 10 feet away?

## METRONOME
**915 B'way (At 21st St.)**
**505-7400**

### ALL MAJOR CREDIT CARDS

This upscale and artistically impressive dinner club offers live jazz nightly with a prix fixe hors d'oeuvres menu for $19.95. The beautiful décor and soothing music makes up for the overpriced drinks and non-polished service. A small bar off the elegant dining area offers an extensive wine and cocktail list to a thirtysomething yuppie crowd. On the weekends however, the place completely transforms into a bridge-and-tunnel hellhole. Scantily clad women and guys in muscle tees and gold chains pack the dance floor and VIP lounges and are on the prowl, big time! We're talking full-blown New Jersey meat-market. Cover on the weekend is $20 and drinks, if you can get one, are expensive.

## MEXICAN RADIO
**250 Mulberry St. (At Prince St.)**
**343-0140**

### ALL MAJOR CREDIT CARDS

Tucked away on a quaint street in Little Italy is teensy gem. The colorful votive candles in the window and the brightly colored walls play a part in making this a cozy spot to chill out. There is a limited beer selection (only 5 bottles), but the reason to come here is the spectacular Mexican food (the best in thearea) and the funky crowd. If you are lucky enough to stumble upon this place, try the Flautas, they kick butt.

### MICA BAR AND LOUNGE
**252 E. 51st St. (bet. 2nd & 3rd Aves.)**
**888-2453**

*ALL MAJOR CREDIT CARDS*

For quiet conversation in a Zen-like setting, the Mica is perfect. The all-wood space has an Asian-inspired décor with its melange of bonsai trees and simple candles. Two levels give customers the choice of a lounge area on the first floor, or small tables with square velvet stools on the second. The staff at Mica is ultra-cool and friendly, without being too kiss-ass.

### MICHAEL JORDON'S STEAK HOUSE
**Grand Central Terminal's balcony**
**23 Vanderbilt Ave.**
**655-2300**

*ALL MAJOR CREDIT CARDS*

In the wake of Grand Central's facelift sprouted this swank little number located on the balcony overlooking Grand Central Station. A beautifully appointed bar area with a young commuter crowd, Michael Jordan's is the closet thing to a SoHo lounge in midtown. With a balcony that overlooks the bustling terminal below, the view is spectacular. Drinks are pricey but strong and the service is quick and friendly. Great place to knock back a few before heading up to the burbs. Or, if you happen to work in the area, this spot beats most.

### MICKEY MANTLE'S
**42 Central Park South**
**668-7777**

*ALL MAJOR CREDIT CARDS*

Welcome to T.G.I.Mickey Mantle's. The ultimate sports theme bar and restaurant attracts mostly a crowd of tourists looking for a bite to eat after their Broadway show. The drinks are relatively cheap for the area, with beer starting at $4.75, and top shelf at $5.95 and the food is typical American grill fare. The waiters wear striped umpire uniforms, so it feels like you're at the Footlocker. As you can imagine, the walls are adorned with every bit of Mickey memorabilia possible and there's even a merchandise room where you can buy anything with the number "7" on it. Considered the most popular sports bar in Manhattan, Mickey Mantle's is a great place for a burger and a beer and a sports fix.

## MILADAY'S
**160 Prince St. (At Thompson St.)**
**226-9340**

One of the few local and unpretentious bars left in SoHo, Milady's has been in the neighborhood forever and caters to an older and not-so-chic crowd. This cluttered space with small tables draped in trashy plastic tablecloths makes ordering something like a martini or cosmopolitan out of place. An imported beer, for that matter, may turn some heads. For entertainment, there's a decent jukebox and a pool table in the back, but most come here to wash down a burger and fries.

## MILANO'S
**51 Houston St. (bet. Mulberry & Mott)**
**226-8632**

### CASH ONLY

This is as close to an urban saloon as you'll get. This long and thin bar, with its tin ceilings and a floor right out of a Grand Central Station bathroom, opened its doors over 90 years ago and has been a fixture in Little Italy ever since. The walls are covered with pictures of some of the patrons who have passed through as well as an array of Frank Sinatra snapshots. This is a real bar for people who want to drink. Though hygiene is not a priority here, you will be hard pressed to find a more authentic Italian pub in the city.

## MO'S CARIBBEAN
### 1454 2nd Ave. (At 76th St.)
### 650-0561

### *ALL MAJOR CREDIT CARDS*

There's a lot of energy going on at this tropical theme bar equipped with palm trees, three large screen TVs and a host of drink specials. The food is pretty good and the tropical drinks, though somewhat embarrassing to order, are tasty. If you liked Senor Frogs when you were on spring break in Cancun, you'll love this place. The crowd is young and recently received their BAs, but there is a lot of fun energy here. Monday is lobster madness with $11 for the first crustacean and $6 thereafter.

## MOJO'S
### 161 E. Houston (At Allen St.)
### 228-4143

### *CASH ONLY*

When you get bored of watching your Chia Pet grow, head on over to Mojo's where the *real* excitement takes place. It's small, dark and extremely unpopular. That could be because there's no beer selection to speak of and the music is so loud you can't even hear yourself think. But the locals who frequent Mojo's will most likely disagree—they like their neighborhood joint and keep coming back, especially for the daily happy hour specials.

## MONA'S
### 224 Ave. B (bet. 13th & 14th Sts.)
### 353-3780

### *CASH ONLY*

Around for 24 years, this decrepit East Village hole-in-the-wall offers a no-frills drinking experience at a really cheap rate. Named after the owner's dead cat, the drinks are strong, cheap and even cheaper on Thursday nights when a pint of Guinness is a measly two bucks. Shoot some pool while the jukebox pumps out the Ramones, Patti Smith, Jesus and

Mary Chain, Fat Boy Slim and some authentic Irish tunes. Monday nights bring in live Irish bands and a great local Irish crowd. It may be a dive, but Mona's has some of the best bartenders in the East Village. They remember what you're drinking, have your drink waiting on the bar as you walk in the door, and often buy back drinks. Except for the lost yuppie looking for the Music Box located across the street, Mona's loyal customers range from dirty, intellectual East Villagers to the occasional stray dog.

**MONKEY BAR**
**60 E. 54th St. (bet. Mad. & Park Aves.)**
**838-2600**

***ALL MAJOR CREDIT CARDS***

Located in the beautiful Hotel Elysee, this New York staple remains one of the more elegant and sophisticated bars in midtown. In the 1940s, this was indeed the place to see and be seen as evidenced by the old Hollywood style that oozes from every nook and cranny of the piano bar and adjoining restaurant. Original paintings of whimsical monkeys from the '40s still cover the walls, adding to the charm. The bar area is clean and is usually filled with a very professional after-work crowd. In the late evenings the older generation replaces the mayhem to take in some live music. Drinks are expensive and the crowd tends to be a meat-market, but it's worth a trip if you have never been here. A great date place and restaurant for the 30+ crowd. Oh, and gentlemen, jacket and tie are required.

**THE MONKEY'S PAW**
**57 Christopher St.**
**(bet. 7th Ave. & Waverly Pl.)**
**206-0303**

Once the Lion's Head, a favorite haunt for old school NYC alcoholic writers and musicians, this West Village bar is now home to a mixed bag of regulars soaking up the cozy, subterranean atmosphere. There's comedy all nights (except Tuesdays and Thursdays) in the dark, stageless side room, and the low-ceilinged, basement-like ambience makes you feel like a political subversive. The place doesn't really get rocking until late so you're better off showing up around 1am.

## MONSTER
**80 Grove St. (At Waverly Pl.)**
**924-3558**

*CASH ONLY*

This festive, old school gay bar puts the glitz and the glamour back in the bar scene with its beautiful floral arrangements and dark, seductive lighting. The older crowd that frequents here looks to have been around the block one too many times, but they're here to have a good time and The Monster practically guarantees it. Enjoy the live piano music at the main bar or get your groove going to the old disco tunes downstairs. The Monster hosts different theme parties each night of the week so call ahead. With a daily happy hour and $4 Cosmopolitans, the Monster is a welcoming recess for older, hip gay men.

## MOOMBA
**133 7th Ave. S. (bet. Charles & 10th Sts.)**
**989-1414**

*ALL MAJOR CREDIT CARDS*

"Moomba," Swahili for "meeting ground for pretentious assholes" remains, even after two years, one of the most popular celebrity haunts in the city. For all you Moomba fanatics, you'll be happy to know that since Leonardo DiCaprio decided to frequent Veruka instead, one actually has an inkling of a chance getting in! Like so many of these upscale restaurants, the people who come here are shallow and have cash to burn. A small ultra-chic bar makes for a good place to get a drink with your better half on slower nights if, and only if, you can make it past the clipboard militia that stands outside. It's nonetheless a beautiful raw space that, despite its pretentious air, is romantic and comfortable. Don't look for shot specials here—Moomba is the type of place where the ice in your drink looks clean and heavy almost to the point of being artistic.

**MOONLIGHTING (AKA 511)**
**511 Amsterdam Ave. (At 84th St.)**
**799-4643**

*ALL MAJOR CREDIT CARDS*

If you want to boogie this weekend at Moonlighting, be sure to wear your deodorant. The dance floor is about 12'x15', and you will get elbowed in the ribs and you will get pissed off. This place caters to a young, professional singles crowd that's on the prowl. Geometrically shaped copper sheets serve as décor behind the bar upstairs while downstairs a mini-bar usually caters to someone's private party. A neat-o tropical nook offers a cheap alternative to a trip to Miami where you can chill under faux palm trees and kick back with a cocktail. Don't be intimidated by the velvet ropes and buff bouncer—if you're nice, you're in.

**MORAN'S (EDWARD MORAN'S)**
**World Financial Center**
**200 Vesey Street (At Hudson River)**
**945-2255**

*ALL MAJOR CREDIT CARDS*

Where do fraternity brothers who have have recently graduated, retired their lacrosse sticks, and landed jobs on Wall Street go to let loose after a long day of buying low and selling high? Moran's, of course! Moran's is Wall Street's most popular after-work spot. During the summer season the yuppies that swarm the place consume more beers than Yankee stadium sells in a season. Half price beer specials on Thursdays are the big draw at this meat-market made up of horny men in suits and cheap women. Overwhelming "cheese factor" aside, it offers a spectacular place to drink outdoors in the summer.

**MORGAN'S (@ THE MORGAN HOTEL)**
**237 Madison Ave. (bet. 37th & 38th Sts.)**
**726-7600**

*ALL MAJOR CREDIT CARDS*

Located in the lower level of the Morgan Hotel, Morgan's is without a doubt one of the swankiest lounges in midtown. Hipsters line both sides of an illuminated bar (sans bartenders) while cocktail gals emerge serving up traditional martinis and cosmopolitans by the light of flickering candles. This is a beautiful people Mecca with loud music and expensive drinks. Expect some overflow from their ultra swanky next-door neighbor, Asia de Cuba, who visit pre- and post-dinner to drop even more cash. It's a great date spot and an even better singles scene.

## MOLLY'S
**287 Third Ave. (bet. 22nd & 23rd Sts.)**
**889-3361**

*ALL MAJOR CREDIT CARDS*

For a nice Guinness in a friendly atmosphere there's no place that beats Molly's. This traditional Irish pub has a reputon of having the best Guinness pour in the city. Get an authentic taste of Ireland as you walk on the sawdust-covered floors and warm up next to the working fireplace. The crowd is a mix of old-timers and yuppies that gather around to watch sports or listen to the jukebox. If you're hungry, don't miss out on their bacon cheeseburger that rivals the Corner Bistro.

## MOTHER
**432 W. 14th St. (At Washington St.)**
**366-5680**

*ALL MAJOR CREDIT CARDS*

Let the skeletons out of your closet and join the sadism at NYC's most dark and decadent dance club. Prepare for the strict dress code at the door: Leather, fetish, cyber, Victorian, etc. There are no exceptions so don't even think about donning that white T-shirt and jeans! The cover charge differs per night as does the theme and the acts, so call ahead. On Tuesday night, a $5 cover charge gets you into Jackie 60. Walk into the eerie, theatrically lit, wallpapered, incense-filled bar in front and be served by Hatti of the old school

Pyramid Club days. The main dance floor gets hot, sweaty and crowded when DJ Johnny Dynell spins hard but funky New York house. Dare to join the brilliantly named cyber-fetish party on Saturday nights at "Click and Drag." Pay a $10 cover and enter into a mixture of "Buffy the Vampire Slayer" and technological fetishism. Feast your eyes on the array of gothic Robert Smiths and Marilyn Mansons. Watch dance moves out of "Desperately Seeking Susan" as DJ Saint James beats the main dance floor with industrial, Goth and techno. Venture into the dungeon of a basement into a small, eerie bar/lounge lit only by TV sets playing fetish vampire flicks. On Thursday nights, Mother hosts The Fang Club where DJ Delchi spins Goth and Industrial. Weekly performances are put on at The Fang Club including chicks singing "Cry Me a River" in coffins. Owned by Chi Chi Valenti and Johnny Dynell, Mother certainly invites the freaks to come out at night. Devoid of any morals, Mother is a definite must for those who need to fill their quota of sleaze, humiliation, and odd experiences in their life.

## MOTOR CITY BAR
**127 Ludlow St. (bet. Rivington & Delancey)**
**358-1595**

### CASH ONLY

This theme bar has ample seating, a Centipede video machine, and tons of automobile paraphernalia. Drinks are cheap and the crowd is local. There's a list where you can leave your friend a free drink (you buy it, obviously) which we thought was quite suave. Relax and grab a seat at the old tire table, or play Pac Man with a friend. Motor City makes for a good place for guys to hang out and shoot the breeze in a non-sports environment.

## MOTOWN CAFÉ
**104 W. 57th St. (bet. 6th & 7th Aves.)**
**581-8030**

### ALL MAJOR CREDIT CARDS

Open since 1995, this theme restaurant/bar packs in the tourists. With live entertainment nightly, this place is a great scene for young out-of-towners. This Motown-lovers dream has gold saxophones lining the walls, 45's lining the steps and an oversized record revolving from the balcony. The crowd eats typical American fare while soothing sounds of The Four Tops and other Motown wonders play in the background. Like all other theme bars in New York, Motown Café also offers specialty drinks with names like, "Do You Love Me," "My Guy," "My Girl" and "ABC" which go for $13.75 a pop and are served in a souvenir glass. It's worth a look if you're a young tourist hoping to branch out from the Hard Rock Café.

## MUDVILLE 9
**126 Chambers St.**
**(bet. Church & W. B'way)**
**349-0059**
*ALL MAJOR CREDIT CARDS*

Don't let the classy name fool you, this place makes most dives in New York feel like the Rainbow Room. Mudville is the type of bar where you can safely bet your life savings that someone, at some point, is going to get beat up. The white trash décor makes a perfect backdrop for "America's Most Wanted." If you don't mind having the bartender threaten to kill you for ordering an imported beer, then it's a great place to grab a Bud and drink by the soothing light of a neon Quick-Draw sign.

## MULDOON'S IRISH PUB
**692 3rd Ave. (bet. 43rd & 44th Sts.)**
**599-2750**

*ALL MAJOR CREDIT CARDS*

There are about as many Irish pubs in New York as there are potholes and hobos put together, but this one really stands out...not! This is one of the dumpiest and most depressing locales in midtown. When every other bar is packed to the gills, standing room only, you can rest assured there is a bar stool with your name on it at Muldoon's. It's only one block from Grand Central and two blocks from the UN, and it still can't bring in a crowd. Even the 8 beers on tap at $4.75 a pop isn't worth it. The old timer bartenders are very

nice considering they have to serve a sketchy group of patrons all day long. If European soccer matches and hurling
are your bag you can crash here and watch it on the tube.

## MULLIGAN'S
**267 Madison Ave. (bet. 39th & 40th Sts.)**
**268-0207**

### ALL MAJOR CREDIT CARDS

A good pub choice if you're looking to throw back a few
after work brewsky's in midtown. Surprisingly, this Irish bar
seems to attract more decent-looking females than most
places in this area. It must be the advertising firms in the
neighborhood that hire all of the high-class tail. There are a
few TVs that air all the popular sporting events. The mood
is upbeat and friendly and happy hour specials help lighten
the strain on your wallet.

## MURPHY'S PUB
**977 2nd Ave. (At 52nd St.)**
**751-5400**

### ALL MAJOR CREDIT CARDS

Just another Irish bar on the 2nd Avenue strip that offers
drink specials and a friendly atmosphere. The green walls
engulf everyone and add to the cheery Irish atmosphere.
Soccer matches may be viewed on one of the few TVs and
the music is up to your discretion via the jukebox. The crowd
is mostly a mix of Upper East Side young women and former
frat boys turned brokers.

## MUSEUM CAFÉ
**366 Columbus Ave. (At 76th St.)**
**799-0150**

This bar/restaurant exudes coziness with its romantic candlelit greenhouse dining area. People watching and first dates
rank high here where drinks are fairly priced: Wine, $4.50;
beer, $4; cocktails, $4-$5. Happy hour on Wednesday-Fri-

day is hopping from 5-7pm with fortysomethings inhaling free nachos and quesadillas. The 20 to 30-somethings move in around 9pm to kick off a night of bar hopping. You may spot Maya Angelou or Seinfeld here so keep your eyes peeled.

## MUSICAL BOX
**219 Avenue B (bet. 13th &14th Sts.)**
**254-1731**

*CASH ONLY*

If you ever see a confused bunch of people looking lost on Avenue B, they're definitely searching for Musical Box. With no sign and red curtains blocking out the riffraff, this neighborhood lounge attracts a mixed crowd of gay and straight college grads and trendy types who don't mind trekking through the colorful neighborhood. The long bar area in front is beautifully decorated with classic rock photos on the walls, comfortable living room chairs, and thoughtfully placed candles. Lounge in the back room on comfy overstuffed couches or play a game of pool on the black top pool table. During the summer, one can take a breather and enjoy the East Village air on the back patio. Drinks are moderately priced while the music varies depending on the bartender. You will hear anything from Bob Dylan and the Beatles to Jane's Addiction and Corner Shop. While the atmosphere is warm, friendly and welcoming, it gets jam-packed on the weekends, so get there early.

## MUSTANG
**1632 2nd Ave. (At 85th St.)**
**744-9194**

*ALL MAJOR CREDIT CARDS*

This popular, sophisticated Upper East Side restaurant is a breath of fresh air. In addition to its Tex-Mex menu, Mustang boasts two Upper East Side anomalies: A well-stocked cigar bar and a chic lounge. Aside from the Santa Fe facade that strips it of its New York hipness, Mustang is a great place to people watch and a well-known pickup spot.

**MUSTANG HARRY'S**
352 7th Ave. (bet. 29th & 30th Sts.)
268-8930

*ALL MAJOR CREDIT CARDS*

Harry's is one of a few decent Madison Square Garden area bars. It's very long and narrow and jampacked with televisions and people. The after-work suits and event goers throng here for the comfortable atmosphere. The sets are always tuned to the racetrack or some other random sporting event. If the crowd gets too overwhelming for the downstairs, the upstairs bar is opened. It's also available for private functions. Harry's serves a full menu of steaks, sandwiches, and salads. The tables are quite busy especially during happy hour, but if you're in the neighborhood it's worth a trip.

**MUSTANG SALLY'S SALOON**
324 7th Ave. (bet. 28th & 29th Sts.)
695-3806

*ALL MAJOR CREDIT CARDS*

Another one of the "Mustang" family, Sally's is a long crowded Irish bar in the vicinity of Madison Square Garden and attracts event goers and local business people to its friendly pub atmosphere. There are a bunch of TVs, good music, good food, and a pretty good-looking crowd. Sally's is open Monday-Sunday from 8:30am to 4:30am. There are 11 beers on tap and always a jovial Irish bartender to talk to.

**~**
**N**
33 Crosby St.
(bet. Broome & Grand Sts.)
219-8856
*CASH ONLY*

Authentic tapas and sangria are what will bring you back to this Spanish SoHo bar while the bartenders aloof, "I will

199

deal with you when I'm ready" attitude may keep you away. Catering to a young, intellectual, good-looking and predominantly European crowd, N is barely an arm's length wide. With hard-to-score bar stools and a couple of comfy tables, the polka-dot walls may remind you of the interior of "Pee Wee's Playhouse." We would be careful about flirting while your date is in the bathroom—there are two-way mirrors on the doors. The music is funky with a European flair which could easily inspire you to samba the rest of the night away.

## NAKED LUNCH
**17 Thompson St. (At Grand St.)**
**343-0828**

### *ALL MAJOR CREDIT CARDS*

A place to dance that's not a club and really more of a bar is probably the best way to sum up this hip little dance space in SoHo. Their signature drink, "Tanqueray Tea," keeps this 25 to 30-something crowd in good spirits. With one glance at the unique lighting on the facade and interior, you'll realize that this bar was inspired by William Boroughs' book, *Naked Lunch*. The crowd changes nightly from eclectic artists and after-work suits during the week, to the dreaded bridge-and-tunnelers on the weekend. You'll be tempted to lock lips at the chrome-and-stone bar in the back that's open Friday and Saturday evening. Bring a group of friends, snag a seat on the semicircular couch and try one of the many wines. The music is excellent and will definitely get you moving. Owned by the same people who own the Gemini Lounge in the East Village, Naked Lunch is a martini-sipper's jive house. There's a DJ every night with a $5 cover that kicks in at the bar's discretion. Great place to dance the night away.

## NEGRIL
**362 W. 23rd St. (bet. 8th & 9th Ave.)**
**807-6411**

### *ALL MAJOR CREDIT CARDS*

Work got you down? Need a vacation but you can't leave the city? Take a jaunt over to the closest thing to a weekend getaway in the Caribbean you'll find within the confines of our concrete jungle. Negril has a spicy reggae beat that transports you to an imaginary island paradise. The huge tropical fish tank behind the bar makes you feel as if you are underwater. The food is seasoned well and very flavorful. Munch on some jerk chicken and grab a seat at the bar to enjoy a wonderful, colorful find.

## NEVADA SMITH'S
**74 3rd Ave. (bet. 11ᵗʰ & 12ᵗʰ Sts.)**
**982-2591**

*ALL MAJOR CREDIT CARDS*

If you want to keep that good old Hoboken feel without stepping foot on the Path train, come to Nevada Smith's. This fraternity headquarters has all the necessities: A pool table, a collection of baseball caps, and lots of TVs. It's loud, full of energy and packs in a crowd that is under 30 and obviously has a drinking problem. There's a strict ID policy and a cover charge.

## NEVER
**245 E. Houston St. (At. Norfolk St.)**
**674-7788**

*ALL MAJOR CREDIT CARDS*

Off the beaten path, this hip new sushi bar/lounge is proof that almost anything can be transformed into a bar. Once a tombstone store, Never is now an ultra-futuristic getaway for those who need to escape from the real world. With its shiny, galvanized steel walls, flashing television sets, and a round steel bar, it practically propels you into the new millennium. At night, a DJ plays unobtrusive club music while a mixed crowd of East Villagers, SoHo-ites and Upper East Siders lounge in cozy nooks or at candlelit tables. Take your pick from over 60 beers, 25 wines, 7 champagnes, 9 beers on tap and of course lots of sake—all at very reasonable prices. When was the last time you drank a Sake Cosmo or a Sake Martini? Probably...*never*! Try it, you'll get hooked. Other drink specials include the "Never Let You Sweat" made with Tobasco sauce, Sake, and pickled peppers. The sushi, served from 6pm - 2am during the week and until 3am on the weekends, is delicious and affordable. Open from 6pm - 4am, this night spot brings in various promoters with an array of music as well as drink and sushi specials. With its relaxing atmosphere and warm staff, you'll "never" want to go home.

## NIAGARA
**112 Ave. A  (At 7th St.)**
**420-9517**

*ALL MAJOR CREDIT CARDS*

This is the bar that the stars of "Swingers" were looking for and couldn't find in LA. Finally an answer to your '50s, swing-esque prayers have been answered! A sight for sore eyes, Niagara's swank interior and '50s-style bar brings you back to the days of zoot suits and wallet chains. Beautiful women in leopard print jackets and men in hip leather jackets with pompadours mingle at the bar and in the back room. Well-dressed bartenders will light your cigarette as you drink Cosmopolitans from classic '50s glassware. Despite the heavy smokers at the bar, the air is crisp and clean and the place is spotless. Take a walk downstairs to the Tiki room and bask in the warmly lit atmosphere of palm trees and a huge colorful fish tank. While drinks are a bit pricey, it is worth it for this classy experience. A toast to the owners, Jessie Amlin and Jonny T.!

## NIGHTINGGALE'S
**213 2nd Ave. (at 13th)**
**473-9383**

*CASH ONLY*

This is a rock concert T-shirt and dirty jeans crowd tempered by Polo shirt-wearing types. Most of the patrons either play in a band, or know somebody who does. If you like live bands, you'll want to stop by this spot. A no-frills venue complete with a pool table, darts and a bar that hasn't been dusted in years, bands perform every night at floor level (there's no stage) and the crowd is usually jumping and sweating right in there with them. Although there's usually a $5 cover charge, you'll be able to hear from the street if you like the music. Enter the bathrooms at your own risk.

**9C**
**700 E. 9th St. (At Ave. C)**
**358-0048**

*CASH ONLY*

Stop into the last of the neighborhood squatter bars on the up-and-coming Avenue C. Swill cheap beer with a host of pierced, anti-conformists who hate the world. 9C offers a 2 for 1 happy hour, Monday-Thursday from 8pm to 10pm and Friday-Sunday from 4pm to 8pm. The pinball machine and customized low rider prints and satanic Vargas girl paintings covering the wall will make you feel like you have stepped into the social class of the homeless Greasers. With a mixed Rock & Roll jukebox, certain nights bring in a live DJ who spins early heavy metal such as Black Sabbath and Blue Oyster Cult. Buy the DJ a drink and she will spin your favorite headbanging tune with a smile. The heavy handed, heavily tattooed bartenders, Rock & Roll, squatters and aimless dogs makes this hidden, out of the way bar a dive lover's gold mine.

**NIVA**
**188 Allen St**
**(bet. Houston & Stanton Sts.)**
**254-9360**

Just on its feet, Niva (Israeli for "elegance") is attempting to cater to a pre-club crowd while entertaining the idea of being a classy martini lounge with plans to expand its walls into a club. Uh, can you say identity crisis? This tiny, tiny lounge is minimally decorated with concrete floors, dim candlelight and nothing-to-write-home-about couches and tables. Each night boasts a different theme: Fridays, a DJ play '80s classics while Saturdays draw in the house music-loving crowd. While drinks are reasonably priced ($5 shelf, $4 bottled beer), they make the big bar faux pas of charging $1 more per drink on the weekends. It's really a miracle that Niva doesn't get inundated by the B&T crowd that infests most LES bars on the weekends so revel in it while it lasts. Hopefully, Niva will pick a theme and find a drink price and stick with it!

## NO IDEA
**30 E. 20th St. (Park Ave S./B'way)**
**777-0100**

*ALL MAJOR CREDIT CARDS*

Every night is a different theme at No Idea. The weekend attracts a 25 to 35-year-old, preppie, after-work crowd to enjoy weak drinks served in pint-sized glasses. Beers are $4, while mixed drinks range from $4 to $6. Pop music such as the Counting Crows plays over the jukebox, while a couple of TVs highlight the day's sports events. Although there is no happy hour, No Idea is a great place to get a drink after a long day at work.

## NO. MOORE
**234 N. Moore St. (At W. B'way)**
**925-2595**

*ALL MAJOR CREDIT CARDS*

This large, loft-like space offers a laid-back alternative for those who want to avoid its glamorous next door neighbor, the Bubble Lounge. Huge windows offer a relaxed feeling that compels after-work Wall Street patrons to loosen their ties and set their lemming souls free. On the weekends, No. Moore attracts the decked out bridge-and-tunnel scene and rejects from next door. If you're hungry, you can order food for delivery from some of the nearby restaurants.

## NORTH RIVER BAR
**145 Hudson St. (At Hubert St.)**
**226-9411**

*ALL MAJOR CREDIT CARDS*

A pre- and post-Wetlands bar, the North River is a real bar with pool, video games, a jukebox and free popcorn. Pete's Wicked Ale, Bass, Guinness, Sam Adams, and of course, Bud are at your tap service. With a 20 to 30-something crowd, it's a great bar to load up on cheap test tube shots or grab a few beers before a show or after work. Happy hour is from 11am-6pm daily with 2 for 1 drinks, including champagne. How's that for catering to the unemployed? Pints are $3 after 6pm, and Sun.-Wed. gets you a pitcher for around $8. Pool prodigies love this place, where teams convene for full-scale competitions on Monday night.

## NORTH STAR PUB
**93 South St. (At Fulton St.)**
**509-FOOD**

As the name implies, this is a faux-mariner joint for Wall Street types after a hard day pillaging the high seas of corporate finance and landlubber tourists on the weekends. There's a modest, full bar that fills up quickly, and four booths clustered by the window that overlooks the South Street Seaport. The North Star prides itself on being a genuinely "British" pub; the décor above the bar is resplendent with blow-up sheep and a framed photo of the Queen Mum. No American beer, but a dizzying selection of British ales on tap, as well as 86 (!) single malt scotches. The pub puts out a whimsical newsletter/menu for its patrons with such hard-hitting articles as "101 Ways to Cook Spam." The menu itself boasts, among other Brit-treats, fish and chips, as well as venison pie. Keep in mind that in America, "pub" is a euphemism for "cramped, loud, and smoky."

## NOVECENTO
**343 W. B'way (bet. Grand & Broome Sts.)**
**925-4706**

*ALL MAJOR CREDIT CARDS*

Argentinean-owned NoveCento is a two-level bar/restaurant that tries hard to encourage a sophisticated crowd to party with the Euro-trash it attracts. This popular and trendy spot in the heart of SoHo boasts an upstairs retreat for cozy groups to gather for dinner. In the past, the attic was transformed into a wildly popular late night dance spot but they have since lost their cabaret license and have therefore lost the crowds. Be sure to check out the extensive wine list.

## NOWBAR
**22 7th Ave. So. (At Leroy St.)**
**293-0323**

### *ALL MAJOR CREDIT CARDS*

Among the many gutted underground spaces in NY, this damp, dark and smoky space has had a few lives. Its predecessors were a speakeasy jazz club, The Milk Bar, an after hours venue and a French restaurant. It has been thriving as the NowBar for more than three years and now offers a little something for everyone. Morality and sobriety are not the mottos of this joint, for sure. With two levels of curious vibe and a visually stimulating clientele, the DJ spins house, classic soul, jazz and Disney songs in Japanese. Thursday and Saturday, women and transvestites get in for $5 while men get in for $10. (Sometimes it really *does* pay to be a woman.) Wear your hippest wig and you just might get noticed.

## NV /289 LOUNGE
**289 Spring St. (bet. Varick & 6ᵗʰ Ave.)**
**929-6868**

### *ALL MAJOR CREDIT CARDS*

Two big and scary bouncers stand guard at this modern, designer club. With its two levels, the gothic and industrial 289 Lounge and dance floor of NV pleasantly convene. The quasi-futuristic club draws a young, hip, and trendy crowd who are in for a big night in the city from the outer-boroughs and Jersey. Upstairs boasts a large dance floor where you can boogie to the grooves spun by the DJ while loving yourself a little too much for your own good. Wednesday is hip-hop night so be sure to keep an eye out for Puffy in the crowd. The door policy is your usual pain in the ass (with a full pat down and pocket inspection) and the $10 cover charge is a little extreme for what you get. Nonetheless, it's one of New York's better looking places.   289 Lounge is stunning and merits a visit.

## NW3
**242 E. 10<sup>th</sup> St. (bet. 1<sup>st</sup> & 2<sup>nd</sup> Aves.)**
**260-0891**

*ALL MAJOR CREDIT CARDS*

Even though the name sounds like a rap group it really stands for Northwest 3, a postal code in London. After the British owners sold the place two years ago, the name remained. Located steps away from the well-known Tenth Street Lounge, NW3 receives much of the overflow. There are no surly bouncers to contend with and no cover charge. A cool, mellow vibe consistently engulfs this teeny-weeny red velveteen bar. Thursdays, Fridays and Saturdays, guest DJs spin hip-hop, breakbeat, and drum and bass. Beers are $5.50 and mixed drinks run about $7, but considering there is no cover charge and the music is really hip, it's not so bad. The crowd is a mix of young East Village artsy types and sweater set wearing uptown girls.

## 101 BAR
**101 7th Ave. S. (At W. 4<sup>th</sup> St.)**
**No Phone**

No cover and half price drinks before 9pm every night of the week...is that possible? This live music venue is a great alternative for people who love live music but don't feel like necessarily paying for it.  An array of tables set up by a small stage makes for an intimate evening. On Friday nights, tables are filled with a young, funky, couple crowd.  Pick up a flyer from one of the just-out-of-rehab guys working the door and check it out sometime.

## 119
**119 E. 15th St. (bet. Irving Pl. & Union Sq.)**
**777-6158**

*CASH ONLY*

Believe it or not, an actual dive does exist in glitzy Gramerc
Park and it's called 119. This not-as-popular-as-it-used-to
be hangout is filled with a surprisingly non-divey, predomi
nantly single crowd. The front room, which looks like it's
New York City police station, has a round-the-clock occu
pied pool table and a few flea market couches and chair
spread around. The back room has a bar and a few booth
where beer and tequila shots are consumed by a crow
that digs the alternative melodious tunes of Pearl Jam
Smashing Pumpkins and Prodigy.

## 147
**147 W. 15th St. (bet. 6th & 7th Aves.)**
**929-5000**

### ALL MAJOR CREDIT CARDS

Like with all things good and trendy, the bridge-and-tunne
folk eventually find their way to it and cause its tragic de
mise. Yet 147 remains one of the nicer looking glam spot
in the city and it is still a great place for an after-work cock
tail or post-dinner drink.  The bartenders are good-looking
friendly, and mix drinks that are well worth the steep prices
Located in an old fire station, the large space is inviting and
is always packed with a beautiful, professional crowd. Even
the 37" bar is worthy of an Oscar. (We couldn't help leaving
that mistake in...it's so "Spinal Tap.") Come with a date for
drinks but skip the food; it leaves little to be desired.

## OFF THE WAGON
**109 McDougal St. (bet. W. 3rd & Bleecker Sts.)**
**533-4487**

### ALL MAJOR CREDIT CARDS

Off The Wagon is what happens when AA members don't
complete their 12 steps.
Watch as New Jersey boy and Frat boy meet, drink and
feed each other's testosterone levels with lots of beer. Frat
Heaven never had it so good: Pool tables, foosball, darts,
an ATM machine, sports playing on a satellite TV, hamburgers, pizza, fries and an extra special Wednesday night special—Ladies' Night. Yeehaw! Free domestic beer for ladies

all night long! No need to travel all the way to the underage clubs of Mexico for attention, ladies, just come to this West Village spot to be groped, harassed and maybe even puked on. This two-level, wall-to-wall lesson in immaturity has a daily happy hour from 5pm to 8pm serving ½ price drinks and shots. Open daily from 3pm - 4am.

## O'FLAHERTY'S ALE HOUSE
**334 W. 46th St.(bet. 8th & 9th Aves.)**
**581-9366**

*ALL MAJOR CREDIT CARDS*

This is a fantastic Irish pub in the heart of "Restaurant Row." It has a mixed crowd, which makes it perfect for shooting pool, downing a couple of pints or just hanging out with friends before a broadway show. The menu is a typical pub menu consisting of shepards pie and cheese and crackers. This is a fun place to hang and chill. Especially on their outdoor patio.

## O'FLANAGAN'S
**1215 1st Ave. (bet. 65th & 66th Sts.)**
**439-0660**

*ALL MAJOR CREDIT CARDS*

O'Flanagan's *feels* like a lodge with its roaring fireplace and dark brown wood. But you'll soon discover that this spot is not conducive to quiet conversation. With seven televisions (2 of them big screen) blasting the likes of Guns 'n' Roses' "Sweet Child O' Mine," the lodge-like feeling will disappear quickly. The booths lining the north side of the bar tend to draw the heavy drinkers who consist of a mixture of men and women in their early twenties to late thirties, many of whom are couples. On some nights decent live music motivates the drunkenly crowd to stumble onto the dance floor. Other than that, don't expect too much from this place.

**THE OAK ROOM (@ THE PLAZA HOTEL)**
**768 5th Ave. (At 59th St.)**
**546-5330**

*ALL MAJOR CREDIT CARDS*

If you are a woman of the night, or are just looking for one, you will want to visit The Oak Room at the Plaza Hotel. Owned by Ivanna Trump, this stuffy and touristy old bar is overrated and overpriced. The ancient and personality-free bartenders serve criminally weak martinis and cosmopolitans (for $10) to scantily dressed tourists who mingle with overdressed and overstuffed socialites under dim lighting and clouds of cigar smoke. The energy here is as dead and ancient as the staff. You can either lounge at tables, or have a seat at the bar with escorts and their dates. Although the Plaza is beautiful, The Oak Room lacks character, charisma and life.

**THE OAKS**
**49 Grove St. (at Bleecker St.)**
**243-8885**

This Judy Garland haunt that's been open for over 40 years caters to fabulous drag queens. The lovely Lene and Ruby Rims will greet you at the door. Feel free to take a table— you don't have to eat, but the food is good. The bar does not offer a very good view of the piano, but the bartenders are classic, with friendly service, awesome wit, and a heavy pour. Everyone here is a star or at least acts like one. There's an open mike, so feel free to bring your sheet music and perform like the Diva you know you are! Drinks are $4.50 and there is never a cover.

**OASIS LOUNGE**
**121 St. Marks Place (At Ave. A)**
**358-8402**

Owned by the proprietor of the now defunct Downtown Beirut, Oasis Lounge could be considered an oasis if you really dig your parent's living room. With a spacious front bar and two decently sized lounge areas in the back with old, worn-out couches, curtains on the window-less walls and mini plastic vases on dirty glass tables, all this place needs is your parent's Zenith without the remote! The hanging Christmas lights, young raver types and wafting assortment of smoke create the perfect "Dazed and Confused" meets 1999 ravers sort of vibe. Certain nights are quiet with a few locals hanging out listening to a jukebox playing Neil Diamond, The Police and The Saturday Night Fever soundtrack. Saturday nights a DJ delights youths clad in oversized clothing and day glow necklaces with Jungle, House and Trance music. Drinks are pretty cheap and often served in the back room by an old Polish woman who has seen better days. A daily happy hour offers great drink specials from 5pm - 8pm. ($1 Rolling Rock mugs, $2 well drinks, and $3 Kamikazes) Open from 5pm - 4am.

## OBECA LI
**62 Thomas St. (bet. W.B'way & Church)**
**393-9887**

***ALL MAJOR CREDIT CARDS***

One of the best looking spots in New York, this TriBeCa restaurant and lounge is an unexpected fantasyland tucked away on a nondescript street. A "loungified" sake bar overlooks a mini Shangri-La that is manicured and feng shui'd to the max. If you happen to be down in that area, it's definitely worth stopping in to take a look. Serious cash was invested in this truly spectacular space.

## ODEON
**145 W. B'way (At Thomas St.)**
**233-0507**

***ALL MAJOR CREDIT CARDS***

When Odeon first hit the practically abandoned TriBeCa area in 1980, the owners probably didn't realize what a goldmine they had. Now almost 20 years later, Odeon is one of the most popular bistros in New York City. Everyone from locals to upper east siders to out-of-towners flock here for the very happening bar scene and the delicious French fare. What's unbelievable is Odeon has yet to be rivaled by another restaurant that has comparable popularity and cuisine. The locals are probably screaming for a new place to eat! (And a better bang for your buck.) Warm and inviting with a deco interior that every bar in town has mocked, this is a perfect place to bring your date or a large group of friends. During the day it's practically empty but expect to wait a while at night and on the weekends if you don't make a reservation—it's jam-packed.

## OHM
**16 West 22nd (bet. 5th & 6th Aves.)**
**229-2000**

### ALL MAJOR CREDIT CARDS

A more appropriate name for this multiplex mega club formerly known as Les Poulets might be, "Ohm I God, I can't believe I'm wasting my Friday night in hell." After standing in an unruly and generally unnecessary line with surly bouncers who handpick patrons in this manner..."Four girls, one guy," and then paying $20 hard earned greenbacks to enter, you'll stand in the middle of a humongously daunting, yet empty room pulsating with international something or others, wondering what the hell that line was for in the first place. It seems that Ohm's line out front is specially orchestrated for the sole purpose of faking the unsuspecting B&T crowd into thinking there are a bunch of really crazy party people in there rocking out. The 20,000 square foot, pseudo chic loft space was transformed into a restaurant, three bars, two dance floors and a restaurant. Guest DJs perform here always, so call in advance to see if your musical preference will be touched upon the evening you go. Generally house, R&B and Latin music prevail.

## OLD TOWN BAR
**45 E. 18th St. (bet. Park Ave. & B'way)**
**529-6732**

### *ALL MAJOR CREDIT CARDS*

This fixture on 18th Street is a dark and primitive saloon. With 14' ceilings and stained glass, Old Town has retained its original character since it opened in 1892. Families, trendy locals and Bowery bums can be spotted here, as well as an occasional celeb. The chatter of the crowd and one small TV fills the quiet void in the bar that would normally be filled with music (there is none). A brass rail bar runs the entire length of the restaurant and guards the 2-ton, original cash registers. Dark wooden booths are separated by high wood and glass dividers each adorned with their own charming stained glass tulip lamps. Bar fare is served until closing at 1:30am.

## BOX CAR LOUNGE (AKA OOPS)
**168 Ave. B (10th & 11th St.)**
**473-2830**

Engaged in a ceaseless quest for new methods of spending an overflow of cash, Soho-ites and Upper-East-Siders mix with East Villagers at Box Car Lounge. In the midst of Alphabet City is where you'll find this intimate, tiny wine and beer lounge flooded with beer, great sakes, fantastic sangria and exotic wines. Lounge around on cushioned couches while listening to unobtrusive jazz, Brazilian and better-than-mainstream music. With corrugated metal walls, deep red painted bricks and dim lighting, Box Car provides a charming and quaint relief from the typical bars with attitude. Open daily from 7pm until 4am, this tiny space is chic yet has no dress code, no velvet rope and no doorman. Yes! The drinks are inexpensive and very soothing for those in search of the perfect thirst quencher. A beer is about $3, a glass of wine is $5, and a bottle of wine is about $18 - $22. Make sure to check out their new outdoor garden in the back.

**OPALINE**
85 Ave. A (bet. 5ᵗʰ & 6ᵗʰ Sts.)
475-5050

*ALL MAJOR CREDIT CARDS*

Tucked underground along the Avenue A strip, this easy to miss venue is a pleasant and unexpected surprise. Under a wall of slanted plate glass lies a moderately sized, always crowded and smoky lounge section with a mishmosh of seating and very little space to stand. If you're not up for drinking in cramped quarters, move to the huge rustic bar/restaurant tucked away in the back with its skylight, thick green leather seats and old ceiling fans. A tidy and formal bar offers an excellent selection of wine by the glass to a mix of non-East Village yuppie types who enjoy the beautiful space that is "sans attitude." The food here is also tasty and reasonable, making it an ideal date spot.

**OPERA**
539 W. 21ˢᵗ St. (bet. 10ᵗʰ & 11ᵗʰ Aves.)
229-1618

*ALL MAJOR CREDIT CARDS*

Whoever designed the furniture in this place was either heavily influenced by "Alice in Wonderland," or marijuana. From the attitude you get at the door, to the oversized interior furnishings—everything about Opera is big. The space itself is impressive with its floor-to-ceiling framed mirrors, cigar bar, and sweeping, velvet emerald sitting couch big enough to sit you and 20 friends. Cocktail waitresses in white mini-dresses mill about what appears to be a predominantly bridge-and-tunnel clientele. Beware of the clipboard-armed militia that stands outside and make sure to thank them for deciding that you're cool enough to fork over the $10 cover charge. If you've got friends in from out of town, why not take them someplace special, like to the Opera?

**OPIUM DEN**
**29 E. 3rd St. (bet. 2nd Ave. & Bowery)**
**505-7344**

*CASH ONLY*

This gothic cave is cool, comfy, and dark. Despite its trendiness, consider it one of the better and smaller lounges in the East Village. Everything from disco to Trip-Hop plays within this setting which looks like an old monastery. With dark brick walls, flickering candles, and statues of monks behind mission-style chairs and benches, it's a good place to kick back and chill with a moderately priced drink. On the weekend it does get crowded, so come early. Bring a date for after dinner drinks.

**ORCHARD BAR**
**200 Orchard St. (bet. Houston & Stanton Sts.)**
**673-5350**

*ALL MAJOR CREDIT CARDS*

Ah, so this is where all the contemporary artists hang after they show off their recent installation! Everyone is so "full of thoughts" and chic as they wander aimlessly through one of the most hip lounges on the Lower East Side. The Orchard Bar looks like a fusion between a terrarium and a poorly lit SoHo loft. The long narrow space is comfortable, soothing, and certainly unique. Over the simple bar hangs a series of glass jars with perfectly formed Granny Smith apples displayed as if they were oddities. A variety of fish tanks filled with plant life are built into the walls, and a large screen in the back silently plays highlights from the nature channel. A DJ keeps a good vibe throughout the bar and despite a "no dancing" sign, you'll see a few feet tapping.

## ORSON'S
**175 2nd Ave. (bet. 11th & 12th Sts.)**
**475-1530**

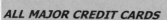 

### *ALL MAJOR CREDIT CARDS*

Don't let the roach motel facade fool you, this place is super cool and hip-looking inside. The icy blue globe-shaped lights hanging from the ceiling look like something out of the 1940s World's Fair and add a certain mystique to the place. The bar is small but accommodating with its mirrored back and sleek, metal design. Open for 7 years, Orson's offers an extensive drink menu, superb food with huge portions, and good music. The crowd is mixed, local and laid back.

## OTIS
**754 9th Ave. (bet. 51st & 52nd Sts.)**
**246-4417**

### *ALL MAJOR CREDIT CARDS*

Walking into this place you can't help but hear the theme from "Shaft" pulse in your mind as you cruise like a cool cat through the dimly lit, vinyl-and-velvet appointed lounge. Otis has that funky/freaky feel about it that makes for an ideal Quentin Tarrentino location spot. Though Otis has made claims to be the representative "SoHo lounge" in Hell's Kitchen, a more accurate description would be a mix between the East Village and inner-city Detroit. With its dim lighting, vintage wrap-around couches and spectacular photographs of musical icons like James Brown and Maria Carey, Otis makes for a great place to bring a group of friends. The food isn't bad and there's a choice of 8 beers on tap. Occasionally there is live music so call ahead for details.

## THE OTHER ROOM
**143 Perry St. (bet. Greenwich & Washington Sts.)**
**645-9758**

This tiny romantic lounge tucked away on one of the most beautiful blocks in the West Village is a fabulous little place to get away from it all. Super friendly bartenders serve an excellent selection of foreign beer and wine to a well-be-haved, clean-cut, artsy crowd. Iron, brick, tea lights and comfy bench seating dominate this perfect perch to meet up with a friend or share a post-dinner drink with a date. Take-out menus are available at the bar.

## OYSTER BAR & RESTAURANT
**Grand Central Station, lower level**
**490-6650**

*ALL MAJOR CREDIT CARDS*

Located in the underbelly of Grand Central lies this fabulous New York Institution. With its 1970s logo and vaulted, tiled ceiling, Oyster Bar offers an extensive seafood menu and an even more elaborate wine menu to midtowners and com-muters alike. The saloon in the back equipped with checked table cloths and a heavy wood bar is old-world and pre-dominantly male. The late night crowd leaves little to be desired—they're mostly married male professionals looking to score with people half their age.

## OZONE BAR & LOUNGE
**1720 2nd Ave. (bet. 89th & 90th St.)**
**860-8950**

*ALL MAJOR CREDIT CARDS*

It doesn't get swankier than The Ozone Bar & Lounge—a nice respite from the Upper East Side frat bars. Deep red curtains, exposed brick and candlelit tables set the stage for a romantic evening at this SoHo-esque lounge. Two years old, it's hard to believe that this handsome space once housed a super cheesy frat bar! Covered in a beautiful Mo-roccan tent, the back lounge, even on a crowded weekend evening, remains virtually smoke-free. With red lighting, candlelit tables and comfy couches, this is the perfect spot to woo your first date. Moroccan rugs are elegantly draped over exposed brick walls while funk and disco music is played nightly by different DJs. Open from 4pm - 4am, a very mel-low, trendy crowd drink martinis, sangria and red wine and smoke the cigars available at the bar. A daily happy hour serves 1/2 price draft bottles and takes $1 off all premium drinks. One of the better looking bars in the area, the Ozone Bar & Lounge is a sight for sore eyes.

## P&G CORNER CAFÉ
**279 Amsterdam Ave. (At 73rd St.)**
**874-8568**

### *CASH ONLY*

Open since 1942, P&G prides itself on having some of the oldest neon beer signs in New York City. The staff could easily be stand-ins for a "Seinfeld" episode and the patrons were undoubtedly members of their high school debate team. This simple, straight forward, traditional-looking pub is, according to Al, a regular who has been frequenting P&G since 1986, "the only classic bar in New York that really does not have a theme and does not appeal to one particular ethnicity or age group." 30 or so regulars congregate here nightly, and most of them claim to be married, divorced or emotionally wounded in some way or another. Nonetheless, the bar is complete with good tunes and more importantly, a Ms. Pac Man machine.

## PADDY REILLY'S
**519 2nd Ave. (At 29th St.)**
**686-1210**

Hot, loud and crowded with NYU nurses dancing to Irish bands, it's no wonder that Paddy Reilly's is the place the infamous band Black 47 got their start. This barn-like venue is usually packed with men in Guinness-stained rugby shirts and women who are too drunk to walk home. There is a happy hour Monday through Thursday from 12pm to 7pm. Friday and Saturday nights charge a $5 cover for very loud bands.

**PAGEANT**
**109 E. 9th St. (bet. 3rd & 4th Aves.)**
**529-5333**

*ALL MAJOR CREDIT CARDS*

Formerly a bookstore, this bar/restaurant is riding on the coattails of the famous Pageant Bookstore where "Hannah and Her sisters" took place. Pageant, owned by the proprietor of Tom and Jerry's, serves a full American/Mediterranean menu from 5 -11 pm while the bar serves pricey cocktails, beer and wine until 4am. Seven days a week, a young, tame NYU crowd trying too hard to be cool, pile in for the evening. On the weekends, expect to see a B&T crowd lined up outside ready to flash their ID and willing to pay the cover. Inside, the upstairs lounge decorated in red velvet and candles is definitely the place to hang out. Lots of dove-like light fixtures illuminate the bar while R&B and rap unobtrusively play in the background. Not much life is breathing in this place but hopefully the soon-to-be industry nights on Monday (promoted by Camel Cigarettes), will bring in a more energetic, interesting crowd.

**PARK AVALON**
**225 Park Ave. S. (bet. 18th & 19th Sts.)**
**533-2500**

*ALL MAJOR CREDIT CARDS*

What first strikes you upon entering Park Avalon is not the large blurry landscape photograph over the bar, nor the high ceilings, but the larger-than-life candle shrine that engulfs the right half of the bar. It's as if Dracula saw this place and decided to permanently set up shop! During the week the clientele is largely yuppies who are tired of going to Angelo & Maxies. On the weekend, the bridge-and-tunnel crew invade for a big night on the town. On Sundays, mellow locals take in smooth jazz over brunch. The bartenders only help you when they feel like it, and prefer to schmooze with the wait staff. Cocktails are pricey.

**PARKSIDE LOUNGE**
**317 E. Houston St. (bet. Aves. B & C)**
**673-6270**

*ALL MAJOR CREDIT CARDS*

Open for 53 years, this Lower East Side dive bar caters to both the old and new school LES clientele. Owned by the proprietor of the Bleecker Street Bar, Parkside Lounge serves super cheap drinks and has the longest happy hour known to man—12pm - 8pm daily. Happy hour specials include $2.50 beers, $3.50 well drinks, and $3 Sky Vodka. With no cover charge, bands, performance art, comedy and poetry readings perform in the cavernous back lounge of this pre-war, decrepit space. A jukebox offers old school favorites like Charlie Parker, Duke Ellington and Ella Fitzgerald. Grab your Miller High Life and play a bowling pin game, shoot some pool or watch some sports on TV. Open daily from 12pm - 4am, there's no need to dress to impress—it's just a bunch of chill Lower East Siders getting together to drink cheap, shoot some pool or listen to some live performances.

**THE PARLOUR**
**250 W. 86th St. (bet. B'way & West End Aves.)**
**580-8923**

*ALL MAJOR CREDIT CARDS*

Fake fireplaces set the ambiance for this new-looking, try-ing to be old-looking, Irish pub. During the week this place ropes in the older crowd, complete with old men wearing fur. On the weekend the vintage, couch-filled basement packs in a younger crowd for live bands such as the killer '80s band, Modern English. An occasional traditional Irish band is thrown in for color every few days. With three full bars, beer and cocktails are reasonably priced.

**PASSERBY**
**436 W. 15ᵗʰ St. (bet 9ᵗʰ & 10ᵗʰ Aves.)**
**206-7321**

Mary Boone meets Steve Rubell at this new bar/gallery in the most up-and-coming part of New York—Chelsea. From the outside, it looks like any nondescript crack den. The inside, however, is a whole different bag of Q-tips. The space consists of two small bar areas with lots of mirrors for effect, and a gallery in the back where you can soak in the installation of the moment. The crowning glory of this hip, trendy hot spot is the flashing lighted dance floor straight out of the '70s. Studio 54 isn't dead yet, it's just 600 sq. ft. The crowd is very in-the-know, so wear your Sunday hippest. Reality is, this review is larger than the bar, but it's a lot of fun.

## PATRIA
**250 Park Ave. S. (At 20th St.)**
**777-6211**

*ALL MAJOR CREDIT CARDS*

Patria is clearly one of the best restaurants on the lower Park Avenue strip. The multi-level dining room packs crowds in daily for a taste of chef Douglas Rodriguez's creative Nuevo-Latino fare. The mosaic murals have a soothing effect on even the most exhausted, hardworking crowd that come here to enjoy an escape to something foreign. If you come here just to enjoy the upbeat bar scene, you mustn't leave without trying the signature drink of the house—the mohito. This wonderfully powerful concoction of sugarcane, rum, and lime juice will certainly knock your socks off if you're not careful. But why be careful, you're here to have fun! Enough good things can't be said about Patria. The entire experience is perfect, from the friendly and competent waiters to the well executed and creative dishes.

## PECULIAR PUB
**145 Bleecker St. (At Laguardia Pl.)**
**353-1327**

Welcome to the Peculiar Pub, where the drinks are cheap and the mood is young. This large pub-like bar really packs it in! With 200 beers to choose from and rock-and-roll playing on the jukebox, this is the place to be if you're young and looking for cheap drinks. A male dominated pick-up scene, preppy college kids flock to grab a table and seem right at home amongst the St. Pauli girl posters, beer advertising mirrors and bumper stickers. There's nothing peculiar about this place at all. In fact, it's quite run-of-the-mill.

## PEGASUS
**119 E. 60th St. (Lexington Ave.)**
**888-4702**

*ALL MAJOR CREDIT CARDS*

This bar is truly beautiful inside. The bar is modern and small, and the decor is very masculine with club chairs and pictures of jockeys and their horses on the wall. Excellent piano players offer a pleasing mix of show tunes and pop music to a distinguished mature crowd in the lounge, while others play in the garden. There is a happy hour daily from 5-9 pm, and on Tuesdays they have kareoke, so come here and sing your heart out!

## THE PENN TOP BAR (@ THE PENINSULA HOTEL)
**700 5th Ave. (At 55th St.)**
**903-3910**

*ALL MAJOR CREDIT CARDS*

The Penn Top Bar, conveniently located in the heart of midtown, offers some of the most breathtaking views of Manhattan. With terraces to both the east and west, impeccably dressed clientele rush here after work to sit outside and catch sundown while sipping one of the elaborate martinis from the menu. With such impressive surroundings, this is a great place to bring a date. However, be prepared to shell out a lot of cash because your drinks will probably be $12 a pop.

## PETER'S
**182 Columbus Ave (bet. 68th & 69th Sts.)**
**877-4747**
*ALL MAJOR CREDIT CARDS*

Once you make it through the gauntlet, you're in for a relatively pleasant surprise. Yes, there is a bar on the Upper West Side where thirtysomethings hang out. The attractive crowd tends to settle in for the night, pleased to spend the entire evening here surrounded by pleasant, approachable people. There's a long front bar and additional back bar and the friendly bartenders, who somehow remember your name, eagerly wait on the patrons and make sure that you're never left wanting for another drink. Peter's gets crowded on Thursdays and weekends, but still has a solid steady crowd in attendance all week. The most notable point about this place is that it is actually difficult to leave here without getting a phone number or being asked out on a date.

### PETE'S TAVERN
**129 E. 18th St. (At Irving Pl.)**
**473-7676**

***ALL MAJOR CREDIT CARDS***

Since 1864, Pete's has been a corner saloon, but during Prohibition it was a speakeasy with a flower shop facade. The food here is mediocre, so stick to the basics. Happy hour on Thursday and Friday serves free unlimited hors d'oeuvres from 4:30-7:30pm. It's not a place to go and get rowdy with the guys over the game unless of course you don't mind watching it on their one TV. Pete's is simply a friendly place to feel cozy, guzzle a mug of brew, and take in some history. The author, O. Henry, is believed to have written "The Gift of the Magi" here so be sure to check out the black wooden booth where he gathered his thoughts.

### PHEBE'S
**361 Bowery (At 4th St.)**
**473-9008**

Across the street from the chic and ultra-trendy B Bar lies its polar opposite—Phebe's. A dive in the truest sense, Phebe's was around long before the East Village was considered cool. If you don't mind the sticky floors and ratty seats, you can enjoy pitchers of Bud for $5.50 and tasty

Blackjack burgers and fries. There's classic rock on the jukebox and plenty of room for you to bring a large group of friends. Last year they made a huge investment and had doors put on the bathroom stalls. What more could you want from an establishment this cheap? Open 364 ½ days a year.

## PIECES
**8 Christopher St. (Greenwich Ave.)**
**929-9291**

### *CASH ONLY*

Happy hour starts at 2pm so come in and get it going early. This popular gay bar offers a different theme every night of the week. Stop by for "Mailbox Night" where boys actually send mail to each other anonymously. On Monday nights, join in the Broadway show tunes sing-a-long with Jim Allen. Boys range from 18 to 80 and it's very popular with the outer-borough crowd. One of the only gay bars where waiters serve mud-slide shots in glass test tubes.

## PIERROT
**28 Ave B (At 3rd St.)**
**673-1999**

### *ALL MAJOR CREDIT CARDS*

An oasis of elegance with a touch of frivolity has recently added color to the dreary corner of Third Street and Avenue B. The idea behind this convivial and warm bar/restaurant started along the young owner's adventures through Paris. Pierrot, which derives from a French theater clown from the 1800s, is filled with clowns. Clowns on circus posters, clowns on toy airplanes, wooden toy clowns, clowns, clowns, clowns. The lighting at this rustic setting exudes a mystical calm, making for a very relaxing atmosphere. Great old toys, building blocks, currency and a lot of stuff pulled out of the closet is displayed in the glass encased bar. Catering to a twentysomething neighborhood and uptown crowd who come to see something funky, this place is open daily from 5pm to 4am. Food is served till 2am on the weekends and till 1am during the week. An eclectic and soothing musical selection unobtrusively adds to the amiable ambiance of Pierrot. This is a great place for a first date, a quick drink after work or even a dinner party.

## PLANET 28
**215 W. 28th St. (bet. 7th & 8th Aves.)**
**643-1199**

*ALL MAJOR CREDIT CARDS*

An odd little club nestled in a dark block of upper Chelsea, Planet 28 is odd, dark, and, um, in upper Chelsea. Mostly a dance club farmed out to the DJs and promoters of the day, this place is small, dingy, and covered from floor to ceiling in wood, wood and more wood. Forget doing a split, you could get a splinter right in your sphincter. The dance floor is cramped, and seems more suited to some sort of a ritual you would see on a Geraldo special. With no beers on tap, no menu, and an overall frightening and dreary atmosphere, this place is absolutely..."wonderful."

## POLLY ESTHER'S
**186 W. 4th St. (Barrow/Jones St.)**
**924-5707**

*ALL MAJOR CREDIT CARDS*

Sure it's cheesy, filled with guidos and you'd rather die than than say you've been there, but you'll be hard pressed to find find a better place to dance to songs that you actually like. Known for offering a healthy dose of "New Jersey culture," Polly Esther's is a wildly fun place to dance. It's cheap, it's loud and they play kick ass disco and '80s hits all night long. And because everyone is so damn cheesy it's okay for you to let loose. Who cares how you look, right? Just look at the guy dancing next to you! Prepare yourself for hourly shot specials, smoke machines and overfondled blow up dolls. Weekends bring men in chains, women in bad Nine West shoes and several bachlorette parties. It's best to come here with a group of friends and even better when you're totally intoxicated.

## POTION
**370 Columbus Ave. (bet. 77ᵗʰ & 78ᵗʰ Sts.)**
**721-4386**

### ALL MAJOR CREDIT CARDS

Do you remember Spencer gifts in any mall USA? Well, the Potion's windows are filled with the plastic panels of water and bubbles that fascinated us so much as a child. This trendy little find on the Upper West Side is a breath of fresh air in this frat town. The crowd is a little older (27-35) and a little hipper than the other local watering holes, so leave your rugby shirt and Timberlands at home. Check out the layered drink machine!

## POUR HOUSE
**1710 2ⁿᵈ Ave. (bet. 88ᵗʰ & 89ᵗʰ Sts.)**
**987-3790**

### ALL MAJOR CREDIT CARDS

Smack in the middle of "frat row" is yet another young, "Lets drink till we pass out," boyish bar. Adorned with dart trophies and Jagermeister posters, this pint-size bar boasts housing the best dart team in Manhattan. Every Monday and Tuesday there are dart competitions while serving up cheap drinks and loud top forties jukebox hits. Around for 5 years, Pour House offers $1 off drink specials daily from 5pm to 8pm. Otherwise mixed shelf drinks will run you $4 while drafts and bottles start at $3.50. You collegiate types who like high-energy, loud music and shots galore will feel very welcome at the Pour House.

## PRAVDA
**281 Lafayette St. (bet. Prince & Houston Sts.)**
**226-4696**

### ALL MAJOR CREDIT CARDS

Meaning "truth" in Russian, this trendy bar/restaurant has held elite ground for three years. Below the street in the heart of SoHo, Pravda entertains a mid 20s to 40s professional crowd. Gilded mirrors, Russian lamp posts and an art deco bar takes you out of New York into a secret meeting place for the KGB. There is a dining room and a bar and lounge area where a friendly host greets you and finds you a comfortable place to sit. Dining specials include three different kinds of caviar as well as a pricey assortment of smoked fish and steak frites. The upstairs lounge is very dark, small, and tends to be a bit touristy. Some of Pravda's specialty drinks include Russian Martinis, Russian Marys, Metropolitans, and the Samovar Sling. Pravda is the place to be if you enjoy the fine art of drinking with beautiful people. While there is no happy hour, the kitchen is open until 3:50am on the weekend and until 3:15am during the week. A great place to seal the big deal.

**PROHIBITION**
**503 Columbus Ave. (bet. 84th & 85th Sts.)**
**579-3100**

*ALL MAJOR CREDIT CARDS*

This prefab, industrial space is one of the swankier looking venues on the Upper West Side. Young, cute couples and groups of friends are drawn here for the bar and pool table in the back room. A menu with designer tapas-like fare and a great wine list makes for an inexpensive date or a good place to meet up with friends. Live jazz is offered nightly ("sans" cover) and an extensive $7 martini menu is sure to make the place even more enjoyable.

**PUFFY'S TAVERN**
**81 Hudson St. (At Harrison St.)**
**766-9159**

*ALL MAJOR CREDIT CARDS*

Famous for being one of Manhattan's oldest taverns, Puffy's draws a great mixed local crowd who love to drink and get down to the jukebox's funky '70s disco and rock. The bartender has enough wit to break the most cynical New Yorker and you'll never wait for a drink. There is no happy hour but mixed drinks are only $4. There's a dart board and plenty of people who love to play. If you're hungry, get a pizza at the bar ($4). It's no wonder that Puffy's is one of New York's oldest taverns—they've got great service, great drinks, a quiet location, and an awesome, welcoming, neighborhood crowd.

## PYRAMID CLUB
**101 Ave. A (bet. 6th & 7th Sts.)**
**473-7184**

Believe it or not, the Pyramid Club—a dive and club in one—is still standing tall. Since the '80s, the Pyramid has been home to many age-withstanding drag queens who *still* make an occasional appearance. Once past the attitude-filled doorman, you'll enter a dark, smoky cave of fetish-themed nights filled with nostalgic debauchery. It's the tacky '80s all over again on Friday night at the "1984" gay dance party. Get there early to avoid the long line of men dying to relive the olden days of house music, drag queens and bad hairdos. Saturday nights bring in the best of the goth kids. Dance to Bauhuas, Love and Rockets with a little Morrissey thrown in to lighten the mood. Sunday hosts an array of live rock and punk bands such as "Gringo Starr" and "Kritter." Closed on Mondays and Tuesdays, even without a happy hour, drinks are strong and cheap. Whether you're goth, gay, a drag queen or into hearing live bands, there is a little bit of everything at this East Village relic.

## RACCOON LODGE
**1439 York Ave. (bet. 77th & 78th Sts.), 650-1775**
**480 Amsterdam Ave. (At 83rd St.), 874-9984**
**59 Warren St. (At W. B'way) 766-9656**

*ALL MAJOR CREDIT CARDS*

You couldn't miss the obnoxious neon red sign outside, even if you were blindfolded. If you're meeting friends here, tell them to wear anything but a striped oxford shirt and a baseball cap otherwise you won't find them—*everyone* is dressed like this. The Racoon Lodge, three of them in all, are nice, clean establishments that tend to draw wall-to-wall frat boys. If you're searching for a squeaky clean, heterosexual scene of lacrosse players, look no further. The Racoon Lodge across town is slightly less crowded, but otherwise identical.

## RADIO PERFECTO
**190 Avenue B (bet. 11th & 12th Sts.)**
**477-3366**

*CASH ONLY*

Owned by the proprietors of Opaline, this fairly new kid on the up-and-"yupping" block of Avenue B opened its doors in October of 1999. Minimally decorated in lightly colored wood and a huge garage door at the store's entrance, Radio Perfecto's ambiance is equally simple with low light and quiet music. The space is uniquely decorated with old radios and light fixtures made of old hand drills wired with halogen lights. A huge outside garden always draws in the summer crowd.

## RAINBOW ROOM (CLOSED; THE RAINBOW GRILL OPENS IN OCT.)
**30 Rockerfeller Plaza, 65th fl.**
**632-5000**

*ALL MAJOR CREDIT CARDS*

The best view that a bar has to offer in New York, hands down! The flawless Art Deco space offers sweeping views of Manhattan that make you wish you could afford an apartment on the top floor of those annoying high-rises in your neighborhood. If you are lucky enough to get a window seat, don't get caught up in the romantic mood and say something you don't mean. The Rainbow Room is always packed to the rafters with an older, well-dressed crowd made up mostly of tourists who are out for a big night in the Big Apple. The drinks are painfully expensive, but are the best in the city. Don't under- estimate the power of the view, it's a date maker!   A must see.

## RAOUL'S
**180 Prince St. (bet. Sullivan & Thompson Sts.)**
**966-3518**

Raoul's has been, and seems always will be, one of the all-time SoHo trend spots. Who doesn't love its curt French waiters, narrow smoke filled bar, and steak au poivre that's to die for? So chic and hip, Raoul's never loses its flair for dishing out authentic French cooking (they use plenty of lard in most dishes) accompanied by a thoughtful wine list. Please be careful to watch your alcohol intake because the spiral stairs leading to the restrooms could prove hazardous to your health. Come here often because the mood is always bright and you'll never be disappointed.

## RATHBONES
**1702 2nd Ave. (At 88th St.)**
**369-7361**

### *ALL MAJOR CREDIT CARDS*

Welcome to the Ground Round of the Upper East Side Irish bars. Open for 26 years, Rathbones caters to an older, Irish food lovin' crowd. With floors covered in sawdust, paper tablecloths on wooden tables and sports blaring from television sets, you instantly forget you're in New York City. If you favor Shepard's Pie, a top forties jukebox, oppressively bright lighting, an atmosphere dull as the tip of a butter knife, *and* you're Irish, then this is the spot for you. Only open until 1am, Rathbones boasts an impressive Irish brunch on Saturday and Sunday from 12pm – 4pm. Drinks are reasonably priced so the lack of a happy hour is no loss. Don't expect much excitement—it's as mellow and uneventful as it gets.

## THE RAVEN
**194 Ave. A (At 12th St.)**
**529-4712**

### *ALL MAJOR CREDIT CARDS*

Edgar Allen Poe's poem, "The Raven," may have a macabre air to it, but the bar is anything but sinister. Here you'll find one of the most intimate, relaxing and friendly atmospheres in the East Village. This local eatery/bar has brought together teachers from the local high school for breakfast and East Village hipsters for beer and wine in the evening.

Open from 8am till 4am daily, the Raven serves sandwiches, soups, salads and cappuccinos along with an array of beer, wines and sake. Owners Ria and Harold put their heart and soul into this warmly decorated and spacious setting. Sit at the bar and play a board game or play pinball while listening to Sinatra. A few tables and chairs create the cafe atmosphere while church pews and couches provide places to lounge. Food and drink prices are extremely reasonable with specials nightly. Asahi beer is $2.50 and a pint of Budweiser or glass of wine is $3.50 and up. Happy hour is offered daily from 4pm till 8pm which offers 1/2 price tap beer. Wednesday nights is ladies' night with half off tap beer.

## RAWHIDE
**212 8th Ave. (At 21st St.)**
**242-9332**

*CASH ONLY*

Cattle call! This isn't any ordinary audition, though. In this part you'll have to pretend that you actually like a bar called Rawhide. Can you do it? If you're into overweight, middle-aged men stuffed into leather and Levis who have not showered for days, you'll love this bar! Nightly drink specials, pool tables and pinball attract a regular crowd that is looking for love at all hours of the day. Walking by, you can smell a mixture of booz and alcohol waft through the door as someone stumbles their way onto the street. Enter at your own risk.

## READE ST. PUB
**135 Reade St. (At Greenwich St.)**
**619-2811**

*CASH ONLY*

The first thing you notice as you walk through this comfortable and friendly pub is a large toy train set with boxcars adorned with the names of neighborhood businesses wrapped around the ceiling. Besides that, it's your typical pub experience: Wooden booths, dart board, TVs, the jovial Irish bartender and good pub food. The crowd is a mix of TriBeCa locals (yuppies to the non-native), some frat types, and blue-collar workers. You won't find god here, but you will find a good burger, a relaxed atmosphere and a nice beer selection. It's a nice change from the yuppy-filled lounge hells popping up all over the neighborhood.

## RE BAR
**127 8th Ave. (At 16th St.)**
**627-1680**

### *ALL MAJOR CREDIT CARDS*

Situated on a dark corner in Chelsea, you will always find a small crowd waiting to get into the Re Bar. This hip little dance spot attracts a different crowd every night with a weekly venue that spans from comedy nights, to hip-hop parties, to Reefer Madness Reggae Dance Hall. Either way, it's a great little dance spot and the later you get there, the better it is. Come with a buzz because the bar is hard to get to and the drinks are a bit pricey. The crowd tends to be an eclectic mix of young, tough kids from the outer-boroughs who know how to dance. Docker-clad yuppies may want to think twice about busting their moves here. The cover and theme changes nightly so call ahead.

## RED BENCH
**107 Sullivan St. (bet. Prince & Spring Sts.)**
**274-9120**

### *ALL MAJOR CREDIT CARDS*

This small lounge located in the heart of SoHo is dark, cozy, hip and serves as a nice break from some of the louder and more mainstream venues. The back hosts an array of velvet couches and chairs where you can curl up with a date or have an intimate conversation with a friend. The crowd is in their 20s, good-looking and laid back. Pop in here after having dinner at Blue Ribbon, next door. On most nights, the music is loud and spectacular.

## RED LION
**151 Bleecker St. (At Thompson St.)**
**473-9560**
### *ALL MAJOR CREDIT CARDS*

This rock 'n' roll bar is a staple among the Bleecker Street watering holes. Adorned with chintzy rock memorabilia and filled with outer-borough rock 'n' roll fans, this dive bar hosts nightly cover bands who, for $5, will play tributes to Kiss, Led Zeppelin, and the Beatles. Between bands, one can amuse themselves by listening to the jukebox or watching sports highlights on one of the three television sets. Kamikaze shots are offered by girls in cute outfits, while a beer will run you $4 and mixed drinks $5. Come here to relive the sounds of the '60s, get loaded, puke on the street, and drive back to New Jersey.

## RED ROCK WEST SALOON
**457 W. 17th St. (At 10th Ave.)**
**366-5359**

For a totally uninhibited, outrageous, liberating, and utterly unparalleled drinking experience, get to Red Rock West as fast as you can. This dingy bar on the very quiet and eerie corner of 10th Ave. plays host to a wonderful mix of personalities and somehow pleases everyone. The POW/MIA banner, skulls hanging from the bar, and bumper stickers posted everywhere just add to the mysterious charm of the place. Where else can you see beautiful bartenders wearing cheerleader style ponytails clad in ultra-mini plaid Catholic schoolgirl uniforms and knee-high black leather boots? For added entertainment there are a whole host of props behind the bar to play with. Wigs, noisemakers, pots and pans, water guns, water balloons, and lots of whipped cream are used to enhance any evening you happen to stop by. The bartenders have special use of a microphone that allows them to address patrons…and they don't always say the nicest things. Be prepared to be mocked and abused, that's what these girls are good at. During some very special songs they will actually get on the bar and do "skit" type dances for the crowd. For instance, when Def Leppard's "Pour Some Sugar on Me" starts playing, both bartenders hop deftly onto the bar, whipped cream and peach schnapps in hand, and begin literally pouring the sugary sweet mixture onto each other and licking it from exposed body parts just the way naughty girls should. Another song leads them to pour

233

pitchers of water all over themselves while dancing. If you don't want to get doused step far away from the bar. If you're looking for a wild and outrageous time that'll never let you down, try Red Rock West

## REGENTS
**315 E. 53rd St. (At 2nd Ave.)**
**593-3091**

### ALL MAJOR CREDIT CARDS

Enter this dual-level antiquity which sports quite the restaurant for the distinguished gentleman downstairs. Upstairs features another English pub and gay bar wannabe with comfy seating and a lovely piano. There is live piano entertainment nightly and the lounge tends to be quite cruisy. Fridays it gets a little younger and a little hipper. No cover.

## REIF'S TAVERN
**302 E. 92nd St. (bet. 1st & 2nd Ave.)**
**426-0519**

### CASH ONLY

Open since 1942, Reif's Tavern has been handed down through the Reif family from generation to generation. This small ex-gangster watering hole is inhabited by faithful locals who come in for the family-type atmosphere. With a small front bar minimally decorated with beer signs and mirrors, the back "lounge" area houses a pool table and a couple of the most scuzzy couches ever seen. The huge outdoor deck attracts the locals who bring their own BBQ food and watch sports on TV. Open daily from 12pm - 4am, a happy hour serves up $2 drafts and $2 well drinks from 12pm to 8pm. With four beers on tap, drinks are pretty inexpensive. A typical top forties jukebox plays the likes of Green Day, Motely Crew, Blind Melon and Dave Mathews. A pretty tame atmosphere, Reif's is big with the locals.

## REMEDY
**462 Amsterdam Ave. (bet. 82nd & 83rd Sts.)**
**No phone**

With the black facade and the scripted red "Remedy" as your first visual, you might expect to see some nudity inside. Two candles burn in the windows facing Amsterdam Ave., giving off a minimalistic and mysterious vibe. The crowd inside is a bunch of lounge lizards who sit motionless on mix-and-match couches watching VH1's "Pop-Up Video." The space itself is rather routine, but if you're looking for a scene free of fraternity brothers and kakki pants, this is your spot. Black clothing is a must.

## REMINISCENCE
**334 E. 73rd St. (bet. 1st & 2nd Aves.)**
**988-6100**

Introducing downtown to uptown, Reminiscence is one of the most non-yuppie, non-frat, chill lounges on the Upper East Side. Owned by the proprietors of downtown's "Shine," this casual lounge has played host to hip and dope bands such as Run DMC and the Sugar Hill Gang. Yes, on the Upper East Side! Besides the Tuesday night acoustic performances, a DJ plays a mix of soul, funk and groove nightly. With exposed brick walls covered with black and white framed photos, there is a definite touch of class in this lounge. Sit up front at the spacious bar and converse with the friendly bartenders or take advantage of waitress service in the comfortable and candle-lit back lounge. Drinks are reasonably priced while a daily happy hour draws in a crowd of early revelers. Don't let the 25 and up, mostly male crowd scare you away, this is not your typical Upper East Side beer drinking crowd.

## RESERVOIR
**70 University Pl. (bet. 10th & 11th Sts.)**
**475-0770**

### ALL MAJOR CREDIT CARDS

This village hangout has been many things before, ranging from a jazz spot to a pub. Today it is a sports bar equipped with a slew of TVs and frat types who come for the drink and chicken wing specials. It looks a little out of place in this sleepy neighborhood, but it's a safe bet if you don't want to travel to the Upper East Side.

## REVIVAL
**129 E. 15th St. (bet. Irving & 3rd Ave)**
**253-8061**

Owned by the proprietors of the Looking Glass, Revival definitely needs a little reviving. Located in the heart of Gramercy, the poorly decorated space plays host to a diverse crowd of twentysomething locals and rowdy salesmen from the local PC Richards. See live bands upstairs or hangout downstairs by the bar. If you dare, hang out in the dingy lounge or on the back porch. Claustrophobics, please avoid the downstairs bar—the ceilings are copper and so low that the cigarette smoke can't rise. Those scared of the dark, beware of the dark lounge in the back room. Finally, if you're not a fan of trailer parks, do not venture to the back deck—the K-mart plastic furniture and sports banners may cause some '80s, NJ shore flashbacks.

## REVOLUTION
**611 9th Ave. (bet. 43rd & 44th Sts.)**
**489-8451**

### ALL MAJOR CREDIT CARDS

The first of the new generation of bars to crop up in Hell's Kitchen, Revolution is perhaps at the top of the list for this area. A loungy nook up front with a fake fireplace provides young 20 to 30-something locals with a place to shoot the breeze. The bulk of the large space is occupied by a long bar and tables that serve American fare along the opposite wall. The service is prompt and friendly and a head bopping DJ spins memorable crowd-pleasing tunes from the past.

## RICHTER'S BAR
**1608 3rd Ave. (bet. 90th & 91st Sts.)**
**722-5405**

### CASH ONLY

The stone exterior and wood door give Richter's a definite cottage feel. But this is no cottage. Ladies drink free here every night from 9pm –11pm. So what's the catch? Maybe it's the fact that the crowd is predominantly male, in their mid-forties and there's not much to do but play fooseball. Gals, keep your distance from this testosterone fest. Guys, find a new place to meet chicks.

## RIVERTON LOUNGE
**187 Orchard St. (bet. Houston & Stanton)**
**388-1288**

### ALL MAJOR CREDIT CARDS

The Riverton Lounge is the token Upper West Side bar on Orchard St. Visually, its high ceilings, large wooden bar, pastoral paintings and comfy old couches add charm, but for some reason this place has about as much soul as a Twinkie. The crowd is young and squeaky clean and either show up really buzzed or are too buzzed to leave. If you need a meeting place for a lot of people, this is a good choice. If you're looking to score and have a romantic moment, go somewhere else. Come play pool in the back to some poorly mixed tapes played on an Aiwa stereo.

## RODEO BAR
**375 3rd Ave. (At 27th St.)**
**683-6500**

### ALL MAJOR CREDIT CARDS

"Urban Cowboy" gone terribly, terribly wrong. If Tortilla Flats and the late Denim and Diamonds had a child, this would be it. A tremendously huge and scary stuffed bison perches over the front bar while a huge water tank hangs from the ceiling. Peanut shells are strewn all over the floor, and old license plates trim the bar, adding to the old hillbilly charm. Live rockabilly bands perform nightly to a mixed crowd. Expensive but strong drinks are served at the two bars. The back bar is an old trailer covered in chili pepper lights, tin sidings and even more old license plates. The front of the Rodeo Bar attracts a mainly male crowd of tourists and Jersey-ites who come to listen to music with a country edge. It's definitely not the place to meet the beautiful people, but it's a great place to bring a crowd and drink until you fall on the floor and get peanut shells embedded in your arm.

## THE ROOM
**144 Sullivan St. (bet. Houston & Prince)**
**477-2102**

*CASH ONLY*

There's *no* room at the Room, especially on a weekend night when it's swamped. This narrow, two-room lounge offers a tremendous beer selection served in large glasses. During the week, the gothic space makes for a comfortable and almost romantic spot. On weekends, it becomes swamped with an uptown crowd who's decked and psyched to be hanging out in SoHo. If you're looking for a mellow alternative, check out The Other Room in the West Village.

## THE ROXY
**515 W. 18th St. (bet. 10th & 11th Aves.)**
**645-5156**

*CASH ONLY*

This mega club hit NYC in the early '80s and is still dosing New Yorkers with action-packed disco dancing and techno clubbing. On Friday nights, the Roxy presents a Latin fiesta of 18 and older hootchied-out Latinas . DJs spin the booming sounds of salsa, merengue, house and reggae. Straight Friday nights feature a very steamy, hormone-indulgent, $1000 male/female bikini contest. Look out for the angry Mike Tyson-esque body guards—one wrong move and these guys could do some serious damage. And leave all of your weapons at home; in order to enter the club, you need to go through metal detectors and you will be thoroughly frisked, felt up and made to feel like a suspected terrorist. Saturday nights fill up the Roxy with fun-loving Chelsea boys. The atmosphere is of a rollicking disco extravaganza. DJ Victor Calderon helms the main dance floor spinning progressive style house while Andy Anderson spins retro pop upstairs in the lounge. Relive the '70s and break out your sneaker skates on Roller-skating Wednesdays. Pay a $10 cover before 9pm ($12 after 9pm) and roller disco from 8pm to 2am. Drink prices are typically overpriced: $6.60 a beer and $7.50 a mixed drink in plastic cups. Admission charges as follows: $20 for men, $15 ladies, $5 extra for those wearing sneakers (?) and reduced admission with passes or if you are on a guest list. It is rumored that Latin Friday nights will transform into Guido night, so polish up your gold chains and aqua net the hair...Brooklyn's gonna be in the house!

**RUBY'S TAP HOUSE**
**1754 2nd Ave. (bet. 91st & 92nd St.)**
**987-8179**

*ALL MAJOR CREDIT CARDS*

Beer, beer and more beer is what has placed Ruby's Tap House in the "Good Beer Guide." Boasting the freshest tap system around, Ruby's offers 26 beers on draft, 45 bottled beers and 16 single malt scotches along with 22 different types of hamburgers. Open for 20 years, this Upper East Side beer joint is decorated with its 26 beer taps lined up behind the bar. Hand-painted murals line the walls relaying the story of the old-fashioned English beer brewing system throughout time. The tavern-like atmosphere brings in the 25 and up crowd on the weekends who listen to DJ'd rock and roll, play pool and of course, drink beer. Sunday through Wednesday, the bar honors a policy of "First draft is on us" whenever you buy a hamburger or chicken salad. The friendly

239

atmosphere and great beer turns Ruby's into the Cheers of the Upper East Side.

## RUDY'S BAR & GRILL
627 9th Ave. (bet. 44th & 45th Sts.)
974-9169

Rudy's is a small slice of hell on earth. A place where you are not only afraid to drink out of the glasses, but afraid to even sit down. For some reason, Rudy's has become wildly popular to a host of shallow people who think it's "cool" to hang out in a place that's downright disgusting. If you thought that sports bar on that backroad of West Virginia was bad, you ain't seen nothing! Despite the drizzle of a few Hell's Kitchen hipsters, the crowd is predominantly seedy, young and skuzzy beyond repair. Beer is cheap and they serve up free hotdogs which causes a smell inside that will not only make your mouth water, but your eyes as well.

## RUSSIAN VODKA ROOM
265 W. 52nd St. (bet. 8th Ave. & B'way)
307-5835

### ALL MAJOR CREDIT CARDS

Don't be put off by the hole-in-the-wall entrance, and get over the tacky, hotel lobby décor because you're about to sample the best drinks around. Owned by Russians, staffed by Russians and frequented by Russians, the Russian Vodka Room is a seriously cool place and a refreshing change from the other predictable bars and lounges today. With a menu of over 70 vodkas, stunning flavored martinis, and caviar that rivals Petrossian's, this place will win you over in no time. You can order an iced rack of 6 infused vodkas of your choice, or try some of their homemade specialties like tarragon, ginger, peach, horseradish...and the list goes on. That outdated wood paneling and hunter green, wall-to-wall carpeting will fade into the distance as you sip your super-chilled, Granny Smith apple-infused Cosmo. Watch out for happy hour when the flavored vodkas are half price from 4-7pm, after which the piano guy comes in and plays mellow, jazzy tunes till midnight. If you're afraid of the strong stuff, try one of their Eastern Bloc beers from Estonia or the Czech Republic. The vibe is international (but not pretentious), with an age range of 30-45. Good for after work or late night with friends, the RVR makes us happy to see the Cold War a thing of the past.

## RYAN'S IRISH PUB
**151 2nd Ave. (bet. 9th & 10th Sts.)**
**979-9511**

*ALL MAJOR CREDIT CARDS*

With live Irish music on Sunday night and a free buffet during happy hour, this pub tries to offer more than your typical dive bar. Its outdoor space is really the one plus that sets this place apart from the rest. The crowd is local and the beer is pretty cheap. You've seen this place at least a million times before.

## 7B (VAZAC'S)
**108 Ave. B (At 7th St.)**
**473-8840**

*ALL MAJOR CREDIT CARDS*

This East Village relic is one of a dying breed, especially in the trendy and over-loungified East Village. It's loud, it's smoky, and it's always packed with a slew of 20 to 30-some-things screaming to hear each other over the jukebox. Whether alongside the wooden horseshoe-shaped bar, or stuffed into one of the many rickety tables and booths, you'll find all walks of life here—everything from your skuzzy pierced punk rocker to docker-clad urban yuppie. Skanky decor aside, 7B remains a neighborhood favorite that serves up cheap pints of Guinness and ice cold beer. Bouncers are about as warm and fuzzy as a bag of broken glass and they're strict on the ID, so beware.

## SAINTS
**992 Amsterdam Ave (At 109th St.)**
**222-2431**      *CASH ONLY*

After several months of controversy featuring some hefty opposition from the local community, the Morningside Heights/Columbia University area finally has its own gay bar. Outside, it's your typical shady gay bar of yore, sporting small darkened windows, closed windows shades and a heavy door that bears no sign other than the street address. Inside, it's a festive and friendly cross-section of gay New York representing about every color of the rainbow flag. Customers sit at the long wooden bar or at one of the many booths, shoot some pool or just stand around while the bartenders call out random happy hours much to the crowds delight. If you want to avoid a cruisy, drippy and pretentious crowd, this is the place.

## SALA
**344 Bowery (At Great Jones St.)**
**979-6606**

### *ALL MAJOR CREDIT CARDS*

Sick of Heineken, gin-and-tonics or the newly dreaded martini fad? Welcome to Sala, where Sangria rules and tapas are king. This NoHo newcomer has all the makings of a cool spot without the attitude. A hip crowd, a great looking space, distressed walls and serene lighting should add some Spanish flair to any date going flat (the sangria helps a bit too). For those looking for a mix of Spain and lounge, a downstairs lounge will be available in October, so don't work yourself into a "Rat Pack" panic. The weekend sports a DJ and a more party-oriented crowd, so choose your times carefully. This is a definite all around Shecky pick.

## SAN FRANSICO REST.
**544 6th Ave. (bet. 14ᵗʰ & 15ᵗʰ Sts.)**
**924-9125**

### *CASH ONLY*

Is "rest." How they spell restaurant in San Francisco or did the owners not want want to shell out the extra dough to spell out "restaurant"? Truly weird. This is a dive-o-rama catering to a predominately local Hispanic crowd with a couple of Chester-the-Molesters drooling over the underage-looking and underdressed bartenders. A wall adorned with photos of patrons doing such things as stripping, straddling a pool table and licking whip cream seductively off a champagne glass is sure to build an appetite. The decor offers artistic breakthroughs like a Bud Light blimp and St. Pauli's Girl posters Scotch-taped to the wall. And as if all this wasn't entertaining enough, there's a very scary sign in the back that advertises mud wrestling.

## SAPPHIRE LOUNGE
**249 Eldridge St. (bet. Housten & Stanton Sts.)**
**777-5153**

*CASH ONLY*

Is acid-wash still *okay* to wear in NYC? What was once a great neighborhood disco has turned into a most dreaded and, at times, even scary tourist trap. Sweater vests, leggings, teased hair and purse backpacks? There is simply no excuse for this! Spinning a mix of reggae, disco, R&B and funk, the DJ turns this tiny bar into a hot and sweaty dance-a-thon on the weekend. Although the drink prices are relatively cheap, the $5 cover charge is unwarranted. What is even more unwarranted is the attitude at the door. But to be fair, bars *do* need to weed out the unfashionable out at the door, right? So, if you don't wear your cut-off shorts and Chuck Connors, then you're probably not getting in. On Sundays the door is complimentary before 11pm and 99 cents thereafter. Happy hour drinks everyday from 7pm-10pm. Luckily, the crowd during the week is local. It's time for a makeover, guys.

## SAVOY LOUNGE
**355 W. 41ˢᵗ St. (At 9ᵗʰ Ave)**
**947-5255**

*CASH ONLY*

Across from the bus depot, this Hell's Kitchen dive was previously home to young gay hustlers. In 1997, the Savoy changed its tune to jazz, although it still looks more like a blues joint. An average-sized local bar, you can enjoy $2 tap and bottled beers, $2.50 imports, and cheaply priced cocktails. Keep an eye on the bartender's dangling ciga-rette ashes that come a little too close to falling into your drink. There is live jazz nightly with a $5-$10 cover Fridays and Saturdays. Sunday is blues night. Locals who work the night shift hang out here starting at 8am and the local musicians who come to jam stay till closing at around 4am. Come for the music or check out one of the best jazz juke-boxes in the city which includes Bird, Trane, Miles and Monk. Call ahead for a list of events.

## SCHARMANN'S
**386 W. B'way (bet. Spring & Broome)**
**219-2561**

### *ALL MAJOR CREDIT CARDS*

This extremely comfortable, large space in SoHo is a coffee house by day and a laid-back bar by night. The lofty space is draped with funky local art and filled with garage sale chairs and couches. Although it has lounge-like qualities, Scharmann's doesn't quite make lounge status—it's more like a large living room. The loft setting is filled with a di-verse crowd that is looking to hang loose and head bob to the cool tunes spun by the DJ. There's live music on Tues-days and Thursdays. On the weekend, it becomes tourist central, flooded with Euro-trash and Americans in sneakers and fanny packs. During the off-peak hours, it's a nice place to hang with a date while grabbing a drink and dessert.

## SCRATCHER
**209 E. 5th St. (bet. 2nd & 3rd Aves.)**
**477-0030**

### *CASH ONLY*

Step down into this underground comfort zone to find a fun and lively crowd that's happy to see that there isn't a re-upholstered vintage couch in sight! This very welcoming and popular Irish bar is a fantastic little nook that seems to have drawn its clientele via word-of-mouth. A wall of dark wooden tables offers plenty of seating to a dressed down, 20 to 30-something crowd. The bartenders are very friendly and they have a good variety of beers on tap.

## THE SCREENING ROOM
**54 Varick St. (At Canal St.)**
**334-8209**

*ALL MAJOR CREDIT CARDS*

Here's a unique spot where you can grab a drink, a meal and a flick, all in one sitting! Around for three years, The Screening Room caters to an indie crowd and filmmakers who need somewhere to talk shop. Take a film client for a prix fixe dinner that includes a three-course meal and a film, or hang out at the bar for a pre-movie martini. This large space is draped in art deco décor with two stories of cozy seating. The long, beautiful bar is elegantly illuminated with candles and theatrical lighting that transports you back to the glitz and glamour of old Hollywood. A live jazz band playing on the balcony somehow completes the effect. Open daily until 11pm and until 1am on the weekends, view such classics as "Breakfast at Tiffany's" or one of the new indie flicks.  Although on the expensive side, this is a great place to take a date or throw a premiere or wrap party. Reservations are recommended.

## SCULLY ON SPRING (CLOSED)
**203 Spring St. (at Sullivan)**
**965-0057**

## SESSION 73
**1359 First Ave. (At 73rd St.)**
**517-4445**

*ALL MAJOR CREDIT CARDS*

What a welcome surprise to the Upper East Side. Sessions, newly opened this year, provides a lounge with live jazz and blues every night to a neighborhood starving for something new and different. Sessions has a slightly cosmopolitan feel and attracts a well-dressed crowd of late 20 to early 30-somethings. You can enjoy the music relaxing in one of the booths in the front, or mingle along the incredibly long, cigar friendly bar. It also offers an extensive Tapas menu in the restaurant area, as well as outside café-style seating.

## SHADE
**241 Sullivan Street (At 3rd St.)**
**982-6275**

*ALL MAJOR CREDIT CARDS*

This brand-new café and bar is small, cozy, and screaming for you to bring a date. Great lighting and exposed brick have transformed this small space into a comfortable, romantic dining spot. Shade boasts a simple contemporary American menu and a decent wine list. Average price of a glass of wine is $5. Beers are all $4. Don't expect much of a bar crowd except for those looking for a late night gourmet snack. The kitchen is open until 4am and they deliver until 3am. Stop by in the afternoon and schmooze with fellow grad students over a good cup of coffee.

## SHARK BAR
**307 Amsterdam Ave. (At 74th St.)**
**874-8500**

*ALL MAJOR CREDIT CARDS*

This predominantly African-American crowd is young, good-looking and searching for love. The bar swarms with 20 to 30-somethings who enjoy everything from the soul food, to the groovin' tunes. Although there is no dancing allowed, the atmosphere has a lot of vitality. Try the chicken wings as an appetizer and snag a seat at the bar. Shark closes at 2am. It's best on Fri. and Sat. nights.

## SHINE
**285 W. B'way (At Canal. St.)**
**941-0900**

*ALL MAJOR CREDIT CARDS*

Formerly the New Music Café, Shine is an ultra-lounge with an ego the size of Montana. Since they haven't reached "velvet rope status" yet, they have a scrutinizing door policy and an unwarranted cover charge instead. Inside the large space there are several nooks, including a super comfy pillow area with a '70s-style patchwork backdrop. The crowd is young and self-conscious and cling to each other like velcro by the bar. There is also a cabaret stage in the center of the room where live performances are hosted nightly by a very funny MC. All in all, Shine seems like a diamond in the rough.

## SHINBASHI
**280 Park Ave.  (At 48th St.)**
**661-3915**

### ALL MAJOR CREDIT CARDS

"Irasshimasse! Irasshimasse!" If you are wondering what the hosts are saying as you walk in, it's simply, "welcome!" (Or at least that's what they told us.) Stepping into Shinbashi is the equivalent of taking a trip to Tokyo. This super deluxe and expensive Sushi restaurant, open for lunch from 11:30am to 2:30pm and dinner from 5:30pm to 10pm, caters mainly to a native Japanese crowd. Mr. Sato, the bartender, says he had to stop drinking due to doctor's orders. Now he lives vicariously through his customers, offering a variety of delicious Japanese whiskeys ($7-10) and wonderful sake ($7-15). If you are patient and can simply smile when you just don't understand what anyone is saying, you'll probably get a chance to enjoy the most delicious whiskey and sake otherwise unavailable in the West.

## SHIP OF FOOLS
**1509 2nd Ave. (bet. 82nd & 83rd Sts.)**
**570-2651**

### ALL MAJOR CREDIT CARDS

If you can't catch the game on one of the 15 television sets, try starting your own game inside this large bar. Once known as Easy Street, Ship of Fools could easily be called Playland for Adults. After midnight on a given Friday, you will find a selection of Upper East Side yuppies and their visitors partaking in the bar's selection of games like pool and darts. The quasi-cafeteria setting with basic wooden tables and chairs in the back makes this place ideal for mass consumption of large quantities of domestic beer and fried pub fare. This is by far the nicest sports bar on the Upper East Side.

## SIBERIA
**50th & Broadway
(In the downtown 1/9 subway station)
333-4141**

*CASH ONLY*

The dark and very well hidden Siberia provides NYC with the ultimate underground scene. Just walk downstairs as if you're taking the 1/9 downtown and at the bottom you'll find an old Kung Fu video store turned Russian bar. With windows draped in old newspapers, the only sign of bar life is a torn, cardboard sign on the front of the door displaying the name of the bar. Covered in painted graffiti, the walls are draped in posters of Karl Marx, Russian books, Russian memorabilia, Russian pictures, Russian relics, Russian dressing. Apparently when this underground dive was discovered, there were Russian passports, books, etc., found within the walls—thus the Russian theme. Open daily from 3pm till 4am, the music on the jukebox is as eclectic as the crowd. Bowie and Velvet Underground please a very diverse crowd from theatre and writer types to East Village hipsters to musicians and Russians from Brooklyn. It's teeny, but they serve cheap drinks, have a couple of video games and offer a slew of different vodkas. Definitely not a pickup joint, but a real gem if you are looking for an inconspicuous dive.

## SIDEWALK CAFE & BAR
**94 Ave A (At 6th St.)
253-8080**

*ALL MAJOR CREDIT CARDS*

This quintessential East Village café/bar is a staple for all anti-Soho, non-conformist types. For the neighborhood locals, this grungy bar that serves cheap drinks is home. Take a walk into the back room for some live music, open mike night or a poetry reading. Down in the basement you'll find a lone pool table and next door there's the 24 hr. cafe where you can get a cheap meal while listening to Helmut or Guns

'N' Roses. There's a daily happy hour from 2pm-6pm (buy one, get one free).

### SIMONE
**134 1st Ave. (At St. Marks Pl.)**
**982-6665**

*ALL MAJOR CREDIT CARDS*

It's hard to believe that this place used to be a dirty, dreary dry cleaners. The beautiful Chinese decor with elegant crystal chandeliers creates the perfect mood for a first date. While jazz quietly fills the air, French waiters serve wine and espresso with a delicious array of sandwiches and desserts. Designed by the owner, the Eurasian setting has a black marble bar, classically-molded ceiling, and red Chinese wall paper. This cafe/bar is definitely worth a visit.

### S.J. SOUTH'S & SON
**273 Church St. (bet. White & Franklin Sts.)**
**219-0640**

*ALL MAJOR CREDIT CARDS*

This is as close to a real English pub as you can get without leaving TriBeCa and hopping on a Virgin flight to the former motherland. Equipped with a long wooden bar, a stained glass window in the rear, lots of seating, and a friendly bar staff, S.J. South's is a nice retreat from the lounge hells that are popping up all over the city. The food is typical English pub food, consisting of Welsh Rarebit, Shepard's Pie and Fish and Chips. The crowd is a laid-back, local group, and the vibe is just downright friendly.

### SKI BAR (CLOSED)
**1825 2nd Ave. (bet. 94th & 95th Sts.)**
**369-9635**

### SLAUGHTERED LAMB
**182 W. 4th St. (bet. 6th & 7th Aves.)**
**627-5262**

This bar caters to the tourists who meander along the west 4th strip and think it's a true glimpse into New York City life. Well, that couldn't be further from the truth. West 4th and all of its bars are only a poor representation of the city. That brings us to the Slaughtered Lamb, a supposed English tavern replete with yard long beers in many variations, animal heads hanging from the walls, and an overwhelming werewolf theme. The downstairs area is convincingly decorated as a dungeon. A menu of burgers, fries, etc. is served, but stick to the alcohol. Like all the other theme restaurants in NYC, Slaughtered Lamb caters to those who get a thrill out of the macabre. Stop by for a quick look-see, but don't make it your destination

## SMALLS
**183 10th Street (At 7th Avenue)**
**929-7565**

*CASH ONLY*

Located in an unsuspecting nook in the West Village, Smalls is home to a slew of jazz unknowns on the brink of success. Enter the basement through a steep flight of stairs to find Mitch Bordon, the doorman/janitor/owner/only employee. Offering the best deal in town, $10 will keep you swinging every night from 10pm to 8am. The mood is ultra-casual, cramped, and smoky. Although there is no actual bar (except for a free arrangement of juices and snacks), you are more than welcome to bring the liquor of your choice. Every night is a new, and equally impressive group. Mondays hosts the Jason Lindner Big Band, or check out the Omer Avital Group on Thursdays. Feel free to hoot and holler during a hot solo...that's the way it should be.

## SMITHS
**701 8th Ave. (At 44th St.)**
**246-3268**

*ALL MAJOR CREDIT CARDS*

This place has "David Lynch location shot" written all over it! Open since 1910, this New York institution (literally), with its half burned-out neon sign, is downright depressing. Harboring a bus station mosaic of patrons, it is here that you will find the answer to Paul MaCartney's heart-wrenching question from Eleanor Rigby, "All The Lonely People, Where Do They All Come From?" Now, the out-of-date bar is upsetting to the eye, but back in the early '20s it was probably considered "the place to be." It's the type of place where the bartender's friendliness and willingness to do shots with the patrons has probably thwarted a few sui-cides. Worth poking your head in for a snapshot of life in the slow lane, nothing more.

## THE SNUG
**450 Amsterdam Ave. (bet. 81st & 82nd Sts.)**
**595-5670**

*ALL MAJOR CREDIT CARDS*

It's snug, it's bright, and you probably won't be happy here if you've just quit smoking. The name of this joint could have aptly been called "The Slug", with its happy hour that lasts from dusk till dawn. It attracts drinking buffoons from 8am-7pm for $2 beers and $2.50 well drinks. There's a pool table, a rock-and-roll jukebox and a sports TV to keep the male/female ratio (9:1) entertained.

## SOLAS
**232 E. 9th St. (bet. 2nd & 3rd Aves.)**
**375-0297**

*ALL MAJOR CREDIT CARDS*

Home of the late Cafe Tabac, this swanky lounge packs in the 25 to 30-year-old crowd. Solas, Irish for "light," exhudes class and style. Certainly one of the better looking spots in the neighborhood, this chic, two-story lounge is drenched in 1930s style. With deco light sconces, copper-topped tables and velvet-draped windows overlooking 9th street, this is the perfect retreat for cozy groups to gather and have a drink. Lounge upstairs or in the tiny red room off the bar. With red fixtures, red couches, red walls and red curtains, you feel like you are indulging in the good life a la 1930s Paris. Solas boasts the best Guinness around and an entic-ing Mediterranean bar food menu. So grab a Guinness and an appetizer and take in the swank of Solas.

## SOUND FACTORY
**618 W. 46th St. (bet. 11ᵗʰ & 12th Aves.)**
**489-0001**

*CASH ONLY*

Defining the nightlife of NYC, The Sound Factory has remained quite the club icon for years now. Whether you're
gay, straight, goth, yuppie, guido or gender-confused, you
will be swept up in the sky high energy levels here.  DJs
spin hard, crowd-pleasing house music which shakes the
main dance floor, while Honey Dijon spins classics, hip-hop
and R&B in the basement.  On Friday nights, the doors
open at 11pm for those 18 and older.  Young club kids in
oversized phat pants wearing lots of Tommy and Adidas
show off their urban dance moves with abounding energy
and street style.  Saturday nights open at 11pm and stays
open until noon on Sunday.  The after hours evening attracts the 21 and older nocturnal insomniacs and crystal
methors working off angst, stress or are just too friggin'
lonely to call it a night.  There's a $20 cover and like most
clubs, drinks are undersized and overpriced.  Open Friday
and Saturday only.

## SOUNDS OF BRAZIL (SOB'S)
**204 Varick St. (bet. Housten & King)**
**243-4940**

*ALL MAJOR CREDIT CARDS*

This urban, Caribbean bar features bamboo and palm tree
decor with a full-on limbo party attitude.  This Latin American pickup spot hosts an array of musicians nightly.  Whether
it's samba or reggae that you dig, the place is loud and full
of energy. Try the pricey tropical and rum cocktails while
you are chowing down on conch fritters. Open daily from
7pm till 5am, the steep cover varies depending on the band.
Watch out for the enormously thick doormen. The place
gets pretty crowded with a rowdy bunch of bridge-and-
tunnellers who like to mambo the night away.

### SOHO KITCHEN & BAR
**103 Greene St. (bet. Prince & Spring Sts.)**
**925-1866**

*ALL MAJOR CREDIT CARDS*

It's almost impossible to have a bad time here. With a huge wrap-around bar, SoHo K&B is highly recommended for a good, all-around drinking and eating experience, especially with a group. Despite a tendency to draw an out-of-town element, this massive SoHo space offers one of the best beer and wine selections in the city (110 wines/ 40 beers) at moderate prices. Serving "flights" of wine, one can sample 5-6 different world class reds and whites from all regions. During the week, it's popular among the suits that come here after work. The vibe is energetic with a good music selection that you can lip-sync to.

### SOPHIE'S
**507 E. 5th St. (bet. Aves. A & B)**
**228-5680**

*CASH ONLY*

This small, smelly, smarmy, dark, dank, decrepit East Village institution has been around forever. Sophie's is always crowded with a non-specific, dirty crowd and the drinks, like the people, are cheap. There's not much to do here except get on the interminable line for the pool table. You may want to avoid the bathrooms—like a box of chocolates, you never know what you're going to find inside. The jukebox does have some of the best '70s punk classics mixed in with Frank Sinatra. This place will live on long after the cockroach is extinct.

### SPAGHETTI WESTERN
**59 Reade Street (bet. Church & B'way)**
**513-1333**

*ALL MAJOR CREDIT CARDS*

You have just entered the twilight zone. This is where you go after serving a rough day of jury duty to hang with people who look like they walked off the set of "Night of the Living Dead." The ambiance is kind of depressing and the décor is made up of Sergio Leone posters (for the under 30 crowd that's Clint Eastwood's first movies), and a scary looking bar area. However, the drinks are cheap, the sound system is surprisingly top notch and the food is pretty good. They usually close before midnight, but it's a blessing in disguise— after the municipal nightmare you're bound to experience, you'll be ready to hit the road.

## SPEEED
**20 W. 39th St. (bet. 6th & 7th Aves.)**
**719-9867**

*CASH ONLY*

Speeed is as bad as Sandra Bullock's sequel. After a $20 cover charge at the door, you're greeted by a sea of guys wearing khaki Dockers and women wearing the latest Express fashions. The bulk of the crowd is bridge-and-tunnel with a mix of vacationers who heard about the club through their hotel's concierge. The first floor of this triplex houses a coat check and a small smoky lounge where preppy guys and girls dance in place to a techno beat. The energy in this lounge is very low and people walk in and out of the room with a look of confusion. The next floor down contains a larger lounge area with two bars, a stage, some seating and some pillows thrown together on the floor which creates an Egyptian vibe. The DJs turn this lounge into a sea of disco dancing Gap kids. Finally, after descending a final set of poorly lit stairs, you enter the basement where the techno is pumping, the smoke machines are smoking, and the lights are flashing. Here is where your bridge-and-tunnelers let loose and bust their latest dance moves. As expected, drinks are overpriced—a B52 is $9 while a martini is $10. Available by the bottle are Absolut and Dewars for $200, and Hennessey for $250. And for you beer drinkers, plan on shelling out a good $7 to $8 for a bottle of beer. This place is generic and boring and is in no way a good representation of a real NYC club scene.

## THE SPIKE
**120 11th Ave. (At 20th St.)**
**243-9688**

*CASH ONLY*

A New York City landmark, this is probably one of the most famous gay leather bars on the face of the planet. Big hairy men and bikers with tattoos, piercings, Levis and flannel shirts flirt with the tourists who love them. This is the home of the "Famous Mr. New York City Bear Contest." There are pool tournaments, raffle ticket drawings and a happy hour making this the place to meet a big rough-and-tough man. Not for the faint of heart. $5 cover on Fri. and Sat. after 11pm.

## SPIRAL
**244 E. Houston St. (At Norfolk St.)**
**353-1740**

*CASH ONLY*

This live music venue has been around since 1989, hosting everything from rap to rock-and-roll bands. With two pinball machines, hanging Christmas lights, framed, undecipherable black-and-white photos, and two televisions over the bar, this dive bar attracts an alternative, young, East Village crowd. With an occasional charge of $5 (depending on the performance), the long bar and stage area is packed with live music lovers. An incredible happy hour turns this venue into a late night stomping ground for the heavy drinkers. 2-for-1 drinks begins at 2am and ends at 4am on Friday and Sunday! Otherwise drinks are cheap: $3 for a beer and $4 for a mixed drink.

## SPLASH
**50 W. 17th St. (bet. 5ᵗʰ & 6th Aves.)**
**691-0073**

*CASH ONLY*

Hot and sweaty, this club is pumping with a DJ's grooves and bare-chested men working it on the dance floor. The huge round bar in the front gives way to a large and jumping dance floor in the back and a downstairs lounge. With go-go dancers after 10pm and pornos playing above, this place gets packed with cruisy, hot men. A definite meat-market! With cheap drinks and no cover charge, this energy-filled club will keep you dancing all night long.

## SPOON (CLOSED)
12 Ave. A  (1st/2nd St.)
477-9050

## SPRING LOUNGE
48 Spring St. (At Mulberry St.)
965-1774

*CASH ONLY*

This local Little Italy pub with a stuffed shark over the bar is home to an older and laid-back local crowd. A bit out of place for this newly hip area, Spring Lounge manages to retain a feel for the neighborhood culture. The bar is never really crowded during the week, but on a Friday night, you'll be hard-pressed to get a seat. It's a nice respite but the drinks are not as cheap as you might expect.

## SPY
101 Greene St. (bet. Spring & Prince Sts.)
343-9000

*ALL MAJOR CREDIT CARDS*

Warm, velvety and huge, Spy is fashionable and sexy, so dress to impress. This two- level ultra-lounge is Renaissance-like and offers many nooks for a rendezvous. Spy is so spread out that they have "jumelles" (giant binoculars) on the top floor to do some serious "Spy"ing. Drinking cognac is encouraged in the cigar lounge and you might as well try the caviar while you're there. With enormous chandeliers and high ceilings, it looks straight out of the 18th Century. Though the space itself is worth the trip, Spy could have the most obnoxious door policy in the city.

## STANDARD
### 158 1st Ave. (bet. 9th & 10th Sts. )
### 387-0239

Along a street of bodegas and junky-looking thrift stores, the crisp, frosted glass windows of Standard looks out of place. If ever a bar was to appeal to the "Sprockets" from Saturday Night Live, Standard gets the medal with its extremely minimalist, modern European décor. With a smattering of plastic, low-back bar stools and not a thing on the wall to distract your eye, it takes a few minutes to figure out whether you can get comfortable here. A tiny illuminated bar serves the basics (no beer on tap) to a crowd that is made up of East Villagers dressed in SoHo gear. If nothing else, the bartenders are extremely friendly and will chat you up if you're bored.

## STANDARD NOTIONS
### 161 Ludlow St. (At Stanton St.)
### 473-3535

*CASH ONLY*

This place looks a little out of place on the hip Ludlow Street strip. This basic pub-style bar offers interesting food combinations, drink specials and lots of seating. Your world will not be rocked by its vibe, but it's a satisfactory local spot with a mixed crowd. There's a garden in back and plenty of seating in the front (a rarity for this area). Come by any weekday and there's a happy hour from midnight to 3am.

## STARLIGHT BAR & LOUNGE
### 167 Avenue A (bet. 10th & 11th Sts.)
### 475-2172

Formerly Velvet, Starlight is one of the newest gay bars to sprout up in the East Village. This very smart looking bar caters to a mellow, 25 to 35-year-old gay crowd. Low flickering candles illuminate tables and booths in the front of the bar while twisted metal chandeliers pours a dim red light from above. In the back, one can lounge in a very sexy atmosphere on comfy couches. With nine beers on tap, a mixed drink will run you about $5 while beer costs about $4-5. Live DJs and performances occur nightly. Raven O performs weekly while Sunday night is lesbian night. Open daily from 9pm to 4am, Starlight is a nice addition to the neighborhood.

## ST. MARK'S ALE HOUSE
**2 St. Mark's Pl. (bet. 2nd & 3rd Aves.)**
**260-9762**

*ALL MAJOR CREDIT CARDS*

With sports on TVs and college students drinking discounted drinks, the St. Mark's Ale House is a friendly watering hole that serves a good selection of beer with cheap eats. 2 for 1 pasta is offered Monday through Friday from 12pm - 5pm along with buffalo wings and burgers. The comfortable wood-panelled saloon and beautiful old-fashioned bar offers a $2 pint, well drinks and a happy hour Monday - Friday from 5pm -7pm. With 24 beers on tap and a very comfortable setting, St. Mark's Ale House will make you feel at home.

## ST. MARK'S BAR (CLOSED)
**132 1st Ave. (at St. Marks Pl.)**
**505-0290**

## STONEWALL
**53 Christopher St. (At 7th Ave. S.)**
**463-0950**

*CASH ONLY*

On the site of the original Stonewall riots, this place is trying its best, and we wish them luck. Give it a try and relive the nostalgia of victory. The place is your basic pub-style bar with an upstairs dance floor. Happy hour is Mon.-Fri. from 2:30pm-9pm. There's Bingo on Monday nights and a comedy mike on Thursday.

**SUBWAY INN**
**143 E. 60th St. (At Lexington Ave.)**
**223-8929**

*CASH ONLY*

Open for over 65 years, the Subway Bar is one of the first establishments in New York to get a liquor license after Prohibition. It's also probably the last time it had been re-decorated. When you walk inside past the huge neon "BAR" sign you'll feel like you're in every film ever made about a seedy New York bar. It is dark and gloomy with red lights illuminating the liquor bottles. Drinks are cheap at $2.50 for domestic bottles and $1 drafts during the day. Open from 8am to 4am (Sunday's open at noon), the Subway gets one of the most diverse crowds in midtown. You'll find yuppie traders sharing a Bud next to bookseller, and they'll both be across from the Scandinavian couple sucking down $6 Margaritas. After midnight, the place fills up with local restaurant staff from all the upscale digs in the area. The bar staff is seasoned and friendly and the jukebox offers a usual selection of classic rock, Indie crossover hits and a little Billie Holiday for good measure. Don't expect to get picked up—this is where you come to drink.

**SUSPENDERS**
**111 B'way (At Wall St.)**
**732-5005**

*ALL MAJOR CREDIT CARDS*

They say you can never go home again, but this Wall Street bar comes pretty close. From the large spacious drinking area to the stained glass windows that adorn the walls, Suspenders feels more like a local neighborhood haunt than a pit stop in the heart of the financial district. The bartenders never seem to change, the food is pretty consistent and the staff is always friendly. With all of these qualities it's no wonder it has gained such a loyal (mostly male) following. P.S., it's located underground, next to the subway station.

## SUTTON PLACE
**1015 2nd Ave. (bet. 53rd & 54th Sts.)**
**207-3777**

### ALL MAJOR CREDIT CARDS

Looking for a spot in midtown to get an overpriced drink, watch some sports on many large screen TVs and hang out with a homogenous Banana Republic crowd? You've found it! The décor is clean and personality-free and the crowd is about as interesting as a soggy bowl of Rice Crispies. If you just moved to New York, this is a safe place to make a painless transition to NY nightlife. There is an upstairs lounge, plenty of standing room and it's full of twentysomething Wall Street types bragging about their last bonus checks.

## SWAY
**305 Spring St. (bet. Greenwich & Washington Sts.)**
**620-5220**

### ALL MAJOR CREDIT CARDS

"I would rather go two hours out of my way to visit the largest ball of twine than wait five minutes to get into Sway," remarked one agitated survivor of Sway—the new, hip, in-the-know celebrity hangout. Owned by Nur Khan, the former owner of Wax, this Moroccan-esque hot spot is nothing special on the inside—with velvet couches and lounge lighting, Sway is more like a bad takeoff of Chez Es Saada with no food. So what's all the hype about? One can only assume that this overcrowded, pricey, attitude-laden bar has some very good PR people because there is no reason why this place should be filled. If the bouncer and unnecessary guest list don't "sway" you from coming in, maybe the self-important people waiting outside with you will.

## SWEET AND VICIOUS
**5 Spring St. (bet. B'way & Elizabeth St.)**
**334-7915**

Unpretentious, simple and tastefully designed, this accommodating, simple and tastefully designed space is a new favorite for many. The burnt orange walls, exposed brick, silver doors, dark wood benches and dim mosque-like lighting complement each other to create a unique bar experience. Lay your eyes on the steel butterflies that fly behind the bar while you order their delightful and powerful signature drink, Yeni Raki (Turkish liquor), served with water on the side. Tamara and Hakan, the owners, have been blessed with good fortune from "Sweet" and "Vicious," Tamara's cats who inspired the name. A beautiful 700' garden in the back makes this a great pick for summer drinking.

## SWEET MELISSA'S (CLOSED)
**1629 2nd Ave. (84th/85th St.)**
**639-1630**

## SWIFT HIBERNIAN LOUNGE
**34 E. 4th St. (bet. Bowery & Lafayette)**
**227-9438**

***ALL MAJOR CREDIT CARDS***

From the outside, this bar looks like an old English pub. On the inside, it feels more like the castle that Robinhood stormed with his merry men. The heavy wooden decor is accentuated by a large stained glass window and mission-style benches. There is a large candle chandelier that cries for someone to swing from it. A DJ keeps a steady stream of cool acid jazz flowing throughout the bar while NYU types and Wall Street yuppies alike swill one of the many beers and ales from the vast selection. When all is said and done, Swift is a good-looking bar that is worth checking out.

## SWINE ON NINE
**693 9th Ave. (At 48th St.)**
**397-8356**

What do Donald Trump, Mother Theresa and Luciano Pavoratti have in common? Nothing, except that you will never see any of them at this trailer park/bus station of a bar in the heart of Hell's Kitchen. If you're looking for $1 beers, cheap, hard drinks, Patsy Cline blaring on the jukebox, 20 teeth for every 5 people and a giant pig in front of the bar, your mothership has landed. It looks scarier than it is, but don't come here dressed in your Gucci looking for Mr. Destiny—you might just end up with Senor Syphallis.

## SWIM
**146 Orchard St. (bet. Rivington & Stanton Sts.)**
**673-0799**

*ALL MAJOR CREDIT CARDS*

Boys and girls, grab your fishing gear because we're going fishing for a mate. Once you get by the hulking doorman, be prepared for the Lower East Side's pickup bar of the century. This small, two-story sushi bar with a small bar downstairs and a sushi bar upstairs, is packed with young twenty-ish bridge-and-tunnelers working the room. Pounding dance music that could possibly break the sound barrier makes having a conversation nearly impossible. Although the drinks are pricey, the sushi is pretty reasonable and it's the only sushi available in the neighborhood at 2am. It's young, it's crowded and it's cheesy, but hook line and sinker, there are a lot of fish in the sea...or at least there are at Swim.

## SYDNEY B
**202 9th Ave. (bet. 23rd & 22 Sts.)**
**989-2002**

*ALL MAJOR CREDIT CARDS*

A new addition to 9th Avenue and formally known as August, this beautiful, spacious, bar/restaurant draws an upscale, gay/straight crowd who feast on Kumomoto oysters and little necks at the raw bar. Excellent wines, extensive single malts, great bourbons, and awesome Cosmopolitans are served by the knowledgeable and amicable bartender, Emilio. Try the Crescent City Crab Cakes ($7) or Fresh

Calamari ($8), the Morilleau Muscadet ($6) or the Penfolds Semillion Chardonnay ($6), and enjoy the art in the bar's revolving gallery space while you work up your appetite for one of the amazing entrees ($10-$20).

## SYSTEM (CLOSED)
### 76 E. 13th St. (bet. B'way & 4th Ave.)

## 2A
### 27 Ave. A (At 2nd St.)
### No Phone

*CASH ONLY*

This popular, split-level East Village scene offers the best of both worlds. Downstairs, you'll find your basic bar packed with East Village locals. Upstairs, you'll find a more intimate lounge and second bar with the usual fare of comfortable flea market couches and candlelight. Either way, the two-story wall of windows makes this a perfect perch for people watching or grabbing an after-dinner drink with a date.

## 288 BAR (TOM & JERRY'S)
### 288 Elizabeth St. (bet. Houston & Bleecker)
### No Phone

*CASH ONLY*

Tucked away on an unassuming side street in NoHo, you'll find 288, often referred to as "Tom & Jerry's" due to their large collection of porcelain dinnerware that dons that name. This cavernous space could easily have the best bartenders in the city-they're fast, attentive and mix great drinks. Managing to thrive as a local institution without being too trendy, this neighborhood bar gets high marks not only for the refreshingly unpretentious, young and laid-back crowd that it attracts, but also for the rotating local art displayed on the back wall. The jukebox is a crowd-pleaser with everything from the theme from "Shaft" to Liz Phair. If you can score a table, it's a great place to hang out with a group. This is the best all around bar in NYC.

**2I'S**
**248 W. 14th St. (bet. 7th & 8th Aves.)**
**807-1775**

*ALL MAJOR CREDIT CARDS*

Right next door to Nell's, this after-hours bar/dance club draws a young hip-hop crowd and really packs them in after midnight. The long sleek bar at the entrance illuminates bottles of alcohol like magical elixirs that are furiously grabbed, tossed and mixed by sexy bartenders who refuse to smile. Wall-to-wall couches surround a crowded dance floor in the back where a DJ spins everything from acid jazz to old-school. Downstairs there is a smaller bar/lounge area with comfy seating for a mellow, semi-romantic escape. Cover depends on the night, so call ahead.

**TAPAS LOUNGE**
**1078 1st Ave. (At 59th St.)**
**421-8282**

*ALL MAJOR CREDIT CARDS*

Tapas was introduced to the New York pop culture a few years back, but it seems their popularity hasn't quite reached its apex. There are little Spanish snack bars opening all over the place, but this is the only one located on the culturally deprived Upper East Side. Open till 3am, Tapas Lounge is a refreshing change from the standard 1st and 2nd Avenue frat bars. The dim, sexy lighting evokes a calm and sultry mood. Come here when you need a change and try some of the interesting, delicious, and inexpensive treats.

**TAPIKA**
**950 8th Ave. (At 56th St.)**
**397-3737**
*ALL MAJOR CREDIT CARDS*

Perfect for the semi-grown-up, after work crowd, Tapika (from the latino word piquante, meaning "a little spicy") is a sufficiently civilized, fun place to cocktail. With its attractive, simple décor, good lighting and rust-colored walls, it has enough atmosphere to make you want to behave yourself, which you won't after downing a few of the delish drinks. Confidently situated in a quiet corner of midtown for the past four years, this sort-of but-not-really southwestern bar/restaurant stocks 34 tequilas and some mighty fine margaritas. You can smoke at the bar (cigar friendly) and keep yourself out of trouble by ordering off the bar menu...why else is it there? Good for bringing casual clients or a group of friends, it's also nice enough for a pre-date drink.

## TAP ROOM
**3 W. 18th (bet. 5th & 6th Aves.)**
**691-7666**

**ALL MAJOR CREDIT CARDS**

Formerly Zip City, the Tap Room offers a nice range of home-brewed, Austrian-style beers on tap as well as some seasonal brews. The beer is tasty and served in extra large glasses in an atmosphere which looks like the offspring of Sweden and a Ski Lodge. The bar is large and comfortable, but when it gets crowded, don't even think about finding a place to plant it. The somewhat unaccommodating wait staff makes it clear that if you are not going to eat, you are not going to get a table no matter how empty the place is.

## TATOU
**151 E. 50th St. (bet. Lex. & 3rd Aves.)**
**753-1144**

**ALL MAJOR CREDIT CARDS**

This uptown supper club attracts New Yorkers who have money and want to spend it. With a $20 cover at the door, you can dance the night away (until 4am) while ringing out your wallet on expensive drinks and cigars. The decor is decadent and English with plush reds, antique chandeliers and a theatrical, dimly-lit dining room. The dance floor is huge and packs it in with an older crowd who boogie down to '70s disco while tacky-looking chicks with dyed blonde hair and animal print outfits scour the club for a sugar daddy. If you are a bit younger and have a yearning for a Bar Mitzvah-esque party, venture upstairs to the lounge/bar where bad disco pumps and the decor is loud and tacky. Either way, this place is a scene with money. (Not to be confused with a scene with style.)

**TAVERN ON JANE**
**31 8th Ave. (At Jane St.)**
**675-2526**
*ALL MAJOR CREDIT CARDS*

For the more refined and reserved, the Jane Street Tavern is a place where the "easy listening" crowd can feel at home- a place where the only conflict that will cause a stir is whether to play the Steely Dan or the Christopher Cross CD first. This West Village eatery has a fuzzy welcome home feeling about it with its attentive service that lets you doodle with crayons on the table as long as you like. Though there's not as good of a beer selection as one might expect from a place that calls itself a tavern, it's a great place to sit and relax and view some of the better bar photography that New York has to offer.

**TELEPHONE BAR & GRILL**
**149 2nd Ave. (bet. 9th & 10th Sts.)**
**529-5000**
*ALL MAJOR CREDIT CARDS*

This English-inspired bar has been a popular draw in the East Village for 10 years and it is still going strong. The space is large and comfortable with a comfy back room that looks like it's out of an old castle in the English country side. In front are four London- imported, old-fashioned telephone booths. The food is fair and the service is attentive. The crowd changes from night to night but leans towards the cleaner, yuppie types. Though it's not an obvious pickup bar, it actually is.

## TEMPLE BAR
**332 Lafayette St. (bet. Bleecker & Houston)**
**925-4242**

*ALL MAJOR CREDIT CARDS*

Having an affair? Need a dark seductive lounge to discreetly maul a love interest? Temple Bar just might be your spot. This beautiful bar and lounge with its posh, romantic, art deco decor, is a great pick for a date. Free spicy popcorn keeps you ordering pricey and stiff cocktails for hours. This place has "let's go home and get busy" written all over it. Certainly one of New York's top lounging experiences.

## TENTH STREET LOUNGE
**212 E. 10th St. (bet. 1st & 2nd Aves.)**
**473-5252**

*ALL MAJOR CREDIT CARDS*

We'll say it again...10 dollar cover? You have got to be kidding. If you got rid of the entire staff, this place would actually have hope. Visually, the large space is impressive with a beautiful collection of mission-style furniture, romantic candles, and comfortable seating. All the hard work they put into this place, however, is negated by the lousy bartenders, annoying bouncers and bitchy hosts. $10 to hang out with a crowd that has about as much soul as a tub of Cool Whip? I don't think so.

## TERRA BLUES
**149 Bleecker St. (bet. Thompson & Laguardia)**
**777-7776**

*ALL MAJOR CREDIT CARDS*

This small music club serves as a beacon of hope among the often offensive, loud, NYU and Jersey-filled musical spots that line Bleecker street. Small, candlelit tables packed with the young and intellectual make for an intimate setting to watch live music. Be sure to check out the "Niagara's" on Tuesday nights and there's no cover if you are in the doors before 10pm.

**THIRD AND LONG NYC CORNER SALOON**
**523 3rd Ave. (At 35th St.)**
**447-5711**

*ALL MAJOR CREDIT CARDS*

Perhaps the only feature of this bar that draws crowds is its convenient east midtown location and the Thursday and Friday $2-$3 pints from 4pm-7pm. Other than that there is not much to say about this local corner bar. A few stools, a jukebox, and alcoholic beverages, just about sums it up. The crowd is friendly and generally just happy to be finished with the work day.

**THIRTEEN**
**35 E. 13th St. (At University Pl.)**
**979-6677**

*ALL MAJOR CREDIT CARDS*

This tiny dance club off the beaten Union Square path is a hip little spot to drink and dance the night away. Young and decked-out twentysomethings lounge on comfy seating watching others shake their groove thang under tiny flashing lights. The mood changes nightly so call ahead for details. Don't miss the outdoor roof parties that start up in the spring.

**TIME CAFÉ**
**87 7th Ave. S. (At Barrow St.)**
**220-9100**

*ALL MAJOR CREDIT CARDS*

This bar/restaurant is more popular for its brunch than anything else, but they do sport an outside bar/dining area on the roof with great tables, umbrellas and a nice breeze. The bloody marys are excellent, tangy and spicy. The bar downstairs is calm, tranquil and offers single malt scotches, blended drinks, delicious coffee and a great selection of wines. Time Cafe has a young mixed crowd coming from the West Village and Chelsea and is especially popular with NYU students. The staff is cute but without the usual attitude, and service always comes with a smile. A great place to drink outdoors with great American fare.

## TIN LIZZIES
**1647 2nd Ave. (bet. 85th & 86th Sts.)**
**288-7983**

### *ALL MAJOR CREDIT CARDS*

Tin Lizzies debut in January '98 consisted of a slightly older, Sweet Melissa's crowd (aka frat boys). The owners, who also own the now ex-Sweet Melissa's and several other Upper East Side watering holes, are touting it as a classier spot with no frat hats or sneakers allowed. Supposedly, the dress code is strictly enforced and the "undesirables" are turned away at the door. Music is R&B only to go along with the cigar smoking, lounge-lizard crowd they hope to attract. The back bar serves higher-end beverages, including single malt scotches and ports.

## TOAD HALL
**57 Grand St. (bet. W. B'way & Wooster)**
**431-8145**

### *ALL MAJOR CREDIT CARDS*

Toad Hall has a friendly pub-like feel that caters to a relaxed and predominantly male, mid-thirties crowd. The smoky and dark bar sports a pool table and is low on beautiful people. A killer bar mix is served which puts Chex mix to shame. The always-blaring jukebox and television provide for an interesting mix of sports set to James Brown. If you are looking for more of a scene, check out the better-looking crowd at Lucky Strike, right next door.

## TOOL BOX
**1742 2nd Ave. (bet. 90th & 91st Sts.)**
**348-1288**

### *CASH ONLY*

Thrown in between throngs of testosterone-filled frat bars sits one of the only gay bars on the Upper East Side. This

269

tiny, dark and gloomy bar draws in an older, gay crowd. With a pool table and gay pornos playing on the television sets, there is never a cover charge. Open for two years, Tool Box was originally located on 91st Street. As its name suggests, the testosterone level here is as high as the neighboring frat bars though in a slightly different way. Wed. - Sat. nights hosts infamous Go-Go boy nights. Dancing Go-Go starlets keep the Tool Box drinking till 4am nightly. A great happy hour pours up super cheap drinks daily from 8pm to 11pm. Those of you who are over the tired Chelsea scene, take a ride up to the Tool Box to see how the other side lives.

## TORCH
**137 Ludlow St. (bet. Stanton & Rivington)**
**228-5151**

*ALL MAJOR CREDIT CARDS*

Cool and hipper than hell-in-a-handbasket, Torch is without question the best bar/restaurant on Ludlow Street. With its cool modern art deco flavor, live cabaret, and attentive, unpretentious staff, it is not one of the usual suspects found on the Lower East Side. A good place to meet friends and an even better place to bring a date, book a dinner reservation in advance and take in the soothing sounds of "The Girl From Ipanema." A separate raw bar in a snug velvet nook offers lounging/snacking opportunities if you're not up for the full meal. Torch has become a scene on the weekends, so the earlier you get there, the better.

## TORTILLA FLATS
**767 Washington St. (At 12th St.)**
**243-1053**

*ALL MAJOR CREDIT CARDS*

Bring your piñatas, Ernest Borgnine T-shirts and velvet Elvis posters to this happenin' Mexican margarita party in the West Village. Always crowded, this place hosts Monday night bingo, hula-hoop contests and egg tosses. There's always a birthday party going on which makes it loads of fun if you are with the right people. Keep your eye out for models and celebrities who pop in for a drink after the photo shoots next door. Weekends pack it in with the out-of-town scene, but all in all it's a blast! Best in the spring and summer when the outdoor tables emerge. Happy hour on Friday and Saturday from 1am to 3am. During the week from 7pm to 9pm, take $5 off a pitcher of fantastic margaritas and pay a buck per tequila shot. Cuidado!

## TOWN HOUSE
**236 E. 58th St. (At 2nd Ave.)**
**754-4649**

*ALL MAJOR CREDIT CARDS*

This popular venue hosts a mix of distinguished gentleman and their younger, stylish admirers. The front bar, best right after work, hosts a better suit selection than Barney's. Step through the vestibule to the piano bar and experience the joyful warbling of the gay Wall Street set. You might not recognize them, but they have more money than god and probably designed your sheets. Cruise around the club room downstairs and do not forget to put on your best threads-they have a dress code.

## TRAMPS
**51 W. 21st St. (bet. 5th & 6th Aves.)**
**633-9570**

*ALL MAJOR CREDIT CARDS*

Tramps, the long-standing live music bar, is the epitome of the complete, no-frills music bar. Known for packing in huge crowds to see everything from G. Love and Special Sauce to Willie Nelson, Tramps consists of one large square room divided into three areas of activity. In front of the stage are dozens of square wooden tables, directly behind there lies a dance area, and finally, behind that, a long wooden bar. Beers are slightly more expensive than your typical dive-an Amstel, for example, is $6. The crowd is usually a reflection of the headlining musical act.

**TRIAD**
**158 W. 72nd St. (bet. Columbus & B'way)**
**362-2590**

*ALL MAJOR CREDIT CARDS*

This tiny jazz/blues/performance space is a nice venue for the Upper West Side, 35+ crowd. A $5 cover is well worth it on almost any night of the week where some of the city's top acts come to groove. Teeming with New York jazz fans, the simple space has a bar in the front and an intimate performance space in the back. Call ahead for performance information.

**TRIBE**
**132 1st Ave. (At St. Marks Place)**
**979-8965**

*ALL MAJOR CREDIT CARDS*

Can we have a few seconds of silence to pay tribute to the demise of the 24-year-old infamous St. Marks Bar? NO WE CAN'T. Why? Because what has taken over this chunk of history is now an annoyingly loud, loud, loud and cheesy bar called Tribe. Show your ID to the doorman and then enter the horror show of screaming drunk, jappy girls, pricey drinks and pretentiously boring DJ-spun '70s tunes. Drink your $6 shelf cocktail while listening to the deafening mix of Dolly Parton/Kansas/Coolio. Huh? If the Stones were dead they would be rolling in their graves. (St. Marks bar was the location of the Stone's "Waiting For A Friend" video.) Your only escape is to stare at the ever-changing opaque lights adorning the back of the bar-a perfect way to tune out the tribespeople. Open from 10:30pm till 4:30am, there are 5 beers on tap, $7 martinis and $5 beers. It's sad but true Dorothy, we're not in the East Village anymore.

**TRILOGY**
**1403 2nd Ave. (At 73rd St.)**
**794-1870**

*ALL MAJOR CREDIT CARDS*

Certainly one of the better looking spots in this part of town, Trilogy seems to try very hard to be hip with its dim lighting, clean rustic decor and exposed brick walls. Though we'll give them points for trying, this is still a frat bar no matter how you slice it. There is a pool table in the back, ample seating, and a 10 to 1 male to female ratio. The door person is very strict checking IDs, so come prepared. Basic food is available and it's good.

**TUNNEL**
**220 12th Ave. (At 27th St.)**
**695-4682**

*CASH ONLY*

Thank god New Yorkers have Peter Gatien in our city! After 12 years, the Tunnel still kicks ass! It's hot and pumping music, colorful people and amazing energy that will keep you up for days, makes the $20 cover well worth it. Once inside, you enter a maze of creatively designed lounges and steamy dance floors packed with a mix of young bridge-and-tunnelers, gay men, transvestites, '80s throw-backs and ultra hip ravers. Three floors, nine different sound systems, eleven bars, a tarot card reader, a coffee bar, candy concession stands and message boards create the perfect haven for the fickle. The main dance floor is cavernous and filled with dry ice smoke, strobe lights, and a mosh of people pulsating to Junior Vasquez's delightful mix of house and techno. Young Brooklynites and ravers create breakdance circles and battle each other to prove their talent. If you are lucky, you will be invited downstairs to "Kerfew" where the energy pumps until noon the next morning! You can visit the hunting lounge where progressive house music vibrates while the chic sit at tables behind sheer black curtains. The most fabulous site in the club is in the Kenny Scharf room-the most expensive club-room ever made. It has bubbling fountains, fur-covered walls, glowing algae on the ceiling and waves painted on the floors. With '80s disco, dancing go-go boys, transvestites and shirtless homeboys, it takes you back to the old days. With rap, house, techno, pop, disco, hip-hop, '70s and '80s disco, there is something for everyone at this virtual Disneyland of clubs. Hats off to Gatien for creating what NYC is known for: Truly remarkable nightlife.

**TURTLE BAY**
**987 2nd Ave. (bet. 52nd & 53rd Sts.)**
**223-4224**

*ALL MAJOR CREDIT CARDS*

Established in early 1997, this crowded hangout offers a suit-clad scene during the week and a preppy pickup spot on weekends. Live music plays in the spacious rustic-style lounge upstairs on Tuesdays and Wednesdays, while a disc jockey provides background music to the rest of the bar for those interested in sitting back with chums. Serving food and reasonably priced drinks, this is a good place for after-work or late night. (They serve till 4am.) No matter when you decide to come, you will encounter a crowd of twentysomethings or singles in their early 30s. Cigar-friendly.

**TWIRL**
**201 W. 23rd St. (At 7th Ave.)**
**691-7685**

*ALL MAJOR CREDIT CARDS*

This is one of Chelsea's hippest and hottest gay clubs. Every night of the week is host to an array of hot, built Chelsea boys who love to dance. Mondays, see Hedda Lettuce and her friends for free. The theme Tues.-Thurs. nights varies, so call for info. Fridays, the doors open at 5pm with the incredible and hot Shana a Brazilian super drag diva, who works the runway with go-go boys dancing to the sounds of DJ David Martinez. Saturdays, the doors open at 7pm to let in a flood of go-go boys. Sundays finish the week with a bang as Shequida sings Arias at 10pm for free! This dance space has it all and it's women-friendly.

**TWO POTATO**
**143 Christopher St. (At Greenwich)**
**255-0286**

*CASH ONLY*

A very dark bar catering to an young, Afro-American crowd and their admirers. There are drink specials and wild drag shows. Stop in to see Monday Night Madness with the unequaled Harmonica Sunbeam and Sheila Noxema. Drinks are cheap and the music is pumping. No matter who you are, they are always glad to see you.

**277**
**277 Church St. (bet. Franklin & White Sts.)**
**625-0505**

*ALL MAJOR CREDIT CARDS*

This TriBeCa newcomer is a breath of fresh air in this over-yuppified part of town. Best known for the upstairs restaurant, 277 offers some of the tastiest and most inventive food of 1999, dished up by Delroy Bowen from the Tribeca Grill. After your feast, treat yourself to a drink in the cool and simple lounge right below which is adorned with sleek seating and serpentine-illuminated drink tables. The crowd is hip, trendy and beautiful so dress the part if you want to get in.

**TY'S**
**114 Christopher St. (At Bleecker St.)**
**741-9641**

*CASH ONLY*

Friendly neighborhood gay bar/saloon where you'll fit right in if you are wearing a flannel shirt and have a moustache. This die-hard neighborhood bar caters to a Levis wearin', beer drinkin' crowd. Happy hour lasts for six hours, from 4-10pm Mon.-Fri. Wednesday is "uniform & leather" night, so put on your best, saddle on up and head on over for god knows what. If you didn't know any better, you'd think the crowd wanted to beat you up. Don't worry, that look in their eyes is lust.

**TYPHOON BREWERY**
**22 E. 54th St. (bet. Mad. & 5th Aves.)**
**754-9006**
*ALL MAJOR CREDIT CARDS*

Like most of the big breweries in Manhattan, the decor and feel here is nothing that you have not seen before. Its comfortable/minimalist style, with wooden seating and large copper casks of beer in view, is inviting with an inescapable Colorado Mall feel. After work, it tends to draw a typhoon of yuppie suits. The weekend evenings may remind you of the waiting room in a funeral home so don't bring your drunk posse here. All said and done, the beer is excellent and the food ain't bad either-it's just in a weird part of town.

## UNION BAR
**204 Park Ave. So. (bet. 16th & 17th Sts.)**
**674-2105**

*ALL MAJOR CREDIT CARDS*

With its clean and sleek wrap-around bar and modern aluminum and wood decor, the Union Bar is one of the better bar scenes on the Park Avenue South strip. Catering to young Wall Streeters, trendoids, and Jersey Folk on the weekend, the crowd is predominantly male and on the prowl. If you are looking for something trendy and slick looking, Union might be your best bet. Bartenders sport heavy 'tude but you can't really blame them when you see the patrons that they deal with. Girls, plan on feeling much like a piece of steak when entering this establishment. Thursday nights is a meat-market comprised of some of New York's horniest Wall Street singles. During the weekend the Jersey folk stake their claim. Come for the beer and the gourmet pizza.

## VAIN (CLOSED)
**9 Ave. A (bet. 1st & 2nd Sts.)**
**253-1462**

## VANDAM
**150 Varick St. (At Vandam St.)**
**352-9090**

*ALL MAJOR CREDIT CARDS*

Is it medically safe for a girl who weighs less than 90 pounds to have a 36C chest? Why yes, according to the desired physical standards embraced at Vandam., not only is it normal, it's downright encouraged! Brace yourself for star-tac phones, fake boobs, air kisses, Portofino tans and men who still think it's cool to wear sunglasses at night. Vandam is the place where god's gifts to the world come to compare themselves to a backdrop of models, actors and music execs. Although the food is quite good, most patrons don't even notice because they're either too busy checking each other out, staring at themselves in any reflective surface they can find, or obsessing about their anorexia. The actaul bar area in on the small side and can be uncomfortably jammed, but if you're lucky (or know someone, rather) you can score one of those "that's total bullshit that it's reserved!" tables off to the side. If you're looking for a good-looking but painfully shallow LA scene, the buck stops here. Drinks are pricey but worth it and although the crowd can shake your confidemce it makes for a nice late dinner spot.

## VANITY
**28 E. 23rd St. (bet. B'way and Park Ave. S.)**
**254-6117**

*ALL MAJOR CREDIT CARDS*

Looking for a place that's loud, attracts men in gold chains and muscle tees, and full of people dancing to a 35-minute version of "What is Love? (Baby Don't Hurt Me)"? Try Vanity! This two-floor version of a club is as bridge-and-tunnel as they come. The first floor consists of a small loung-like room with comfortable modern chairs and couches, but the true beauty of this venue is the second floor where the DJ spins early '90s favorites to a cramped, loud dance floor full of eager and horny patrons looking to score. Bring your hairspray, your fake Gucci shoes and hand over $10 to enter a guido meat-market from hell.

## VELVET LOUNGE
**223 Mulberry St. (bet. Prince & Spring)**
**965-0439**

*ALL MAJOR CREDIT CARDS*

This prefab lounge/restaurant with overstuffed couches,

gilded mirrors and chessboards, tries hard to add a touch of hip to this former mafia strip in Little Italy. The theme changes nightly: On Sundays, classic movie lovers flock for screenings. On Wednesdays, a DJ spins hip-hop grooves upstairs (which, by the way, looks like your grandmother's living room). Other nights there are live bands. Decorated with smoky gold mirrors, red velvet screens, fresh flowers and antique Chinese rugs spread over hard wood floors, the mood is relaxing and cozy. Drinks are a bit expensive: $5-$6 for a beer and $6-$8 for a mixed drink. Call before making your way to the Velvet Room because hours vary. It closes early on slow nights.

## VELVET ROOM
**209 E. 76th St. (bet. 2nd & 3rd Aves.)**
**628-6633**

This Upper East Side wine bar desperately wants to be down-town. The velvet couches and upholstered walls and ceil-ings (is this place a fire hazard or what?) cry SoHo, but the older not-so-hip clientele remind you of your location. The tables are for food-eaters only and there isn't much room at the bar, so don't come by unless you want to dine. Serv-ing mainly tapas for around $8, some entrees for $12, wine, port, champagne and beer starting at $5, the Velvet Room is a good place to take your conservative relatives for a little "downtown" action without the cab fare. They will feel chic and love you for it.

## VENUE AND THE LAVA LOUNGE
**505 Columbus Ave. (bet. 84th & 85th Sts.)**
**579-9463**

*ALL MAJOR CREDIT CARDS*

Just as Kevin Bacon turned his lame-ass town into a frenzy of footloose dance freaks, Venue has introduced the idea of "dance" and "lounge" to the Upper West Side. This den of dark nooks is spacious with its multi-levels equipped with plush couches and pillow-covered surfaces. Three full bars serve mixed drinks that are pushing $9 a pop. Descend to the lower levels for the Lava Lounge and experience everything covered in velvet. Oil wheels slither on the walls along with neon paintings, a crop of lava lamps, and faux-fur walls. This, my friends, is texture at its best! A twinkling bed of lights illuminate the ceiling while guys and gals move to the beat. Though Venue tends to draw those who dwell in the area codes of 516, 201 and 914, the majority are city dwellers.

## THE VENUS ROOM
**1074 1st Ave. (bet. 58th & 59th Sts.)**
**207-3858**

*CASH ONLY*

A much-needed swanky cool lounge has recently popped up on the East Side to give midtown drinkers an alternative to "Cheese-Bar Row. The Venus Room offers a cozy atmosphere for sipping martinis, fancy cocktails or ice-cold beer while listening to classic jazz, blues and swing music. The Venus Room is a cool lounge without the pretense. Open 4-2am, Sun-Wed and 4pm-4am, Thursday - Saturday.

## VERMOUTH
**355 Amsterdam (At 77th St.)**
**724-3600**

*ALL MAJOR CREDIT CARDS*

Is it a bar? Is it a restaurant? It needs to decide, if only for space considerations. This Upper West Side establishment took over the old territory of Wildlife, but changed the decor drastically into a more subtle, darker lounge/restaurant. Although it is not quite the hormone-ridden pickup nirvana of its former tenant, there is still a sense of singles, slightly better dressed, looking for love (at least for the night). The narrow bar has difficulty accommodating those who have come to choose from the extensive martini and cocktail menu. A better bet is to come for dinner and sample the eclectic appetizers and get a table outside.

**VERUKA**
**525 Broome St. (bet. Thompson & 6th)**
**625-9561**

*ALL MAJOR CREDIT CARDS*

And on the 8th day, god created obnoxious, annoying , soul-less, rude and overpriced lounges...like Veruka. This two-floor lounge/restaurant is trying as hard as it can to be as swanky and star struck as Moomba, but just doesn't make it. (Although why would anyone want to piss off as many people as Moomba has?) The décor is simple and tastefully done with modern and casual furniture (same interior de-signer as Moomba) but the lousy attitude at the door and the rude managerial staff make this overpriced poser hell a no-go. The door policy is one of the most ruthless in NYC. Avoid it like the plague unless you want to be treated like shit and pay through the nose for it.

**VICEROY**
**160 8th Ave. (At 18th St.)**
**633-8484**

*ALL MAJOR CREDIT CARDS*

Conveniently located on a busy Chelsea corner, Viceroy is sure to please. A beautifully decorated deco bar and res-taurant with a friendly handsome staff draws a trendy, well-dressed, mixed gay/straight crowd of the martini-sipping genre. Sunday night, Viceroy hosts excellent live jazz acts starting at 9pm. Weekend brunch is a favorite in this re-laxed, elegant atmosphere especially with a delicious Bloody Mary or Lillet on the rocks.

**VICE VERSA**
**325 W. 51st St. (bet. 8th & 9th Ave.)**
**399-9291**

*ALL MAJOR CREDIT CARDS*

"Easy Breezy Cover Girl." That's how you'll feel as you step onto the front terrace and through the glass façade of ViceVersa-the fab, spanking-new bar/restaurant recently opened by Franco Lazzari and Daniele Kucera. Formerly of so very-very San Domenico and Jean Georges, the delightful duo brought chef Stefano Terzi in tow. Welcome to heaven all you pale, bitter, New Yorkers! The Milan-meets-L.A. atmosphere of this subtle, sexy joint will have you running around in white Prada and a tan in no time. And you'll be smiling, too, because although the décor is millennium chic (stainless steel bar, glass and slate, white walls, ebony floors), the vibe is warm and relaxed. This attitude-free zone boasts a selection of 65 wines and gorgeous cocktails perfectly mixed by an attractive, professional staff. Have a beer and still feel fancy as you move through the airy dining room to the adorable, glass-enclosed back terrace, complete with fashionable bamboo plantings, canvas umbrellas, and terra-cotta urns. Feel free to eat at the bar (cigar and cigarette friendly) with the civilized, diverse clientele. Equally suited for a romantic date or just drinks with friends, ViceVersa is definitely worth checking out.

## VICTORY CAFÉ
**1604 3rd Ave. (At 90th St.)**
**348-3650**

*ALL MAJOR CREDIT CARDS*

Victory is one of the very last of an unfortunately dying breed of old-fashioned local bars in New York City where the regulars know each other and the friendly bartenders know everyone's name. (Think "Cheers.") The inside of Victory is like a history book. You are greeted by the original "Victory Cafeteria" sign from the 1920s unearthed during the 1984 construction of this bar. The ceiling and floor tiles are the building's originals from approximately 100 years ago. Photos of the old neighborhood, from the collections of the owner and other regulars, cover the walls. At any given time during the day or night you will find an interesting, eclectic crowd of regulars conversing across the length of the classic wood bar. Most are enjoying the excellent food prepared by Victory's Culinary Institute chef that surpasses anything remotely referred to as bar food. The newest addition to this Yorkville legend is the live music offered on Saturday nights. Cross your fingers...some pretty famous musicians hang out here and have been known to be the

Saturday night surprise act.

## THE VIG BAR
**12 Spring Street (At Elizabeth St.)**
**625-0011**

*ALL MAJOR CREDIT CARDS*

Among the long list of trendy SoHo bars stands the Vig. Despite the lack of attitude at the door and the tacky velvet rope, this bar still mirrors most of the swanky lounges found in the area. The front room plays host to a bar and a few tables and chairs to sit in and look pretty. Follow the winding hall into the back lounge area that's dark and decorated in an art deco flair and full of tables and couches, prime for lounging. The music is quite eclectic-one minute you're humming along to a new age Hare Krishna tune and the next minute you're singing along to Puff Daddy's latest hit. Drink prices are a bit on the expensive side, but what do you expect, it's SoHo.

## VILLAGE IDIOT
**355 W. 14th St. (bet. 8th & 9th Aves.)**
**989-7334**

*CASH ONLY*

At last, a bar for those who long for those honky-tonk nights in Texas. Mosey on in to the Village Idiot, slap on some George Thoregood, and order up a $2 Lone Star or some Yukon Jack on tap. You can watch TNN on one TV, vintage beer commercials on another, or pay 25 cents to feed the "killer" turtles. But beware of the subterranean frat pick-up scene, partner.

## VILLAGE LANTERN
**167 Bleecker St. (bet. Thompson & Sullivan)**
**260-7993**

*ALL MAJOR CREDIT CARDS*

This restaurant/bar prides itself on its Italian chef straight from Capri, Italy. A generic Italian dinner is served nightly until 11pm at which point the place transforms into a bar/club nightmare. Owned by the proprietor of Dakota, this spot plays host to adolescent bridge-and-tunnel kids from upper middle class neighborhoods. Live music during the week evolves into DJ'd R&B music on the weekends. Claiming to be the pre-Life pit-stop for models, drinks are expensive and very, very weak and the only time you will see a model is in the drunken fantasy you will have later that night as you vomit your brains out on Bleecker St. This bar is definitely a meat-market for rejects from the club "Life," right across the street.

## VINTAGE
**753 9th Ave. (bet. 50th & 51st Sts.)**
**242-2666**

*ALL MAJOR CREDIT CARDS*

This fairly large and sparsely decorated space has a front lounge, a medium-sized bar and a full restaurant serving everything from tapas to burgers. Though the vibe inside is relaxed and friendly, there is an uneasiness about the space that is probably due to its non-vintageness. Failing to follow through on its very cool façade, the decor inside is a bit of a disappointment with decorating faux-pas like halogen lamps and tacky McDonald's-style formica tables. The crowd is very mixed in age, gender preference and ethnicity and they appear to be very content here. If nothing more, we recommend dropping by with your date if you happen to be in the area.

## THE VODKA BAR
**Royalton Hotel, 44 W. 44th St. (bet. 5th & 6th Ave.)**
**869-4400**

*ALL MAJOR CREDIT CARDS*

Some things never change, like feeling suddenly sexy every time you make your entrance at the decade-old Royalton Hotel. With its eternally white, cinematic feel, this Delano Mini-Me has a secret: The Vodka Bar. Also called The Round Bar, this tiny sphere is in the lobby behind a round, lacquered wall. With its padded, tan leather interior, and dim, flickering light, it sets the stage for a cozy evening of champagne cocktails and flavored martinis. (Or makes you feel like you're in a really cool insane asylum). Totally styled a la Starck (Phillippe, the famous French, architect-designer of all things shiny), the Vodka Room is a great place to show-off your new Prada dress or Hugo Boss trousers. Don't come unless you feel "gorge"-you'll just be competing with the décor. Offering four homemade flavored vodkas (strawberry, raspberry, pineapple, blueberry), 31 commercial vodkas, a full martini menu, umpteen single malt scotches, 5 grappas, 7 gins, a gillion wines and champagnes, two turtle doves and a partridge in a pear tree, they pretty much know what they're doing. Drinks are expensive (they start at $10 and go up), smoking is permitted (no cigars or pipes), and you can order off the lobby menu. The crowd is 25-40s urban chic, but if you bring 20 friends, you can easily take over this mini lounge.

**VOID**
**16 Mercer St. (At Howard St.)**
**941 6492**

*CASH ONLY*

This place could not have been any cooler when it opened a few years ago. If you knew about it, you were definitely part of the in-the-know crowd. Who knew that a swank art bar was hidden behind the façade of what looks to be a Chinese institute? On this dank street, where even the rats are afraid to scurry, The Void is inconspicuous, loungy and dark with a stark inside that plays silent and very strange art films on large movie screens, including such classics as "My Dinner with Shecky," "When Shecky met Sally" and "Breakfast at Shecky's." You'll feel like you're walking into a house party with music so loud even the neighborhood bum has to wear ear plugs. Wednesday is free feature film night at 8:30pm. Live bands play occasionally. Dress in your Sunday worst...nobody cares.

**VON**
**3 Bleecker St. (At Bowery)**
**473-3039**
*ALL MAJOR CREDIT CARDS*

This small and cozy bar looks like it was put together from a country yard sale. The long and thin space which sports a very good-looking bar, serves coffee, tea, beer, cocktails and one of the best wine selections in the area. The crowd is angst-ridden, local and artsy. It's also a subtle pickup place.

## WALKERS
**16 N. Moore St. (At Varick St.)**
**941-0142**

*ALL MAJOR CREDIT CARDS*

If you yearn for those days of summers past when you went to camp, playing and swimming in clean refreshing lake water, leave the city. If you want a good solid bar to smoke a cigarette, grab a beer, and munch on some top notch bar food, come to Walkers. Hands down, this is the best neighborhood bar in TriBeCa. Locals, models, actors and yuppies all drop in for the laid back atmosphere and the comfortable, loft-like pub feel. The music is easy on the ears, and to help unleash the Picasso in all of us is a glass of crayons at every table. It's almost comforting to know that at one point the late JFK Jr. frequented this place too-how could he resist, it was right next door.

## WALL STREET KITCHEN AND BAR
**70 Broad St (At Beaver St.)**
**797-7070**

*ALL MAJOR CREDIT CARDS*

The thirtysomething suits choose Wall St. K&B for after-work jaunts with friends and co-workers. 50 tap beers, 50 wines by the glass, 100 bottled beers, and flights of vodka, scotch, tequila, beer, and wine make this bar a drinker's paradise. The bi-level bar has dark red walls and funky paint-ings. The upstairs is open Wednesday through Friday to accommodate the throngs of after-work revelers. "Decanter Magazine" named Wall Street K&B the best wine list of NYC bars for 1997. Amicable young bartenders make this a de-lightful meeting place.

## WATERLOO
**145 Charles St. (At Washington St.)**
**352-1119**

*ALL MAJOR CREDIT CARDS*

This is the type of place where if a cell phone rings, chances are that every single hand in the place is going to shoot into a bag or a jacket pocket simultaneously like a well choreographed musical. Swanky, sleek and seductive, Waterloo is sure to get your date in the mood for some lovin'. The small bar area is fun only if you can grab a seat. The bartenders are great, the scene is relaxing, and there is no velvet rope in sight. Catering to funky professionals who shed their advertising and Wall Street suits for a black turtleneck and a martini, the adjoining restaurant is excellent. This is an amazing summer bar and a great place for a first date. Plan to spend an evening from drinks to dinner and back again. We highly recommend it!

## WAX
**113 Mercer St. (bet. Prince & Spring)**
**226-6082**

*ALL MAJOR CREDIT CARDS*

Bouncers. Velvet rope. Attitude. This large gothic space equipped with gargoyles, skulls and mega-candelabras harbors a sea of people who love themselves. It's a shame there aren't any mirrors to accent the narcissistic flavor of the place. Wax is like being in Transylvania one minute and in Italy the next. The blue, pink, yellow and purple gel-covered stage lights evoke visions of bloody fangs and black capes, and the fresco of water nymphs is reminiscent of dreamy Venetian quarters. It's dark, but you better be ready to be seen.

## THE WEB
**40 E. 58th St. (bet. 5th & Madison Aves.)**
**308-1546**

*ALL MAJOR CREDIT CARDS*

A gay Asian discotheque? Who knew? This two-level underground midtown club formerly known as Club 58 has been around for years, drawing a regular crowd of Asian guys and their admirers. Though it functions as a bar for the after-work midtown crowd, it only really gets going at night. On the bottom floor is the dance floor which is usually crowded with festive people bopping along to poppy house music. Upstairs there's a pool room, a few video games, a comfortable lounge with plenty of seating to hang out in, and a bar area that overlooks the dance floor. At night two go-go dancers take turns strutting their g-stringed stuff in the metal cage and on weekends there is sometimes a somewhat lackluster drag show. A dependable, though not terribly exciting place to dance and have fun. Cover varies between $5 and $10. Call ahead for details.

## WEBSTER HALL
**125 E. 11th St. (bet. 3rd & 4th Aves.)**
**353-1600**

*ALL MAJOR CREDIT CARDS*

Formerly the alternative rock club The Ritz, this mac daddy of the New York club scene hosts a four-floor venue and a crowd more diverse than the United Nations Security Council. Thick lines of club kids and Jersyites form a block-long line on the weekend to get in and groove. Each floor sports a different type of music from techno to 80s to 70s disco. If you come with a date, make sure not to lose sight of them, it's a pickup scene and you can get lost in one of the countless nooks. Drinks are expensive, the lines are long and it's so hot inside you can grill chicken on your forehead, but you'll probably have a kick ass time.

## WELCOME TO THE JOHNSONS
**123 Rivington St. (bet. Essex & Norfolk Sts.)**
**420-9911**

*CASH ONLY*

If you grew up in the heart of suburbia or just loved the film, "Welcome to the Dollhouse," you will surely feel at home at this Lower East Side bar/living room. Set away from the LES B&T bars, this tiny bar has been on its feet for only a few months. Trimmed outside with colored plastic patio lights, you instantly get a taste of the bar's personality. Lots of wood paneling and fake masonry adorn the walls along with gold covered mirrors and old pictures of your favorite aunt and uncle. Plastic covered chairs and worn-out couches surround old, abused, Koolade-stained tables. An authentic suburban fridge sits in the lounge area where an old Zenith TV broadcasts Ren & Stimpy. The atmosphere is as relaxed as your parent's basement. Lower East Siders play pool while listening to the jukebox which offers blasts from the past like Kizz, T-Rex, Frampton and the theme from Shaft. Friendly bartenders serve cheap drinks while a daily happy hour begins at 3pm and lasts until 9pm. Yep, 3 to 9 you can get $2 well drinks and $1 pints of Guinness. Like that old wooden sign hanging in front of your neighbor's house says, "Welcome to the Johnsons."

## WESTSIDE TAVERN
**358 W. 23rd St. (bet. 8th & 9th Aves.)**

*ALL MAJOR CREDIT CARDS*

The name says it all-it's a tavern and it's on the West Side. A bit more stylish than your average drinking saloon, Westside has exposed brick walls and black and white photos of old New York. For your added entertainment there is a pool table and a jukebox. The crowd consists mainly of residents of the humongous London Terrace Tower across the street and moviegoers from the two multiplexes down the street.

## WETLANDS
**161 Hudson St. (At Laight St.)**
**966-4225**

*ALL MAJOR CREDIT CARDS*

Since 1989, this hotspot has been supporting bands while also strengthening its idea of eco-consciousness 100%. A venue for Grateful Dead cover bands, as well as a mass of bands that are new, old, dead and alive, Wetlands has lent its wings to Pearl Jam, The Dave Matthews' Band, Oasis, The Spin Doctors, Blues Traveler, etc. The Reserve spirit strongly adheres to fun and activism in unison. Music is mixed, from dance, rhythm, world beat, blues, rock, neo-psychedelic, funk fusion, punk and hardcore. Two levels rally with all types and a friendly staff. Crowd is dependent on the band. Popular Sunday matinees are usually hardcore bands.

## WHISKY BAR (@ THE PARAMOUNT HOTEL
## 235 W. 46th St. (bet. B'way & 8th Ave.)
## 819-0404

### *ALL MAJOR CREDIT CARDS*

Although this trendy, upscale bar is part of the chic Ian Schraeger hotel, The Paramount, it is definitely not a hotel bar. Get there early and snag a seat at one of the comfortable chairs or couches. Otherwise, groups of three or more will find themselves fighting for chairs as only two are allowed at each table. The romantic bar caters to both the after-work and the late night crowds. It's packed from 5:30 to 8pm, followed by a lull from 8-10pm, and then a mad rush from 10pm-3am. The drinks are $8, but by the first sip you will feel like you got a bargain-they are very light on the mixers! The scene is made up of horny yuppies who enjoy watching the underage-looking cocktail waitresses prance around in full-body leotards.

## WHISKEY BLUE
## 541 Lexington Ave. (At 49th St.)
## 755-1200

### *ALL MAJOR CREDIT CARDS*

Located in the ultra-swank W hotel is Rande Gerber's latest watering hole. This beautiful hotel bar offers three separate drinking areas, all of which are jammed on Thursday nights with the young and aggressively horny. The crowd is predominately male, young and work on Wall Street-three ingredients that make for a very intense meat-market. The half naked, beautiful and barely legal bartenders ensure that the drinks flow as furiously as the testosterone does. In the main room is where the action takes place but the two additional areas are just as much of a scene and have the added bonus of elbow room and an appetizer menu. Whiskey Blue is one of the best after-work spots in midtown and for single gals looking for a match, this may be a dating service is disguise.

## WHISKEY PARK
**100 Central Park South (At 6th Ave)**
**307-9222**

### ALL MAJOR CREDIT CARDS

Located on Park Ave. South among Manhattan's most expensive real estate, it's no wonder that everyone at this neighborhood bar is dressed in DKNY. It's nice to walk into a bar with a doorman who warmly greets you hello. Inside, expect it to be crowded with young, rich and beautiful executives sipping Beef-Eater Martinis with olives ($7) or excellent Cosmopolitans ($7) while stretching out on modern comfortable chairs and couches. With views of the park and Sixth Ave., this very unassuming place with low lighting and slick and extremely professional service is open 7 days (Sun.-Wed. from 4 PM-2 AM & Thurs- Sat 4 PM- 4 AM) Whiskey Park offers a needed ambiance shift from what most Manhattanites have come to expect of trendy-expensive bars- from arrogance & attitude to one of class, professionalism and courteous service.

## WHITE HORSE TAVERN
**567 Hudson St. (At 11th St.)**
**243-9260**

### ALL MAJOR CREDIT CARDS

Established in the early 1800s, the White Horse Tavern dishes up a little slice o' history. The old fashioned bar, carved up wooden benches and collection of Dylan Thomas paraphernalia on the walls hearkens back to the beatnik generation- a time when writers came to roost while slowly drinking away their angst. WHT remains a very popular New York staple and draws a mix of regulars and yuppies for their bar food, cheap pitchers of beer and 2 dollar draft happy hours. Weekends, unfortunately, tend to draw the out-of-towners, cheesifying the place a bit. Nonetheless, it's a great bar in a beautiful part of town, especially in the summer when the outdoor picnic tables emerge.

## WHO'S ON FIRST
**1683 1st Ave. (bet. 87th & 88th Sts.)**
**410-2780**

*ALL MAJOR CREDIT CARDS*

Yet another frat bar on the Upper East Side. What a shock. Nothing really distinguishes this place from the rest of the generic, youthful, drink-till-you-drop bars in the area. With two floors, Who's on First has a few skank-filled couches to lounge on and Bud signs to admire. Open from 5pm-4am, there's a happy hour from 5pm - 9pm Monday - Thursday offering $2 well and draft drinks. The prices of the drinks mirrors the quality of the atmosphere: cheap, cheap, cheap. Hysterically, the bartenders claim themselves as being "pro-active"-translating into: bartenders who funnel beer and shots-down alcoholic frat boy's throats. A Monday night dart competition brings in a more competitive crowd while the weekend crowd is very young, loud and drunk. It's a shame that such a giant space with potential has been turned into a beer chugging dump.

## WICKED WOLF
**1442 1st Ave. (At 71st St.)**
**861-4670**

*ALL MAJOR CREDIT CARDS*

This basic bar/pub has been a fixture on the Upper East Side since 1976, serving burgers, fries and beer. The male female ratio is about 5 to 1 and it has a certain sports feel about it. This place oozes testosterone.

## WONDER BAR
**505 E. 6th St. (bet. Aves. A & B)**
**777-9105**
*CASH ONLY*

Wonder Bar is the ultimate playground for the young, hip and glamorous East Village fashion boy and his admirers, his fag hag, and even a couple of his lesbian friends. They all come to schmooze on the low sofas, look cute and have a couple of drinks. Meanwhile, a live DJ spins funk, house and whatever while a small disco ball spins circles around the zebra-striped walls. On weekends, the place is intolerably packed and the crowd often spills out onto the sidewalk and beyond. The customers are easily some of New York's most attractive, and they all seem to know it.

## THE WORKS
**428 Columbus Ave.  (At 81 St.)**
**799-7365**

### CASH ONLY

This gay neighborhood bar attracts a well-to-do crowd. Aiming to be known as a video bar, The Works is still the crowded watering hole that has become a pillar in the gay community. Their Sunday Beer Blast that includes $5 unlimited Rolling Rocks, donates $1 per beer to Gods Love We Deliver. Amazingly, they have raised over $160,000! How many bars can or ever will top anything like that? Happy hour M-F with 2-4-1 drinks. They have pool tables and a pool league on Monday nights, $2 Sam Adams pints on Tuesday from 10pm-2am, Thursdays, 10oz. martinis from 4-10pm for only $4! Thursdays they host a $1 margarita night known as Cute Boy Night. A bar worth going uptown for-especially if you're searching for a husband!

## WRECK ROOM
**116 Macdougal St. (At Bleecker St.)**
**253-1843**

### ALL MAJOR CREDIT CARDS

Warning: Those with the propensity to pass out under extreme heat stress, beware. It is a travesty that people actually pay $10 to enter into this dark, smoky, humid, loud and packed basement club. Home of the old Scrap Bar, this place is in desperate need of some style and color. While bands play during the weekend, a DJ mixes house music and R&B

during the week. After checking your stuff at the coat check, fighting your way to the bar may be worth it for the cheaper-than-usual drinks. If reliving the Glam Rock days of the Scrap Bar is what you intend to do at the Wreck Room, forget it. This mixed Brooklyn, 21-and-over crowd need their heads seriously examined for even entering this firetrap.

## WXOU RADIO
**558 Hudson St. (bet. Perry & 11th St.)**
**206-0381**

*CASH ONLY*

From the outside you would almost never know it's there. In fact, most people cruise right by it. Inside you'll find yourself in a small room with a long wooden bar and tables atop an old fashioned tiled floor. There is a decent juke box and a good beer selection, but for the most part it's no-frills and serves mainly as a safe haven from the weekend tourist-infested White Horse Tavern across the street. A plus: You can almost always get a table.

## XANDO CAFÉ & BAR (UPTOWN)
**2160 B'way (At 76th St.)**
**595-5616**

*ALL MAJOR CREDIT CARDS*

Starbucks, take your Mocha Frappachino and take a hike! This dual-level coffee bar, with a few vintage couches and cool chairs, is one of the larger café/bars around. Summer days, patrons sip their drinks on a front patio. This makes for a spectacular meeting place and it serves up every imaginable creation of coffee products at regular coffee prices. At 4:30, turn in your Java mugs for wine glasses or a drink from the full bar. No glitz, no glam, no paparazzi-just decent drinks. Choose your drug, caffeine or alcohol, and unwind at Xando.

## XANDO (DOWNTOWN)
**504 6th Ave. (At 13th St.)**
**462-4188**
*ALL MAJOR CREDIT CARDS*

Beer with your coffee? Xando, decorated in the manner of MTV's "Real World," has waiters who are painfully cute and a pretty good menu, too. It's a perfect place to chill out, smoke a cigarette, pretend to read Kafka, and scope out the young, good looking, off-the-wall crowd. The coffee menu is enormous and there's a full bar for those who need something more than caffeine to deal with the crushing pain of life. Try the "Make Your Own Smores" desert...it's a real treat.

## XR BAR
**128 W. Houston St. (At Sullivan St.)**
**674-4080**

### ALL MAJOR CREDIT CARDS

If SoHo was ever part of the Old West, The XR Bar would be its hottest saloon. It has a pleasantly odd feel to it-parts of it are down-home and rustic, very "Yes, that is a six shooter in my pocket, and yes, I am very glad to see you," and other parts are more modern, more West Village, more "Do you have any bottled ice to go with this Absolut?" Lots of brick and unpolished wood surround you as you sit on stools, throw back a couple of brews, and wonder why the bar is so damn low. There's no kitchen, but they do have a menu-book on hand for delivery. Blues bands four nights a week, cheap drinks, and a friendly, mellow crowd make the XR Bar a damn fine place to drop your spurs and relax.

## XVI (16)
**16 1st Ave. (bet. 1st & 2nd Sts.)**
**260-1549**

### ALL MAJOR CREDIT CARDS

One of the cooler and larger spaces in the East Village, XVI sports a large bar area in the back. It's a bit on the smoky side, and the crowd consists of hip twentysomethings who check each other out. The bar downstairs opens up later in the evening for dancing and leaves you feeling like you are in Emerald City with its mosaic-mirrored walls. This is a good place to hang with friends or a date and listen to good music. The one drawback is the fluctuating cover at the door that seems to be determined by how much the bouncer likes you.

## YORKVILLE BREWERY AND TAVERN
**1359 1st Ave. (At 73rd St.)**
**517-2739**

*ALL MAJOR CREDIT CARDS*

This Upper East Side bar could be in Anytown, U.S.A. The twentysomethings that this place attracts clearly appreciate the raspberry ale and post-collegiate pickup scene. The restaurant half of the tavern is as crowded as the bar and just as reasonably priced, so don't hesitate to order some foccaccia or fries to go with your blonde brew (the drink, not the girl).

## Z BAR
**206 Ave. A (bet. 12th & 13th Sts.)**
**982-9173**

*CASH ONLY*

Long-haired dirty dudes banging heads to Metallica, Ozzy and Guns n' Roses still reign at Z-Bar-the tattooed staple of the east Village dive scene. The bar is vast, with a long metallic bar, pinball machines, booths to sit in and two pool tables. Despite all this space, the place gets jammed on the weekends and is transformed into a serious grungy pickup scene. If the heavy metal air is too thick for you, travel to the dark and dungeon-like downstairs bar. Sit at drafty, graffiti-covered booths or on skanky, roach-infested couches while listening to a DJ spinning punk rock legends such as the NY Dolls and The Stooges. Friendly, heavily-inked bartenders charge fair prices and offer buy backs. A few words to the wise: Stay off of the pool table unless you are a pro, don't make eye contact with the skanky metal chicks and watch out for flying, sweaty hair. You could lose an eye. Hours: Monday - Sunday, 3pm - 4am.

## ZANZIBAR
**645 9th Ave. (At 45th St.)**
**957-9197**

Hop on your magic carpet and fly over to this Mediterranean delight. Park your rug near the neon-lined bar, grab a reasonably priced cocktail, and pick one of the four large rooms to drink it in. Each room has something different to offer-from plush couches to iron chairs, walls of rustic brick to stark plaster; you even have the choice of sitting under a cloudy skylight or near a large, wood-burning fireplace. Fill your belly with a solid selection of unique appetizers and entrees (Avocado Lasagnette?), and, three nights a week, feast your eyes and ears on live Brazilian bands. A comfortable nightspot with more seating than you can shake your sphinx at, Zanzibar is a pleasing place to spend at least a thousand Arabian nights.

**ZINC BAR**
**90 W. Houston St. (bet. Thompson & Laguardia)**
**477-8337**

This tiny jazz cave tucked underneath Houston Street is a great little place to listen to live jazz or Brazilian music and throw back a couple of drinks. This cozy spot which is the size of a city bus, makes for a great place to take a date, especially on nights when they pop in the Sergio Mendez, Brazilian Jazz CD. Stop by to pick up their monthly music schedule and choose a night to stop in. This is a great out-of-the-way spot that feels like you are on a side street in Paris.

# OOPS, WE ALMOST FORGOT

## EL RIO GRANDE
**160 E. 38th St. (bet. Lex. & 3rd Aves.)**
**867-0922**

"La vida loca" is alive and well at this established Murray Hill watering hole. The large outdoor patio packs in the tank top-clad, miniskirt-wearing, twentysomething, midtown worker bees. If you can stand waiting in a monstrous line that occasionally wraps itself around the block and onto 3rd Ave., it'll be worth your while to see the shenanigans that take place at this drunken meat-market. The cheesy Mexican décor and mediocre fare attracts margarita-swilling young professionals from the area who are out for a good time. El Rio Grande always delivers.

## FAILTE
**531 2nd Ave. (bet. 29th & 30th Sts.)**
**725-9440**

*ALL MAJOR CREDIT CARDS*

"Failte," which means "welcome" in Gaelic, graced Kips Bay Christmas season 1998. This two-floor bar/restaurant is very cozy and the two working fireplaces only add to its authenticity and charm. It's usually filled with a neighborhood crowd of thirtysomethings seated at the lovely wooden bar, just hanging out and drinking Guinness. A full menu of American food along with Irish specialties is available either at the bar or in the upstairs dining room. There is an up-to-date jukebox available during the week, and every Sunday an Irish band plays at 5:30pm.

## GRAMERCY TAVERN
**42 E. 20th St. (bet. B'way & Park Aves.)**
**477-0777**

The award winning wine list and phenomenal food is what draws throngs of Manhattanites to Gramercy Park. If you haven't made a reservation in advance don't even think about grabbing a table in the dining room. For a more informal evening situate yourself at one of the tables in the Tavern Room where the same cordial and knowledgeable staff serves an abbreviated menu in the beautifully appointed Vermont tavern setting.

## HELL'S KITCHEN BAR
**538 9th Ave. (At 40th St.)**
**695-5507**

There are lots of bands nightly at this delightful, hole-in-the-wall, live music venue. Sure, it's in a rough neighborhood but Hell's Kitchen Bar supplies you with live rock, blues and heavy metal with cheap drinks and no cover charge. Friendly bartenders serve strong drinks while a jukebox screams out classic rock-and-roll. It's an authentic dive bar with a long and narrow front bar, a small stage in the back and graffiti-ridden bathrooms. Artists, musicians and neighborhood locals all convene nightly to hear up-and-coming music and play pinball in a very congenial and friendly atmosphere. A great place to hear live music and load up on cheap booze.

## IL BAGATTO
**192 E. 2nd St. (bet. Aves. A & B)**
**228-0977**

### ALL MAJOR CREDIT CARDS

This wildly popular Italian restaurant is also home to a lower level bar/lounge. It seems most patrons come here for the ridiculously inexpensive, amazingly delicious, authentic cuisine. However, if you're tardy for your reservation there is no avoiding being waylaid by the hostess (owner) in restaurant purgatory. So if you don't have reservations in the cute, albeit crowded, dimly lit upstairs room, don't travel out of your way to hang out here.

### INTERNATIONAL BAR
**120 1st Ave. (bet. 7th St. & St. Marks Pl.)**
**777-9244**

Smarmy and dingy, the International Bar has been alive and kicking for 37 years. But just how "international" is this place? Could it be the flashing Christmas lights? The plethora of neon beer signs in the window? How about the globes hanging from the ceiling? The décor alone is enough to mentally transport you to another time zone! Hey, at least the drinks are cheap and the local artist types are all over the "idea" of this place. A small back garden is open in the summer till 11pm while the bar remains open till 4am. With no beers on tap, well drinks go for $3, shelf for $4 and beers range from $2.50 - $3.50. There's no happy hour but who needs one at these prices? A nice selection of music plays on the jukebox: The Velvet Underground, The Stooges and Cypress Hill, and there's always real estate at the bar. Okay, so it's not the Eiffel Tower, but it's a hell of a lot cheaper than going abroad!

### KANA TAPAS BAR & RESTAURANT
**324 Spring St. (bet. Washington & Greenwich Sts.)**
**343-8180**

***ALL MAJOR CREDIT CARDS***

Open for one and a half years, Kana brings a touch of Spain to Manhattan. Tucked away on the outskirts of SoHo, this chic, yet cozy restaurant/bar graciously introduces down-town investment moguls to Prada-wearing SoHo-ites. Ex-uding a typical red velvet charm, Kana serves a full tapas menu for reasonable prices. With lots of exposed brick and warm candlelight, Kana plays host to live Flamenco every Tuesday evening. Open daily at 6pm, there are six beers on tap, moderately priced drinks and an ever-flowing abun-dance of Sangria. Kana, which is Spanish for "a glass of beer," will quench your desire for authentic Spanish food and drink.

## LA MAISON DE SADE
**206 W. 23rd St. (bet. 7th & 8th Aves.)**
**727-8642**

Named after the infamous Marquees De Sade, La Maison De Sade cooks naughty French cuisine with an S&M twist. If you're searching for a sexually uninhibited night out, then this is the place for you. Bound and gagged yuppies scream out in pleasure as the crack of leather on bare skin echoes throughout the room. For $20, you can either get a spanking, go to doggy obedience training, get your feet worshipped or be publicly humiliated. Slither your way up to the bar and suck down one of La Maison's famous $8 shameful martinis with names such as "The Autophliac," "The Masochist" or "The Infantilist." Enjoy public humiliation by the waiters who don minuscule leather Speedos and nipple rings. Every Wednesday night, La Maison hosts "Pingo," an interesting twist on Bingo that could win you a date and a dinner for two with one of New York City's hottest escorts...oh behave, baby! With a $5 cover charge Wed. - Sat., La Maison hosts live shows daily at 7pm and 11pm. If leather, transvestites, whips and hot candle wax make you weak at the knees, follow La Maison's mantra which demands, "If you have reservations, stay at some."

## L'ANGOLO
**108 W. Houston St. (At Thompson St.)**
**260-8899**

*ALL MAJOR CREDIT CARDS*

A slice of the Mediterranean on Houston Street, this elegant, tiny café/lounge creates the perfect setting for romantic evenings. The overall vibe is warm and charming, drawing in crowds of fashionable downtowners. With antique couches and coffee tables illuminated by candlelight, this palazzo-styled nightspot generously pours a selection of wine, tropical cocktails, beer and coffee. With eight beers on tap, L'Angolo's signature drink is the Bellini. If you have a penchant for Mediterranean fare, feast on antipasti, pannini from fresh vegetables and focaccia. A great place for a date, L'Angolo delivers a bit of elegance to Houston St.

## LEOPARD LOUNGE
**85 2nd Ave. (At 5th St.)**
**253-6050**

Formerly known as Svobedo, the Leopard Lounge's overall vibe is sophisticated and funky. Known for their delicious "Leopard Tartinis," The Leopard Lounge is well stocked with 20 bottles of wine, champagne and tequila galore. A mid- to late twenties crowd with cash convene nightly, surrounded by leopard-printed velvet and a second floor view of bustling 2nd Ave. With four beers on tap, one of the friendliest bartenders around pours $5 well drinks, $5 beers and $7-9 specialty cocktails. A full menu is served nightly from the restaurant Sin Sin, while an amazing Sunday brunch from 3pm - 10pm offers up free mimosas with mind-blowing Dj'd tunes. The "it's all about the music" party every Tuesday at 9pm features a DJ spinning House, techno and disco. Owned by the proprietors of Rivertown Lounge, The Leopard Lounge oozes Dean Martin, delivering finesse to the East Village.

## LILY'S
**203 Spring St. (At Sullivan St.)**
**334-3855**

Lily's is a dark, quaint bar that attracts a mellow yuppie crowd. Quietly sipping wine, champagne or scotch, overstuffed suits convene at the small front bar to let loose after a rough day of making millions. Dark, red drapes, scarlet walls, lantern-chandeliers and plush seating make for a very Anne Rice-esque setting. Except for the gold mirrors, a vampire could actually add some blood curdling thrills to this stuffy lounge. With four beers on tap, there is quite an extensive menu of Belgian beers, scotches (including Johnny Walker Blue and Gold), champagne and grappa. A happy hour reduces the drink prices from 1pm - 6pm daily. It's quaint, it's quiet and it's dark, which makes for a nice date spot without too much action.

## LUCY'S
**135 Ave. A (bet. St. Mark's Pl. & 9th St.)**
**No Phone**

Everyone knows Lucy's. A staple of the East Village bar scene, Lucy's has been around for what seems like centuries. This smoke-filled dive is home for most East Village locals who come in to play pool, listen to a rock 'n' roll jukebox and get liquored up on the cheapest booze around. This is a no-frills, down-and-dirty bar where the mood is local, tough and just as cheap as the drinks. Featured in the flick "Hurricane Streets," some of the best pool players from the 'hood show how a real pool game is shot. Open till 4am nightly, Lucy's is part of a dying breed of bars on Avenue A that refuses to be gentrified.

## O'NIEAL'S GRAND STREET
**147 Grand St. (bet. Centre & Mulberry Sts.)**
**941-9119**

*ALL MAJOR CREDIT CARDS*

This half restaurant half lounge, cigar-friendly, Little Italy find serves scrumptious, eclectic American food in a club-like atmosphere. The knowledgeable bartenders steer patrons to the perfect glass of wine or cognac to sip in this appealing and sexy atmosphere. There is always hip "of the moment" music playing at a pleasant level. The stylish black-and-white photos of yesteryear New York complement the comfortable leather couches and provides the perfect backdrop for a relaxing evening with a date or with friends. Get here early on Friday and Saturday evenings before the neighborhood yuppies grab all of the seats.

## PLUG UGLIES
**257 3rd Ave. (bet. 20th & 21st Sts.)**
**780-1944**

"Shuffleboard, anyone?" If bar games and friendly folk are on your agenda this is a good place to stop. Also featured is a pool table, dartboard, and killer jukebox. This is a no-nonsense Gramercy Park bar where you are guaranteed to make a few friends and have a fun time. Friday and Saturday nights are definitely busier than the remainder of the week, but it is still remarkable how few people flock here. Could it be the 10:1 male/female ratio? Perhaps.

**POP**
**127 4th Ave (bet. 12th & 13th Sts.)**
**674-8713**

*ALL MAJOR CREDIT CARDS*

Oh, my, god. This place is sooo Hollywood! (Must be said in a Valley Girl accent.) Filled to the brim with pretentious "310" area code wannabes, this fairly new bar/restaurant is the ultimate poster child for "Beverly Hills 90210." The owners of Lemon-which unfortunately is a lemon-have opened up another restaurant, Pop. Minimally decorated with lots of lightly colored wood, orange lights and a small, sterile, white bar, waiters roam the room in gray mechanic suits. The airport-esque ceiling a la JFK Airport's TWA terminal is inspired by Warhol's "box in a box" concept of creation. Although the LA vibe can be a bit much, Pop offers surprisingly excellent contemporary American cuisine with an Asian flair from 6pm - 12am nightly. Unfortunately, the bar scene doesn't live up to the menu-it's super lame. Martinis go for about $10, mixed drinks are $7 and beer ranges from $6-$8. Pop into Pop for a bite to eat but steer clear of anybody remotely resembling Don Johnson or talking on a cell phone at the bar-it's probably "one of them."

**SIN SIN**
**85 2nd Ave. (At 5th St.)**
**253-2222**

*ALL MAJOR CREDIT CARDS*

Pronounced "Shin Shin" and meaning "That's That" in Gaelic, Sin Sin serves up an extensive Irish menu with warmth and sophistication. Feast your eyes on tantalizing dishes such as Apple Smoked Bacon Risotto and Chocolate Sin. A mid-twenties crowd convenes nightly from 5pm-4am to quench their thirst and on weekends for the Irish brunch. Drinks are affordable with $5-$6 glasses of wine, $7 bottled beers, $5 drafts (7 on tap) and mixed drinks for $5 and up. Sin Sin is a great spot for a romantic dinner date with no attitude.

## THAI VILLAGE
**81 Ave. A (bet. 5th & 6th Sts.)**
**533-2928**

### ALL MAJOR CREDIT CARDS

Simply a Thai eatery with a small run-of-the-mill bar in front, Thai Village is an extremely mellow place bordering on the mundane. A daily happy hour offers wine and beer, ½ price, from 5pm to 8pm. While a big screen TV centered in the middle of the bar plays sports, choose from the four beers on tap, $5 well drinks, $4 beers and $7 shelf drinks. Open from 5pm - 2am during the week and 5pm - 3am on the weekends, food is served in the dining area as well as at the bar until closing. It's a good joint to devour Pad Thai, but a poor choice for a drink.

## 23 WATTS
**23 Watts (bet. W. B'way & Broom St.)**
**925-8966**

### ALL MAJOR CREDIT CARDS

Despite its name change from Chaos, 23 Watts hasn't changed. "I'm too sexy for this lounge" is still the mantra for this ultra sexy diva of lounges. One of the premiere nightspots in the world, 23 Watts caters to the "stand and pose" crowd. This multi-level, bordello-like space has enough red velvet to clothe a small population of pimps. Lots of ultra-comfy lounging areas with overstuffed pillows provide the perfect playground for models and their stalkers. Tuesday nights play host to Rusell Simmons' "Babyfat" parties while Wednesday nights hosts "Candyland." Despite the steep drink prices and the varying cover charges, this poser fest merits a visit. Better dress to impress-ultra chic bouncers, with an eye for fashion, like to keep the riffraff away.

Strike a pose!

# BARS BY NEIGHBORHOOD

## CHELSEA

ADLIB
BAR 85
BARRACUDA
BMW BAR
BOTTINO
BREAK
CAFETERIA
CANDY BAR
CHEETAH
CHELSEA BREWING-COMPANY
CHELSEA COMMONS
CIEL ROUGE
COMMUNITY BAR & GRILL
DOWNTIME BAR
DUSK OF LONDON
EAGLE'S NEST
EAST OF EIGHTH
EL FLAMINGO
FLIGHT 151
FRED'S BEAUTY BAR
G
GASLIGHT
H2K
JUSTINS
KING NYC
LA MAISON DE SADE
LA NOUVELLE JUSTINE
LAVA
LOLA
LOT 61
MCDOOLEY'S
NEGRIL
ONE FORTY SEVEN(147)
PASSERBY
PLANET 28
RAWHIDE
REBAR
RED ROCK WEST
ROXY
SAN FRANCISCO REST
SPEEED
SPIKE
SPLASH BAR
SYDNEY B
TAP ROOM
TRAMPS
TUNNEL
TWIRL
TWO I'S
VICEROY
WESTSIDE TAVERN

## EAST VILLAGE

ACE BAR
ALCHYMY
ANGEL' SHARE
ASTOR
B BAR
BAGATELLE
BAR CODE
BAR NONE
BAR ON A
BARAZA
BARMACY
BEAUTY BAR
BEER HALL
BIG BAR
BLACK & WHITE
BLACK STAR
BLARNEY COVE
BLUE & GOLD TAVERN
BOCA CHICA
BOILER ROOM
BOUSCHE
BOXCAR LOUNGE
BREWSKY'S
BROWNIES
BURP CASTLE
C3 Lounge
CBGB AND OMFUG
CHEZ ES SAADA
CIRCA

CLOISTER CAFÉ
C-NOTE
THE COCK
COCO BAR
CONEY ISLAND HIGH
CONTINENTAL
COYOTE UGLY SALOON
DBA
DECIBEL
DELIA'S SUPPER CLUB
DETOUR
DICK'S BAR
DOC HOLIDAY'S
DRINKLAND
EDGE BAR
ELBOW ROOM
ELEMENT ZERO
ELEVENTH ST. BAR
FLAMINGO EAST
FRANKIE BLUE
GEMINI LOUNGE
GLOBAL 33
GOLD BAR
GRASSROOT TAVERN
HOLIDAY COCKTAIL LOUNGE
IL BAGATTO
INTERNATIONAL BAR
INTERNET CAFÉ
IZZY BAR
JACK DEMPSEY RESTAURANT
JOES
JOLLY ROGER
KASTRO BAR LOUNGE
KGB
KOROVA MILK BAR
LA LINEA
LAKESIDE LOUNGE
LEOPARD LOUNGE
LIBRARY
LIFE CAFÉ EAST
LIQUIDS
LUCA LOUNGE
LUCKY CHENGS
LUCY'S

MANITOBA'S
MARION'S CONTINENTAL
MARZ BAR
McSORLEY'S ALE HOUSE
MEKKA
MERCURY LOUNGE
MONA'S
MUSICAL BOX
NEVADA SMITHS
NIAGRA
NIGHTINGALE
9 C
NW3
OASIS LOUNGE
ODESSA
OOPS
OPALINE
OPERA
OPIUM DEN
ORSON'S
PAGEANT BAR & GRILL
PHEBES
PIERROT
PYRAMID
RAVEN
RYAN'S IRISH PUB
SCRATCHER
SEVEN B (Vasac's)
SIDEWALK CAFÉ
SIMONE
SIN SIN
SOLAS
SOPHIES
SPIRAL
ST. MARKS ALE HOUSE
STANDARD
STARLIGHT
TELEPHONE BAR
TENTH STREET LOUNGE
THAI VILLAGE
TRIBE
2A
WONDER BAR
XVI
Z BAR

## GRAMERCY PARK

ABBEY TAVERN
ALVA
AUBETTE
BAHI
BANK CAFÉ
BARFLY
BELMONT LOUNGE
BLUE WATER GRILL
BULLS HEAD TAVERN
CANDELA'S
CIBAR
COFFEE SHOP
COMFORT ZONE
DUKE'S
EL RIO GRANDE
FAILTE
GALAXY
GLOBE
GLOCCA MORRA
GRAMERCY PARK HOTEL BAR
GRAMERCY TAVERN
GRANVILLE LOUNGE
HEARTLAND BREWERY
JAZZ STANDARD
LEMON
LIVE BAIT
MCCARTHY'S
MCCORMACKS PUBLIC HOUSE
MCSWIGGINS
METRONOME
MOLLY'S
NO IDEA
OLD TOWNE BAR
ONE NINETEEN BAR
PADDY REILEYS MUSIC BAR'
PARK AVALON
PATRIA
PETE'S TAVERN
PLUG UGLY
REVIVAL
RODEO BAR
TURTLE BAY
UNION BAR
VANITY

## GREENWICH VILLAGE

BACK FENCE BAR
BAGGOT INN
BAR 6
BITTER END
BLEEKER STREET BAR
BLUE NOTE
BOTTOM LINE
BOWLMOR LANES
CALIENTE CAB COMPANY
CEDAR TAVERN
CLEMENTINE
COMEDY CELLAR
FIDDLESTICKS
40 FLAVORS
GONZALEZ Y GONZALEZ
GOTHAM BAR & GRILL
GREENWICH BREWING Co
GROOVE
HENRIETTA HUDSON
JACK THE RIPPER
JOHNNY'S BAR
KENNY'S CASTAWAYS
KETTLE OF FISH
THE KEY CLUB
KNICKERBOCKER-
 BAR & GRILL
L'ANGOLO
LIFE / ki club
LION'S DEN
LOOKING GLASS
LOUISANA BAR AND GRILL
L RAY
MARKT
MARYLOU'S
MCBELL'S
OFF THE WAGON
PECULIAR PUB
POP
RED LION
RESERVOIR
SHADE

SLAUGHTERED LAMB
TERRA BLUE
THIRTEEN
TIME CAFÉ
VILLAGE IDIOT
VILLAGE LANTERN
WEBSTER HALL
WRECK ROOM
XANDO (VILLAGE)

KUSH
LANSKY LOUNGE
LIVING ROOM
LOCAL 138
LUDLOW BAR
LUNA LOUNGE
MAX FISH
MEOW MIX
MOJOS
MOTOR CITY BAR

## HELLS KITCHEN

NEVER
NIVA
ORCHARD BAR
PARKSIDE LOUNGE
RIVERTOWN LOUNGE
SAPPHIRE LOUNGE
STANDARD NOTIONS
SWIM
TORCH
WELCOME TO THE JOHNSONS

BAR 9
BIRDLAND
BULL MOOSE SALOON
CARBON
DELTA GRILL
DON'T TELL MAMA
FILM CENTER CAFE
FIREBIRD CAFÉ
THE GAF
HELL'S KITCHEN BAR
KEVIN ST. JAMES
OFLAHERTY'S ALE HOUSE
OTIS
REVOLUTION
RUDYS BAR AND GRILL
SAVOY LOUNGE
SMITH'S BAR
SWINE ON 9
VINTAGE
ZANZIBAR

## LOWER EAST SIDE

ARLENE GROCERY
BABY JUPITER
BANK
BARRAMUNDI
BOB
BUTCHER BAR
THE CORNER
DHARMA
GOOD WORLD BAR & GRILL
IDLEWILD

## LITTLE ITALY

CHIBI'S SAKE BAR
DOUBLE HAPPINESS
MEXICAN RADIO
O'NIEALS
PRAVDA
SWEET & VICIOUS
VELVET LOUNGE
VIG BAR

## MIDTOWN

ANNIE MOORES
AQUAVIT
ASIA DE CUBA
AU BAR
BAR 54
BAR AND BOOKS /-
CIGAR BAR AT BEEKMAN
BARCLAY BAR
BEER BAR - CAFÉ CENTRO
BILL'S GAY NINETIES
BISTRO LATINO
BLACK FIN BAR AND-
RESTAURANT
BREW'S
BRIDGE BAR
BRITISH OPEN
BROADWAY LOUNGE
BRYANT PARK GRILL
BULL & BEAR
CAFE CARLYLE
CAFE PIERRE
CAMPBELL APARTMENT
CAROLINE'S COMEDY CLUB
CHINA CLUB
CLUB MACANUDO
COCO CAFÉ
COMMONWEALTH BREWERY
COPACABANA
D LOUNGE/DELMONICO
HOTEL
DIVINE BAR
DOCKS OYSTER BAR
AND SEAFOOD GRILL

DRUIDS
ELLEN'ODEES
FIFTYSEVEN FIFTYSEVEN
FLOAT
FLUTE
FORTY FOUR
GINGER MAN
HARD ROCK CAFE
HARGLO'S CAFE
HARLEY-DAVIDSON CAFE
HOUSTON'S
HOWARD JOHNSONS'S
IGUANA
JAMESON'S
JEKYLL & HYDE CLUB
JIMMIE'S CORNER
JIMMY WALKERS ALE HOUSE
JUDSON GRILL
JULIE'S
KENNEDY'S
KING COLE BAR
KIT KAT KLUB
LA NUEVA ESCUELITA
LE COLONIAL
MCCOYS
MICHAEL JORDON'S
MICKEY MANTLE'S
MONKEY BAR
MORGAN BAR
MOTOWN CAFÉ
MULDOON'S
MULLIGAN'S PUB
MURPHY'S
MUSTANG HARRY'S
MUSTANG SALLY'S
OAK ROOM (Plaza)
OYSTER BAR
PALIO
PEGASUS
PENN TOP BAR
RAINBOW ROOM
REGENTS
RUSSIAN VODKA ROOM
SHINBASHI

SIBERIA
SOUND FACTORY
SUBWAY BAR
SUPPER CLUB
TAPAS LOUNGE
TAPIKA
TATOU
THIRD & LONG
TOWNHOUSE
TYPHOON BREWERY
VICE VERSA
VODKA BAR
WEB
WHISKEY BAR/
PARAMOUNT HOTEL
WHISKEY BLUE
WHISKEY PARK

## NOHO

ACME UNDERGROUND
BELGO
BOND ST. LOUNGE
DROVER'S TAP ROOM
FEZ@ TIME CAFE
HELENA'S
SALA
SWIFT HIBERNIAN LOUNGE
TEMPLE BAR
288 (TOM&JERRYS)
VON

## SOHO

ANTARTICA
AQUA GRILL
BALTHAZAR
BAR 89
BEST IN NEW YORK
BOOM
BOTANICA
CAFÉ NOIR
CASA LA FEMME
CAVIARTERIA
CIRCA TABAC

CUB ROOM
CULTURE CLUB
DENIAL
DIVA
DON HILLS
EAR INN
EMERALD PUB
FANELLI'S
GRAND BAR -
SOHO GRAND HOTEL
HARMONY
JET 19
JET LOUNGE
JUNNO'S
KANA
KAVEHAUZ
KENN'S BROOM ST. BAR
LILY'S
LUCKY STRIKE
M&R BAR - DINING ROOM
MADAME X
MATCH
MERC BAR
MERCER KITCHEN
MEXICAN RADIO
MILADY'S RESTAURANT
MILANO'S
N
NAKED LUNCH
NORTH RIVER BAR
NOVE CENTO
NV
O'NIEALS
PRAVDA
RAOUL'S
RED BENCH CAFE & BAR
ROOM (THE)
SCHARMANN'S
SOB'S
SOHO KITCHEN & BAR
SPRING LOUNGE
SPY
SWAY
SWEET & VICIOUS

TOAD HALL
23 WATTS
VELVET LOUNGE
VERUKA
VOID
WAX
XR BAR
ZINC BAR

## TRIBECA

BUBBLE LOUNGE
CITY HALL
DENNISONS
EL TEDDY'S
ICE BAR
JUNIPER CAFÉ & BAR
KNITTING FACTORY
KORI
LIQUOR STORE BAR
LUSH
MUDDVILLE 9
NO. MOORE
OBECA LI
ODEON
PUFFY'S TAVERN
RACOON LODGE
READE ST. PUB
SCREENING ROOM
SHINE
S.J.SOUTH'S & SON
SPAGHETTI WESTERN
TWO SEVEN SEVEN CHURCH
VANDAM
WALKERS
WETLANDS

## UPPER EAST SIDE

AMERICAN SPIRITS
AMERICAN TRASH
ATOMIC WINGS
AT THE BEAR BAR
AUCTION HOUSE
AUSTRALIA
BEACON HILL ALE HOUSE
BEAR BAR/ATOMIC-
 WINGSUPPER EAST
BIG SUR
BRADY'S
BRANDY'S PIANO BAR
BROTHER JIMMY'S-
 BAIT SHACK
CARNEGIE HILL-
 BREWING CO
THE CLUB CAR
COMIC STRIP LIVE
COWBOY BAR
CROSSROADS
DAKOTA BAR & GRILL
DANGERFIELD'S
DECADE
DOC WATSON'S
DORIAN'S
DT/UT
ELAINE'S
ELSIE'S OKE DOKE
FINNEGAN'S WAKE
FITZPATRICK'S
FLIGHT 1668
GAF BAR
GREAT HALL BALCONY
HEADLINER'S-
 BAR & LOUNGE
HI-LIFE LOUNGE-
 & RESTAURANT
HOGS & HEIFERS NORTH
IGGY's
J L SULLIVANS
KINSALE TAVERN
LEXINGTON BAR & BOOKS

LIVE PSYCHIC
LUKE'S BAR & GRILL
LUV BUZZ
MAD HATTER
MADISON'S PUB
MAD RIVER BAR & GRILL
MADISONS
MARTELL'S
METROPOLITAN MUSEUM
MICA BAR
MO'S CARIBBEAN -
BAR & GRILL
MUSTANG
O'FLANAGANS
OZONE BAR & LOUNGE
POUR HOUSE
RACOON LODGE
RATHBONES
REIF'S
RICHTERS
RUBY'S TAP HOUSE
SESSIONS 73
SHIP OF FOOLS
SUTTON PLACE
TIN LIZZIES
THE TOOL BOX
TRILOGY
VELVET ROOM
VENUS
VICTORY CAFÉ
WHO'S ON FIRST
WICKED WOLF
YORKVILLE BREWERY AND TAVERN

## UPPER WEST SIDE

ALLIGATOR ALLEY
BEAR BAR
BOOMER'S SPORTS CLUB
BURBON STREET
CANDLE BAR
CHAZ & WILSONS
CITRUS BAR AND GRILL
CITY GRILL
CREAM

DIVE 75
DRIP
EMERALD SALOON
EVELYN'S
EXILE
FIREHOUSE
Four Twenty Lounge
FUJIYAMA MAMA
GIN MILL
INDIGO
IRIDIUM ROOM
IVY NIGHT CLUB &CIGA
JAKES DILEMMA
MALACHY'S
MASON'S
MCALEERS PUB
MENDY'S WEST
MERCHANTS
MOONLIGHTING
MUSEUM CAFÉ
P&G CORNER CAFÉ
PARLOR
PETER'S
POTION
PROHIBITION
RACOON LODGE
REMEDY
SAINT'S
SHARK BAR
SNUG (THE)
TRIAD
VENUE
VERMOUTH
WORKS BAR
XANDO

## WALL STREET

THE BEEKMAN
COMMUTER CAFÉ
DELMONICO'S
DIVINE BAR
DONALD SACKS
FRAUNCES TAVERN RESTAURANT
GREATEST BAR ON EARTH
JEREMY'S ALE HOUSE
JOHNNY'S FISH GRILL
LET'S MAKE A DAIQUIRI
MORANS
NORTH STAR PUB
SUSPENDERS
WALL ST. KITCHEN & BAR

## WEST VILLAGE

ART BAR
ARTHUR'S TAVERN
AUTOMATIC SLIMS
BAKTUN
BAR AND BOOKS
BAR D'O
BARROW STREET-
 ALE HOUSE
BLIND TIGER ALE HOUSE
BOOTS AND SADDLES
BOXERS
BRAQUE
CAFÉ REMY
CHICAGO B.L.U.E.S.
CHUMLEY'S
CODY'S
COOLER THE
CORNELIA STREET CAFE
CORNER BISTRO
COWGIRL HALL OF FAME
CUBBY HOLE
DOWN THE HATCH
DUGOUT
DUPLEX
EIGHTY EIGHT'S
FIFTY FIVE BAR & GRILL

GARAGE RESTAURANT
GRANGE HALL
HALO
HANGAR BAR
HELL
HOGS & HEIFERS
HOG PIT
INO
JA
JEKYLL & HYDE PUB
JULIUS
KARAVAS TAVERN
KAVA LOUNGE
LURE BAR
MARIES CRISIS
MARKT
MONKEY'S PAW
MONSTER
MOOMBA
MOTHER
NOWBAR
OAKS (THE)
ONE HUNDRED ONE
OTHER ROOM
PIECES
POLLY ESTERS
SMALL'S
STONEWALL
TAVERN ON JANE
TORTILLA FLATS
TWO POTATO
TY'S
WATERLOO
WHITE HORSE TAVERN
WXOU RADIO

**GAY BARS**

BARRACUDA
BOOTS AND SADDLES
BREAK
BRIDGE BAR
CANDLE BAR
CANDY BAR
THE COCK
COMFORT ZONE
CUBBY HOLE
DUPLEX
EAGLE'S NEST
EIGHTY EIGHT'S
HENRIETTA HUDSON
KING NYC
LURE BAR
MEOW MIX
MONSTER
PIECES
RAWHIDE
SAINT'S
SPIKE
STARLIGHT
STONEWALL
THE TOOL BOX
TOWNHOUSE
TWO POTATO
TY'S
WEB
WONDER BAR
WORKS BAR

**POOL TABLES**

ACE BAR
ALLIGATOR ALLEY
AMERICAN SPIRITS
AMERICAN TRASH
ANTARTICA
ATOMIC WINGS AT
THE BEAR BAR
AUSTRALIA
B BARBANK CAFÉ

BAR NONE
BARFLY
BARRACUDA
BARROW STREET ALE HOUSE
BEACON HILL ALE HOUSE
BEAR BAR
BEAR BAR/ATOMIC WINGS
BLACK STAR
BLEEKER STREET BAR
BLUE & GOLD TAVERN
BOILER ROOM
BOOMER'S SPORTS CLUB
BRADY'S
BREAK
BRIDGE BAR
BULL MOOSE SALOON
BULLS HEAD TAVERN
CANDLE BAR
CBGB AND OMFUG
THE CORNER
COWBOY BAR
CROSSROADS
DICK'S BAR
DOC HOLIDAY'S
DOWNTIME BAR
DRINKLAND
DUGOUT
DUPLEX
EAGLE'S NEST
EDGE BAR
ELLEN'ODEES
GEMINI LOUNGE
GIN MILL
GLOCCA MORRA
HANGAR BAR
HEADLINER'S BAR & LOUNGE
HENRIETTA HUDSON
HOGS & HEIFERS
HOGS & HEIFERS NORTH
HOG PIT
IGGY's
INDIGO
JA

314

JACK DEMPSEY RESTAURANT
JAKES DILEMMA
JIMMY WALKERS ALE HOUSE
JOES
JOLLY ROGER
LEXINGTON BAR & BOOKS
LOOKING GLASS
LUCY'S
MAX FISH
MILADY'S RESTAURANT
MONA'S
MUDDVILLE 9
MUSICAL BOX
NEVADA SMITHS
NO IDEA
NORTH RIVER BAR
OFF THE WAGON
PIECES
PLANET 28
RACOON LODGE
RACOON LODGE
RACOON LODGE
RAWHIDE
RED ROCK WEST
REIF'S
RICHTERS
RIVERTON LOUNGE
RUBY'S TAP HOUSE
SAN FRANCISCO REST
SHIP OF FOOLS
SNUG (THE)
SOPHIES
SPIKE
TOAD HALL
THE TOOL BOX
TRILOGY
WELCOME TO THE JOHNSONS
WESTSIDE TAVERN
WHO'S ON FIRST
WORKS BAR
Z BAR

## LIVE MUSIC

ACME UNDERGROUND
ALCHYMY
ARLENE GROCERY
ARTHUR'S TAVERN
BABY JUPITER
BACK FENCE BAR
BAGATELLE
BAGGOT INN
BAR 9
BAR AND BOOKS
BAR AND BOOKS /
CIGAR BAR AT BEEKMAN
BAR D'O
BILL'S GAY NINETIES
BIRDLAND
BISTRO LATINO
BITTER END
BLUE NOTE
BMW BAR
BOOM
BOTTOM LINE
BRANDY'S PIANO BAR
BROADWAY LOUNGE
BROWNIES
CAFE CARLYLE
CBGB AND OMFUG
CHICAGO B.L.U.E.S.
CLEMENTINE
THE CLUB CAR
C-NOTE
CONEY ISLAND HIGH
CONTINENTAL
COOLER THE
COPACABANA
CORNELIA STREET CAFE
CREAM
CROSSROADS
DENNISONS
DETOUR
DHARMA
DON HILLS
DON'T TELL MAMA
DOWNTIME BAR

DUPLEX
EAR INN
EIGHTY EIGHT'S
ELBOW ROOM
FAILTE
FEZ@ TIME CAFE
FIDDLESTICKS
FIFTYSEVEN FIFTYSEVEN
GARAGE RESTAURANT
GROOVE
HELENA'S
HELL'S KITCHEN BAR
INTERNET CAFÉ
IRIDIUM ROOM
JACK THE RIPPER
KANA
KENNY'S CASTAWAYS
KNICKERBOCKER BAR & GRILL
KNITTING FACTORY
LAKESIDE LOUNGE
LEXINGTON BAR & BOOKS
LION'S DEN
LOLA
LOUISANA BAR AND GRILL
LUNA LOUNGE
MANITOBA'S
MARIES CRISIS
MERCURY LOUNGE
METRONOME
MONKEY BAR
MOTOR CITY BAR
MOTOWN CAFÉ
OAKS (THE)
O'FLANAGANS
ONE FORTY SEVEN(147)
ONE HUNDRED ONE
OTIS
PARKSIDE LOUNGE
PYRAMID
REBAR
RED LION
RUSSIAN VODKA ROOM
RYAN'S IRISH PUB

SESSIONS 73
SHINE
SMALL'S
SOB'S
SPAGHETTI WESTERN
SPIRAL
TERRA BLUE
TORCH
TRAMPS
TRIAD
TURTLE BAY
VICTORY CAFÉ
WETLANDS
WRECK ROOM
XR BAR
ZANZIBAR
ZINC BAR

# DANCING/CLUBS

BAKTUN
BANK
BAR 85
CAFÉ REMY
CARBON
CHEETAH
CHINA CLUB
COOLER THE
COPACABANA
CREAM
CULTURE CLUB
DON HILLS
EL FLAMINGO
40 FLAVORS
GEMINI LOUNGE
GONZALEZ Y GONZALEZ
GREATEST BAR ON EARTH
IGUANA
IVY NIGHT CLUB &CIGAR
THE KEY CLUB
KIT KAT KLUB
LA NUEVA ESCUELITA
LIFE / ki club
LIVE PSYCHIC

MADISONS
MOTHER
NV
OHM
OPERA
PASSERBY
POLLY ESTERS
PYRAMID
REBAR
ROXY
SOUND FACTORY
SPEEED
SPLASH BAR
SUPPER CLUB
THIRTEEN
TUNNEL
23 WATTS
TWIRL
VANITY
WEBSTER HALL
WRECK ROOM
XVI

# DIVE BARS

9 C
ABBEY TAVERN
ACE BAR
ALLIGATOR ALLEY
AMERICAN TRASH
AUSTRALIA
BAR CODE
BARROW STREET ALE HOUSE
BEAR BAR
BLARNEY COVE
BLUE & GOLD TAVERN
BOILER ROOM
BOTANICA
CBGB AND OMFUG
COMMUTER CAFÉ
COYOTE UGLY SALOON
DICK'S BAR

DOC HOLIDAY'S
EDGE BAR
ELEMENT ZERO
ELSIE'S OKE DOKE
EMERALD PUB
EMERALD SALOON
GAF BAR
GLOCCA MORRA
GRASSROOT TAVERN
HELL'S KITCHEN BAR
HOG PIT
HOGS & HEIFERS
HOGS & HEIFERS NORTH
HOLIDAY COCKTAIL LOUNGE
HOWARD JOHNSONS'S
IGGY's
INTERNATIONAL BAR
JIMMIE'S CORNER
JOES
KETTLE OF FISH
KGB
LOOKING GLASS
LUCY'S
LUNA LOUNGE
MALACHY'S
MARZ BAR
MASON'S
MCCOYS
MCDOOLEY'S
MENDY'S WEST
MILANO'S
MOJOS
MOLLY'S
MONA'S
MUDDVILLE 9
MULDOON'S
NIGHTINGALE
OASIS LOUNGE
ONE NINETEEN BAR
PARKSIDE LOUNGE
PLANET 28
RED ROCK WEST
RUDYS BAR AND GRILL

SAN FRANCISCO REST
SAVOY LOUNGE
SEVEN B (Vasac's)
SIBERIA
SMITH'S BAR
SOPHIES
SPIRAL
SPRING LOUNGE
SUBWAY BAR
SWINE ON 9
THE TOOL BOX
THIRD & LONG
TWO A (2A)
VILLAGE IDIOT
Z BAR

## FRAT

ALLIGATOR ALLEY
AMERICAN SPIRITS
ATOMIC WINGS
AUTOMATIC SLIMS
BAR NONE
BEAR BAR/ATOMIC WINGST
BLACK FIN BAR AND REST
BROTHER JIMMY'S -
BAIT SHACK
BURBON STREET
DORIAN'S
DOWN THE HATCH
FIREHOUSE
FITZPATRICK'S
FLIGHT 1668
GIN MILL
J L SULLIVANS
JACK DEMPSEY RESTAURANT
JAKES DILEMMA
JEREMY'S ALE HOUSE
JOHNNY'S FISH GRILL
JOLLY ROGER
MARTELL'S
MCSWIGGINS
MO'S CARIBBEAN BAR & GRILL
NEVADA SMITHS

PADDY REILEYS MUSIC BAR'
PECULIAR PUB
POUR HOUSE
RACOON LODGE
RACOON LODGE
RACOON LODGE
SNUG (THE)
WHO'S ON FIRST

## HOTEL BARS

BARCLAY BAR
BROADWAY LOUNGE
BULL & BEAR
CAFE CARLYLE
CAFE PIERRE
D LOUNGE/DELMONICO -
HOTEL
FIFTYSEVEN FIFTYSEVEN
FORTY FOUR
GRAMERCY PARK HOTEL BAR
GRAND BAR - SOHO GRAND-
HOTEL
KING COLE BAR
MERCER KITCHEN
MONKEY BAR
MORGAN BAR
NV
OAK ROOM- PLAZA HOTEL
PENN TOP BAR
WHISKEY BLUE
WHISKEY BAR

## NEIGHBORHOOD
## BARS

ABBEY TAVERN
ALCHYMY
ANNIE MOORES
ANTARTICA
ARTHUR'S TAVERN
BABY JUPITER
BAGGOT INN
BAHI
BANK CAFÉ
BAR 54
318 BAR ON A

BARFLY
BARRAMUNDI
BEACON HILL ALE HOUSE
THE BEEKMAN
BIG BAR
BLIND TIGER ALE HOUSE
BMW BAR
BOCA CHICA
BOUSCHE
BOXERS
BRADY'S
BREW'S
BULLS HEAD TAVERN
BUTCHER BAR
CARNEGIE HILL BREWING CO
CEDAR TAVERN
CHAZ & WILSONS
CHELSEA COMMONS
CHIBI'S SAKE BAR
CHUMLEY'S
CITY GRILL
CLOISTER CAFÉ
THE CLUB CAR
COCO BAR
CODY'S
COMMONWEALTH BREWERY
COMMUNITY BAR & GRILL
CORNELIA STREET CAFE
THE CORNER
CORNER BISTRO
DAKOTA BAR & GRILL
DBA
DOC WATSON'S
DOCKS OYSTER BAR -
AND SEAFOOD GRILL-
THIRD AVE
DONALD SACKS
DRIP
DROVER'S TAP ROOM
DRUIDS
DT/UT
DUGOUT
DUKE'S

EAR INN
EL RIO GRANDE
EL TEDDY'S
ELEVENTH ST. BAR
ELLEN'ODEES
FAILTE
FANELLI'S
FIDDLESTICKS
FINNEGAN'S WAKE
FRANKIE BLUE
FRAUNCES TAVERN -
RESTAURANT
GALAXY
GARAGE RESTAURANT
GASLIGHT
GINGER MAN
GLOBE
GOLD BAR
GOOD WORLD BAR & GRILL
GREENWICH BREWING Co
HANGAR BAR
HARGLO'S CAFE
HEADLINER'S BAR & LOUNGE
HEARTLAND BREWERY
HI-LIFE LOUNGE & REST-
AURANT
HOUSTON'S
INDIGO
INTERNET CAFÉ
JAMESON'S
JOHNNY'S BAR
JULIE'S
JULIUS
KARAVAS TAVERN
KASTRO BAR LOUNGE
KAVA LOUNGE
KENNEDY'S
KENN'S BROOM ST. BAR
KEVIN ST. JAMES
KINSALE TAVERN
LET'S MAKE A DAIQUIRI
LIBRARY
LIFE CAFÉ EAST

319

LIQUOR STORE BAR
LIVE BAIT
LOCAL 138
LUCKY STRIKE
LUKE'S BAR & GRILL
M&R BAR - DINING ROOM
MAD HATTER
MADISON'S PUB
MALACHY'S
MANITOBA'S
MARION'S CONTINENTAL
MAX FISH
MCALEERS PUB
MCBELL'S
MCCARTHY'S
MCCORMACKS PUBLIC -
HOUSE
McSORLEY'S ALE HOUSE
MEXICAN RADIO
MILADY'S RESTAURANT
MONKEY'S PAW
MORANS
MULDOON'S
MURPHY'S
MUSEUM CAFÉ
MUSTANG SALLY'S
NEGRIL
NIVA
NO IDEA
NO. MOORE
NORTH RIVER BAR
NORTH STAR PUB
OASIS LOUNGE
ODESSA
OFLAHERTY'S ALE HOUSE
O'FLANAGANS
OLD TOWNE BAR
P&G CORNER CAFÉ
PARLOR
PETER'S
PETE'S TAVERN
PHEBES

PLUG UGLY
PUFFY'S TAVERN
RAOUL'S
RATHBONES
RAVEN
READE ST. PUB
REIF'S
REVIVAL
RIVERTON LOUNGE
RUBY'S TAP HOUSE
RYAN'S IRISH PUB
SAPPHIRE LOUNGE
SCRATCHER
SHARK BAR
SIDEWALK CAFÉ
S.J.SOUTH'S & SON
SOHO KITCEN & BAR
SPAGHETTI WESTERN
ST. MARKS ALE HOUSE
STANDARD NOTIONS
SUSPENDERS
SUTTON PLACE
SWIM
SYDNEY B
TAP ROOM
TAVERN ON JANE
TELEPHONE BAR
THAI VILLAGE
THIRD & LONG
TIME CAFÉ
TOAD HALL
TRILOGY
TURTLE BAY
2A
TWO EIGHTY EIGHT BAR -
(TOM&JERRYS)
TWO TWO TWO (222)
TYPHOON BREWERY
VERMOUTH
VICEROY
VICTORY CAFÉ
VILLAGE LANTERN
VON

WALKERS
WELCOME TO THE JOHNSONS
WESTSIDE TAVERN
WHITE HORSE TAVERN
WXOU RADIO
XANDO
XANDO (VILLAGE)
YORKVILLE BREWERY -
AND TAVERN

## SPORTS

BLEEKER STREET BAR
BOOMER'S SPORTS CLUB
BOWLMOR LANES
BULL MOOSE SALOON
JIMMY WALKERS ALE HOUSE
MAD RIVER BAR & GRILL
MENDY'S WEST
MULLIGAN'S PUB
RESERVOIR
RICHTERS
SHIP OF FOOLS
WICKED WOLF

## SWANKY LOUNGES

ALVA
ANGELO & MAXIE'S
ANGEL' SHARE
AQUA GRILL
AQUAVIT
ART BAR
ASIA DE CUBA
ASTOR
AU BAR
AUBETTE
AUCTION HOUSE
B BAR
BALTHAZAR
BAR 6
BAR 89
BAR 9
BAR AND BOOKS
BAR AND BOOKS -
CIGAR BAR AT BEEKMAN
BAR D'O
BARAZA
BARCLAY BAR
BEER BAR - CAFÉ CENTRO
BEER HALL
BELGO
BELMONT LOUNGE
BIG SUR
BILL'S GAY NINETIES
BISTRO LATINO
BLACK & WHITE
BLACK STAR
BLUE WATER GRILL
BOB
BOND ST. LOUNGE
BOOM
BOTTINO
BOXCAR LOUNGE
BRAQUE
BRITISH OPEN
BRYANT PARK GRILL
BUBBLE LOUNGE
BULL & BEAR
C3 Lounge
CAFE CARLYLE
CAFÉ NOIR
CAFE PIERRE
CAFETERIA
CAMPBELL APARTMENT
CANDELA'S
CASA LA FEMME
CAVIARTERIA
CHEZ ES SAADA
CIBAR
CIEL ROUGE
CIRCA
CIRCA TABAC
CITRUS BAR AND GRILL

CITY HALL
CLEMENTINE
CLUB MACANUDO
COCO CAFÉ
COFFEE SHOP
CUB ROOM
DECADE
DECIBEL
DELIA'S SUPPER CLUB
DELMONICO'S
DENIAL
DETOUR
DIVA
DIVE 75
DIVINE BAR
DIVINE BAR
DOUBLE HAPPINESS
DRINKLAND
DUSK OF LONDON
EAST OF EIGHTH
ELAINE'S
EVELYN'S
EXILE
FIFTY FIVE BAR & GRILL
FIFTYSEVEN FIFTYSEVEN
FIREBIRD CAFÉ
FLAMINGO EAST
FLOAT
FLUTE
FORTY FOUR
Four Twenty Lounge
FRED'S BEAUTY BAR
FUJIYAMA MAMA
G
GLOBAL 33
GOTHAM BAR & GRILL
GRAMERCY PARK HOTEL BAR
GRAMERCY TAVERN
GRAND BAR - SOHO-
 GRAND HOTEL
GRANGE HALL
GRANVILLE LOUNGE

GREAT HALL BALCONY
HALO
HARMONY
HELENA'S
HELL
H2K
ICE BAR
IL BAGATTO
INO
IRIDIUM ROOM
IZZY BAR
JA
JET 19
JET LOUNGE
JUDSON GRILL
JUNIPER CAFÉ & BAR
JUNNO'S
JUSTINS
KANA
KAVEHAUZ
KING COLE BAR
KNICKERBOCKER -
BAR & GRILL
KORI
KOROVA MILK BAR
L'ANGOLO
LA LINEA
LAKESIDE LOUNGE
LAVA
LEOPARD LOUNGE
LE COLONIAL
LEMON
LEXINGTON BAR & BOOKS
LILY'S
LIQUIDS
LOLA
LOT 61
L RAY
LUCA LOUNGE
LUDLOW BAR
LUNA PARK
LUSH
LUV BUZZ

G
MADAME X
MARKT
MARYLOU'S
MATCH
MEKKA
MERC BAR
MERCER KITCHEN
MERCHANTS
METRONOME
METROPOLITAN MUSEUM
MICA BAR
MICHAEL JORDON'S
MONKEY BAR
MOOMBA
MOONLIGHTING
MORGAN BAR
MUSICAL BOX
MUSTANG
MUSTANG HARRY'S
N
NAKED LUNCH
NEVER
NIAGRA
NOVE CENTO
NOWBAR
NW3
OBECA LI
ODEON
O'NIEALS
ONE FORTY SEVEN(147)
OOPS
OPALINE
OPIUM DEN
ORCHARD BAR
ORSON'S
OTHER ROOM
OTIS
OZONE BAR & LOUNGE
PAGEANT BAR & GRILL
PALIO
PARK AVALON
PATRIA

PEGASUS
PENN TOP BAR
PIERROT
POTION
POP
PRAVDA
PROHIBITION
RAINBOW ROOM
RED BENCH CAFE & BAR
REGENTS
REMEDY
REVOLUTION
ROOM (THE)
RUSSIAN VODKA ROOM
SALA
SCHARMANN'S
SCREENING ROOM
SESSIONS 73
SHADE
SHINBASHI
SHINE
SIMONE
SIN SIN
SOLAS
SPY
STANDARD
SWAY
SWEET & VICIOUS
SWIFT HIBERNIAN LOUNGE
TAPAS LOUNGE
TAPIKA
TATOU
TEMPLE BAR
TENTH STREET LOUNGE
TIN LIZZIES
TORCH
TRIBE
TWO I'S
TWO SEVEN SEVEN CHURCH
UNION BAR
VANDAM
VELVET LOUNGE
VELVET ROOM

VENUE
VENUS
VERUKA
VICE VERSA
VIG BAR
VINTAGE
VODKA BAR
VOID
WALL ST. KITCHEN & BAR
WATERLOO
WAX
WHISKEY BAR/PARAMOUNT HOTEL
WHISKEY BLUE
WHISKEY PARK
ZANZIBAR
ZINC BAR

## THEME BARS
BARMACY
BEAUTY BAR
BEST IN NEW YORK
BREWSKY'S
BURP CASTLE
CALIENTE CAB COMPANY
CHELSEA BREWING COMPANY
COWBOY BAR
COWGIRL HALL OF FAME
DELTA GRILL
FILM CENTER CAFE
FLIGHT 151
HARD ROCK CAFE
HARLEY-DAVIDSON CAFE
IDLEWILD
JACK THE RIPPER
JEKYLL & HYDE CLUB
JEKYLL & HYDE PUB
KUSH
LA MAISON DE SADE
LA NOUVELLE JUSTINE
LANSKY LOUNGE
LOUISANA BAR AND GRILL
LUCKY CHENGS

MICKEY MANTLE'S
MOTOR CITY BAR
MOTOWN CAFÉ
OYSTER BAR
RODEO BAR
SLAUGHTERED LAMB
TORTILLA FLATS

## DATE SPOTS-ROMANTIC
ABBEY TAVERN
ALVA
ANGELO & MAXIE'S
ANGEL' SHARE
AQUA GRILL
AQUAVIT
ART BAR
ASIA DE CUBA
AU BAR
B BAR
BAGATELLE
BAHI
BALTHAZAR
BAR 6
BAR 89
BAR AND BOOKS
BAR AND BOOKS /
CIGAR BAR-
 AT BEEKMAN
BIG SUR
BILL'S GAY NINETIES
BIRDLAND
BLACK & WHITE
BLUE NOTE
BOND ST. LOUNGE
BOOM
BOWLMOR LANES
BOXCAR LOUNGE
BRANDY'S PIANO BAR
BUBBLE LOUNGE
CAFE CARLYLE
CAFÉ NOIR
CANDELA'S

CANDY BAR
CAROLINE'S COMEDY CLUB
CASA LA FEMME
CAVIARTERIA
CHEZ ES SAADA
CIBAR
CIEL ROUGE
CIRCA
CIRCA TABAC
CITRUS BAR AND GRILL
CITY HALL
CLEMENTINE
THE CLUB CAR
COMIC STRIP LIVE
CORNELIA STREET CAFE
CREAM
CUB ROOM
DECADE
DECIBEL
DELIA'S SUPPER CLUB
DETOUR
DHARMA
DIVA
DOUBLE HAPPINESS
DRUIDS
EAST OF EIGHTH
EL RIO GRANDE
EL TEDDY'S
ELEVENTH ST. BAR
EXILE
FEZ@ TIME CAFE
FIFTYSEVEN FIFTYSEVEN
FIREBIRD CAFÉ
FLUTE
FRED'S BEAUTY BAR
G
GOTHAM BAR & GRILL
GOTHAM COMEDY CLUB
GRAMERCY TAVERN
GRAND BAR -
SOHO GRAND HOTEL
GREAT HALL BALCONY

GREATEST BAR ON EARTH
HARMONY
HELENA'S
HELL
H2K
ICE BAR
IDLEWILD
IL BAGATTO
INO
IRIDIUM ROOM
JA
JAZZ STANDARD
JET 19
JUNIPER CAFÉ & BAR
JUNNO'S
KANA
KORI
L'ANGOLO
LA LINEA
LANSKY LOUNGE
LEOPARD LOUNGE
LE COLONIAL
LEXINGTON BAR & BOOKS
LILY'S
LOLA
LOT 61
L RAY
LUCA LOUNGE
LUDLOW BAR
LUNA PARK
LUSH
MARION'S CONTINENTAL
MARYLOU'S
MERC BAR
MERCER KITCHEN
MERCHANTS
METROPOLITAN MUSEUM
MEXICAN RADIO
MORGAN BAR
MUSEUM CAFÉ
MUSICAL BOX
MUSTANG
N

NEGRIL
NEVER
NIVA
NW3
OBECA LI
ODEON
O'NIEALS
ONE FORTY SEVEN(147)
OPALINE
OPIUM DEN
ORCHARD BAR
OZONE BAR & LOUNGE
PAGEANT BAR & GRILL
PARK AVALON
PATRIA
PENN TOP BAR
PIERROT
POTION
POP
RAINBOW ROOM
RAOUL'S
RED BENCH CAFE & BAR
ROOM (THE)
ROXY
RUSSIAN VODKA ROOM
SCHARMANN'S
SCREENING ROOM
SESSIONS 73
SHADE
SHINE
SIMONE
SIN SIN
SOB'S
SOLAS
SPY
SWEET & VICIOUS
TAPAS LOUNGE
TATOU
TEMPLE BAR
TENTH STREET LOUNGE
TORCH
TWO SEVEN SEVEN CHURCH
VERUKA

VICE VERSA
VON
WATERLOO
WAX
WHISKEY BLUE
XVI
ZINC BAR

# GARDENS-OUTDOOR-SPACES

AQUA GRILL
AUSTRALIA
B BAR
BARRAMUNDI
BEACON HILL ALE HOUSE
BELMONT LOUNGE
BOXERS
BOXCAR LOUNGE
BROTHER JIMMY'S BAIT-
 SHACK
CHELSEA BREWING-
 COMPANY
CHELSEA COMMONS
CIBAR
CODY'S
DBA
DIVINE BAR
DOC WATSON'S
DRUIDS
EL RIO GRANDE
EL TEDDY'S
EXILE
FLAMINGO EAST
GIN MILL
HEARTLAND BREWERY
HELENA'S
INTERNATIONAL BAR
INTERNET CAFÉ
KANA

LIQUOR STORE BAR
LUCA LOUNGE
LUNA PARK
M&R BAR - DINING ROOM
MARKT
MARTELL'S
METROPOLITAN MUSEUM
MICA BAR
MUSICAL BOX
NIAGRA
OBECA LI
OFLAHERTY'S ALE HOUSE
ORSON'S
PROHIBITION
RAOUL'S
REIF'S
SCHARMANN'S
SESSIONS 73
SIN SIN
SWEET & VICIOUS
TELEPHONE BAR
THIRTEEN
TIME CAFÉ
TORTILLA FLATS
VICTORY CAFÉ
WHITE HORSE TAVERN

## CIGAR FRIENDLY

ALVA
ANNIE MOORES
AUBETTE
BAGATELLE
BAR 9
BAR AND BOOKS
BAR AND BOOKS -
CIGAR BAR AT BEEKMAN
BELGO
BISTRO LATINO
BLACK FIN BAR AND
 RESTAURANT
BLARNEY COVE
BROADWAY LOUNGE

BUBBLE LOUNGE
BULL & BEAR
CARNEGIE HILL BREWING CO
CAVIARTERIA
CHELSEA BREWING COMPANY
CHELSEA COMMONS
CIBAR
CIRCA TABAC
THE CLUB CAR
CLUB MACANUDO
COMMONWEALTH-
 BREWERY
DECADE
DELMONICO'S
DIVE 75
DIVINE BAR
DIVINE BAR
DUSK OF LONDON
FLAMINGO EAST
FRANKIE BLUE
GASLIGHT
GINGER MAN
GRAMERCY TAVERN
GRANVILLE LOUNGE
GREAT HALL BALCONY
GREENWICH BREWING Co
HARMONY
HEADLINER'S BAR & LOUNGE
HELENA'S
HELL'S KITCHEN BAR
H2K
ICE BAR
IVY NIGHT CLUB &CIGAR
J L SULLIVANS
JOHNNY'S BAR
KANA
L'ANGOLO
LA MAISON DE SADE
LEOPARD LOUNGE
LEXINGTON BAR & BOOKS
LILY'S
LUCA LOUNGE
MAD RIVER BAR & GRILL

MANITOBA'S
MATCH
MONKEY BAR
MOONLIGHTING
MUSTANG
NEVER
NIAGRA
9 C
NIVA
OAK ROOM (Plaza)
ODESSA
OFF THE WAGON
OZONE BAR & LOUNGE
PAGEANT BAR & GRILL
POP
PRAVDA
REIF'S
RUBY'S TAP HOUSE
SCREENING ROOM
SESSIONS 73
SIN SIN
S.J.SOUTH'S & SON
SOLAS
SPY
SWIM
TEMPLE BAR
TIN LIZZIES
TRIBE
23 WATTS
VANDAM
VICTORY CAFÉ
WALKERS
WAX
WHISKEY BARL
WHISKEY BLUE
WHO'S ON FIRST
ZANZIBAR

## BEST BEER & WINE SELECTION
ALVA

ANGELO & MAXIE'S
ANGEL' SHARE
AQUA GRILL
ASIA DE CUBA
ASTOR
AUBETTE
BAGATELLE
BALTHAZAR
BAR AND BOOKS
BAR AND BOOKS -
CIGAR BAR AT BEEKMAN
BARROW STREET ALE HOUSE
BEER BAR - CAFÉ CENTRO
BEER HALL
BELGO
BLIND TIGER ALE HOUSE
BLUE WATER GRILL
BMW BAR
BOND ST. LOUNGE
BOTANICA
BOXERS
BOXCAR LOUNGE
BREW'S
BREWSKY'S
BUBBLE LOUNGE
BULL & BEAR
BURP CASTLE
CAFE PIERRE
CANDELA'S
CANDY BAR
CARNEGIE HILL BREWING CO
CAVIARTERIA
CHELSEA BREWING COMPANY
CHELSEA COMMONS
CHEZ ES SAADA
CIBAR
CIRCA TABAC
CITRUS BAR AND GRILL
CLEMENTINE
CLUB MACANUDO
COMMONWEALTH BREWERY
DBA
DECADE

DELMONICO'S
DIVE 75
DRUIDS
DUSK OF LONDON
EL TEDDY'S
ELAINE'S
FAILTE
FIFTYSEVEN FIFTYSEVEN
FLUTE
GINGER MAN
GOTHAM BAR & GRILL
GRAMERCY TAVERN
GRAND BAR - SOHO -
GRAND HOTEL
GRANGE HALL
GREENWICH BREWING Co
HEARTLAND BREWERY
HELENA'S
IRIDIUM ROOM
JACK THE RIPPER
JEKYLL & HYDE PUB
JUDSON GRILL
JUNIPER CAFÉ & BAR
JUSTINS
KENNEDY'S
KINSALE TAVERN
LANSKY LOUNGE
LEOPARD LOUNGE
LE COLONIAL
LEMON
LEXINGTON BAR & BOOKS
LILY'S
LOLA
LOT 61
LUSH
M&R BAR - DINING ROOM
MARKT
MERCER KITCHEN
MERCHANTS
MICKEY MANTLE'S
MONKEY BAR
MOOMBA

MURPHY'S
MUSTANG
NEVER
NORTH RIVER BAR
OAK ROOM (Plaza)
OBECA LI
OPALINE
OTHER ROOM
OZONE BAR & LOUNGE
PALIO
PATRIA
PECULIAR PUB
POTION
POP
PRAVDA
PROHIBITION
RAINBOW ROOM
RAOUL'S
ROOM (THE)
RUBY'S TAP HOUSE
SIMONE
S.J.SOUTH'S & SON
SLAUGHTERED LAMB
SOHO KITCEN & BAR
SPY
TAP ROOM
TENTH STREET LOUNGE
TORCH
TWO SEVEN SEVEN CHURCH
TYPHOON BREWERY
UNION BAR
VERMOUTH
VON
WALL ST. KITCHEN & BAR
WATERLOO
YORKVILLE BREWERY AND
TAVERN

# ANNOYING-
# DOOR POLICIES

ASIA DE CUBA
AUBETTE
B BAR

BAKTUN
BALTHAZAR
BELMONT LOUNGE
BISTRO LATINO
BOND ST. LOUNGE
BOOM
CHEETAH
CHEZ ES SAADA
CHINA CLUB
CLEMENTINE
COOLER THE
CREAM
EVELYN'S
FLOAT
GEMINI LOUNGE
IDLEWILD
JA
JET 19
JET LOUNGE
LANSKY LOUNGE
LIFE / ki club
LOT 61
METRONOME
MORGAN BAR
MOTHER
NAKED LUNCH
NV
PAGEANT BAR & GRILL
POP
PRAVDA
PROHIBITION
ROXY
SHINE
SPEEED
SPY
THIRTEEN
23 WATTS
TWIRL
VANITY
VERUKA
WAX
WHISKEY BLUE

## SHECKY'S PICKS

ACE BAR
ACME UNDERGROUND
ALVA
ANGEL' SHARE
AQUA GRILL
AQUAVIT
ARLENE GROCERY
ART BAR
BAR 89
BAR AND BOOKS
BAR CODE
BAR D'O
BARAZA
BARRACUDA
BLACK & WHITE
BLIND TIGER ALE HOUSE
BOTTINO
BOWLMOR LANES
BUBBLE LOUNGE
CAROLINE'S COMEDY CLUB
CAVIARTERIA
CIRCA
DBA
DHARMA
DIVINE BAR
DRINKLAND
EVELYN'S
FIFTYSEVEN FIFTYSEVEN
FLAMINGO EAST
FLUTE
FRESSON
GLOBAL 33
GOTHAM BAR & GRILL
GOTHAM COMEDY CLUB
GRAMERCY TAVERN
GRAND BAR - SOHO GRAND HOTEL
GREAT HALL BALCONY
HELENA'S
HELL
HELL'S KITCHEN BAR
H2K
ICE BAR

IRIDIUM ROOM
JA
JOHNNY'S BAR
JUNIPER CAFÉ & BAR
KORI
LA MAISON DE SADE
LEOPARD LOUNGE
LE COLONIAL
LEXINGTON BAR & BOOKS
LIBRARY
LUCA LOUNGE
MANITOBA'S
MERCHANTS
MICA BAR
MONA'S
MUSICAL BOX
MUSTANG
N
NEVER
NIAGRA
9 C
NW3
ODESSA
O'NIEALS
ONE FORTY SEVEN(147)
OPIUM DEN
ORCHARD BAR
OZONE BAR & LOUNGE
PATRIA
PUFFY'S TAVERN
RAINBOW ROOM
RAOUL'S
RED ROCK WEST
REVOLUTION
SCREENING ROOM
SESSIONS 73
SHIP OF FOOLS
S.J.SOUTH'S & SON
SOHO KITCEN & BAR
SWEET & VICIOUS
TORCH
TUNNEL

TWO EIGHTY EIGHT BAR-
   (TOM&JERRYS)
TWO I'S
WALKERS
WATERLOO
WELCOME TO THE JOHNSONS
WHISKEY BAR
ZINC BAR

# AFTER WORK-
# SPOTS
ABBEY TAVERN
ACE BAR
ALLIGATOR ALLEY
AMERICAN TRASH
ANNIE MOORES
ANTARTICA
AUSTRALIA
B BAR
BAHI
BANK CAFÉ
BAR 6
BAR 89
BARROW STREET ALE HOUSE
BEER BAR - CAFÉ CENTRO
BLARNEY COVE
BLEEKER STREET BAR
BLIND TIGER ALE HOUSE
BOXERS
BRAQUE
BREWSKY'S
BROTHER JIMMY'S BAIT SHACK
BRYANT PARK GRILL
CAMPBELL APARTMENT
CHELSEA COMMONS
CHUMLEY'S
CIRCA TABAC
CLUB MACANUDO
COFFEE SHOP
COMMUTER CAFÉ
CORNER BISTRO
COWGIRL HALL OF FAME

CUB ROOM
DOCKS OYSTER BAR -
AND SEAFOOD GRILL -
DONALD SACKS
DRUIDS
EAR INN
EL RIO GRANDE
EL TEDDY'S
FIREHOUSE
FLUTE
GOTHAM COMEDY CLUB
HARMONY
HEARTLAND BREWERY
HELENA'S
HENRIETTA HUDSON
HOGS & HEIFERS
HOUSTON'S
H2K
ICE BAR
JEREMY'S ALE HOUSE
JOHNNY'S BAR
JOHNNY'S FISH GRILL
JUDSON GRILL
KANA
KINSALE TAVERN
L'ANGOLO
LA MAISON DE SADE
LE COLONIAL
LET'S MAKE A DAIQUIRI
LEXINGTON BAR & BOOKS
LIQUOR STORE BAR
LUNA PARK
LUSH
MADISON'S PUB
McSORLEY'S ALE HOUSE
MERC BAR
MERCHANTS
METROPOLITAN MUSEUM
MEXICAN RADIO
MICA BAR
MICKEY MANTLE'S
MONKEY BAR
MORANS

MULLIGAN'S PUB
MURPHY'S
MUSTANG SALLY'S
NEGRIL
OAK ROOM (Plaza)
PALIO
PETER'S
PETE'S TAVERN
PLANET 28
PRAVDA
RED ROCK WEST
RUBY'S TAP HOUSE
SCREENING ROOM
SESSIONS 73
SIDEWALK CAFÉ
SLAUGHTERED LAMB
SUBWAY BAR
TAP ROOM
TELEPHONE BAR
THIRD & LONG
TORTILLA FLATS
TYPHOON BREWERY
UNION BAR
WALKERS
WALL ST. KITCHEN & BAR
WATERLOO
WELCOME TO THE JOHNSONS
WESTSIDE TAVERN
WHISKEY BAR
WHISKEY BLUE
WHISKEY PARK
YORKVILLE BREWERY
AND TAVERN
WHISKEY BAR

## OLDER SCENES

ADLIB
ANNIE MOORES
ARTHUR'S TAVERN
ASIA DE CUBA
AU BAR
AUCTION HOUSE
BAGATELLE
BAR AND BOOKS

BAR AND BOOKS /CIGAR BAR-
  AT BEEKMAN
BARCLAY BAR
BIRDLAND
BISTRO LATINO
BLACK & WHITE
BLARNEY COVE
BLUE NOTE
BLUE WATER GRILL
BRANDY'S PIANO BAR
BREW'S
BRITISH OPEN
BROADWAY LOUNGE
C3 Lounge
CAFE CARLYLE
CAFE PIERRE
CAVIARTERIA
CHAZ & WILSONS
CHICAGO B.L.U.E.S.
CIBAR
THE CLUB CAR
CLUB MACANUDO
COCO CAFÉ
COPACABANA
CORNELIA STREET CAFE
CUB ROOM
D LOUNGE/DELMONICO HOTEL
DECADE
DELMONICO'S
DENNISONS
DIVINE BAR
DIVINE BAR
DOC WATSON'S
DOCKS OYSTER BAR-
  AND SEAFOOD GRILL -
DON'T TELL MAMA
DUPLEX
EAST OF EIGHTH
EIGHTY EIGHT'S
ELAINE'S
ELLEN'ODEES
EMERALD PUB

EMERALD SALOON
FANELLI'S
FIDDLESTICKS
FIFTYSEVEN FIFTYSEVEN
FIREBIRD CAFÉ
FLUTE
FORTY FOUR
FRAUNCES TAVERN
  RESTAURANT
GASLIGHT
GLOCCA MORRA
GRAMERCY PK. HOTEL BAR
GRAMERCY TAVERN
GRAND BAR - SOHO
GRAND HOTEL
GRANGE HALL
GRANVILLE LOUNGE
GREENWICH BREWING Co
INTERNET CAFÉ
IRIDIUM ROOM
JAZZ STANDARD
JUDSON GRILL
JULIE'S
JUSTINS
KANA
KENN'S BROOM ST. BAR
KING COLE BAR
KNICKERBOCKER BAR
LE COLONIAL
LEXINGTON BAR & BOOKS
LILY'S
LOLA
LOT 61
L RAY
MADAME X
MALACHY'S
MASON'S
MATCH
MCALEERS PUB
McSORLEY'S ALE HOUSE
MERCER KITCHEN
METROPOLITAN MUSEUM
MICHAEL JORDON'S
MILADY'S RESTAURANT
MONKEY BAR

MUSEUM CAFÉ
OAK ROOM (Plaza)
ODEON
OLD TOWNE BAR
ONE FORTY SEVEN(147)
ORSON'S
OYSTER BAR
OZONE BAR & LOUNGE
P&G CORNER CAFÉ
PARK AVALON
PENN TOP BAR
PUFFY'S TAVERN
RAINBOW ROOM
REVOLUTION
SAN FRANCISCO REST
SAVOY LOUNGE
SIN SIN
SMALL'S
SMITH'S BAR
SUPPER CLUB
TAP ROOM
TATOU
TAVERN ON JANE
TOWNHOUSE
TRIAD
VELVET ROOM
WALKERS
WATERLOO
WHISKEY BAR
WHISKEY BLUE
WHITE HORSE TAVERN
WHISKEY BAR

# NEW BARS-
# HOT HIP

23 WATTS
ALCHYMY
BAGATELLE
BLACK & WHITE
BOXCAR LOUNGE
BUTCHER BAR

CAVIARTERIA
CIRCA TABAC
CULTURE CLUB
FAILTE
FLOAT
FRANKIE BLUE
GREENWICH BREWING Co
H2K
HALO
HARMONY
ICE BAR
INO
JA
KORI
LA MAISON DE SADE
L'ANGOLO
LEOPARD LOUNGE
LUCA LOUNGE
LUNA PARK
LUV BUZZ
MANITOBA'S
MARKT
MARKT
NEVER
NIVA
OFF THE WAGON
OHM
OZONE BAR & LOUNGE
POP
RUSSIAN VODKA ROOM
SESSIONS 73
SIN SIN
STARLIGHT
SWAY
SWIM
THAI VILLAGE
THE CLUB CAR
THE COCK
THE CORNER
THE KEY CLUB
TRIBE
TWO TWO TWO (222)
VANDAM

VICE VERSA
WELCOME TO THE JOHNSONS
WHISKEY BLUE
ZANZIBAR

## CLOSED

ANSEO
AVENUE B SOCIAL CLUB
BAILEY'S CORNER
BAR CODE
BLUE ANGEL EXOTIC CABARET
CHAOS
CITY WINE & CIGAR
CONEY ISLAND HIGH
CUCKOO CARIBE
DEADLINE
DENIM & DIAMONDS
E & O BAR
EAST SIDE ALE HOUSE
FASHION CAFÉ
FREDERICK'S
FROLIC ROOM
J L SULLIVANS
KELLY'S CORNER
OOPS
SCULLY ON SPRING
SKI BAR
SPOON
ST. MARKS BAR
SWEET MELISSA
SYSTEM
VAIN

## PICK UP SPOTS

ABBEY TAVERN
AMERICAN SPIRITS
AMERICAN TRASH
ANGELO & MAXIE'S
ART BAR
AUBETTE
AUSTRALIA

AUTOMATIC SLIMS
BAR NONE
BARRAMUNDI
BEAR BAR
BEAR BAR/ATOMIC -
WINGSUPPER EAST
BISTRO LATINO
BLACK FIN BAR AND
RESTAURANT
BLACK STAR
BOB
BOOM
BOTTINO
BROTHER JIMMY'S BAIT
 SHACK
BUBBLE LOUNGE
CHEZ ES SAADA
CHINA CLUB
CIRCA TABAC
CITRUS BAR AND GRILL
CLEMENTINE
THE COCK
CUB ROOM
CULTURE CLUB
DAKOTA BAR & GRILL
DICK'S BAR
DIVA
DONALD SACKS
DORIAN'S
DRINKLAND
DRUIDS
FLAMINGO EAST
FLOAT
FRANKIE BLUE
GEMINI LOUNGE
H2K
ICE BAR
IVY NIGHT CLUB &CIGAR
JA
JOHNNY'S FISH GRILL
JUNNO'S
THE KEY CLUB
KING NYC
L'ANGOLO
LA MAISON DE SADE

LE COLONIAL
LIBRARY
LIFE / ki club
LIQUIDS
LIVE BAIT
LUDLOW BAR
LUV BUZZ
MARKT
MAX FISH
MEOW MIX
MERCHANTS
MONKEY BAR
MOONLIGHTING
MORANS
MULLIGAN'S PUB
MURPHY'S
MUSICAL BOX
MUSTANG
NAKED LUNCH
NIAGRA
NIVA
NV
NW3
OASIS LOUNGE
OFF THE WAGON
OHM
ONE NINETEEN BAR
ORCHARD BAR
PAGEANT BAR & GRILL
POUR HOUSE
PRAVDA
RAOUL'S
RED ROCK WEST
REGENTS
SAPPHIRE LOUNGE
SHINE
SLAUGHTERED LAMB
SOUND FACTORY
SPEEED
SPY
STARLIGHT
SWIM

TAPAS LOUNGE
TELEPHONE BAR
THIRD & LONG
THIRTEEN
THE TOOL BOX
TORTILLA FLATS
TRIBE
TRILOGY
2A
23 WATTS
TWIRL
TWO EIGHTY EIGHT BAR -
(TOM&JERRYS)
VANDAM
WAX
WESTSIDE TAVERN
WHISKEY BLUE
WHITE HORSE TAVERN
WHO'S ON FIRST
Z BAR
ZANZIBAR

# COMEDY CLUBS

CAROLINE'S COMEDY CLUB
COMEDY CELLAR
COMIC STRIP LIVE
DANGERFIELDS
GOTHAM COMEDY CLUB